Marketing Mutual Funds and Limited Partnerships to Your Life Insurance Clients

Marketing Mutual Funds and Limited Partnerships to Your Life Insurance Clients

BRUCE W. SAENGER
CLU, RHU, CFP, CPCU, CIC, ChFC

Farnsworth Publishing Company
a subsidiary of Longman Financial Services Publishing, Inc.

While a great deal of care has been taken to provide accurate and current information, the ideas, suggestions, general principles, and conclusions presented in this book are subjected to local, state, and federal laws and regulations, court cases, and any revisions of same. The reader is thus urged to consult legal counsel regarding any points of law—this publication should not be used as a substitute for competent legal advice.

Published by Farnsworth Publishing Company
a subsidiary of Longman Financial Services Publishing, Inc.

85 86 87 10 9 8 7 6 5 4 3 2 1

Library of Congress Cataloging in Publication Data
Saenger, Bruce W.
Marketing mutual funds and limited partnerships to your investment insurance clients.

1. Investment trusts. 2. Limited partnership. 3. Insurance, Life. I. Title.
HG4530.S24 1985 332.63'27 85-6989
ISBN 0-87863-241-7

Sponsoring Editor: Ivy Lester
Project Editor: Karen Schenkenfelder
Cover and Internal Design: Robert L. Cooley

Table of Contents

This book is dedicated to my wife Cheryl whose unfailing support provided the inspiration necessary to complete this extensive project.

Preface

This text has been written for you, the life insurance sales professional who offers a wider range of financial services than those traditionally attributed to our industry. It has become apparent in recent years that merely becoming licensed to sell mutual funds and limited partnership offerings is not enough. Though a strong technical base of information is helpful in explaining investment concepts to your clients, the appropriate sales procedures have rarely been described. Therefore, this book is designed to provide you not only relevant technical information but also a complete sales procedure that has been used successfully by your peers.

For years policyowners have been caught in the crossfire between life insurance companies and investment firms. Neither side has attempted to reduce the misunderstanding surrounding the purpose of each. The two types of products, insurance and investments, are designed to solve different financial problems. They do not compete but rather complement one another. Investment products can never solve the financial problems that result from untimely death. On the other hand, as life continues and capital accumulation becomes increasingly important, investment products and life insurance each provide separate but essential ingredients for developing a balanced capital accumulation plan.

As a life insurance agent/registered representative, you should view yourself as a financial planner who can help your clients solve their financial problems. You will not be competing with yourself since insurance dollars and investment dollars are taken from "different pockets," so to speak.

Policyowners want and need investment products, yet existing sources for these products are inadequate for their needs. This is one of the main reasons so many life insurance companies have organized broker-dealer firms. As an agent/registered representative, when you offer investment products *and* insurance, you become more important to your clients. In effect, you become a financial center, thereby increasing your effectiveness.

A major misunderstanding among representatives is the notion that the investment products salesperson must be an investment expert. Nothing could be further from the truth. Had a similar perception prevailed in the life insurance industry, only actuaries would feel comfortable in a sales interview. Likewise, a registered representative who is licensed to sell both life insurance and investment products does not need to know the intricacies of the stock and bond markets to sell investment products successfully.

The essential talent of the registered representative is the ability to recognize that an investment is suitable for the client. The main reasons for purchasing managed investments are diversification and the availability of professional investment management. The selection of a particular stock is not within the normal province of the representative. Your role is to be the catalyst, the intermediary between the client who seeks help in making investments and the qualified professional who manages investment portfolios.

It is most important to understand that your role in the sale of investment products is neither one of a regular securities salesperson nor one of an investment analyst. Yet, as experienced life insurance people, you are already accustomed to providing professional services and probably consider yourselves advisors in whom your clients place great confidence.

While many people may feel they own adequate life insurance, few, if any, believe they have enough money. Investment products have proven to be an ideal door opener for those prospects who are reluctant to discuss their insurance program but welcome the opportunity to discuss their total financial situation. The introduction of investment products gives you a completely new inventory of merchandise. Although life insurance continues to be a focal point, the proper introduction of investment products helps to balance financial considerations.

Often, when you are selling investment products to the over-age-forty market, you will find that many of these people have not talked to an insurance agent for a number of years. It is here that new life insurance sales develop to meet changes in lifestyles. Most over-age-forty clients still need more life insurance in addition to revised investment plans. The same investment-product buyers also can introduce you to younger people who are prospects for life insurance.

When compared to the more complex uses of life insurance in programming, estate analysis, and partnership and corporate situations, investment products actually play a relatively simple role in financial planning for most people. Investment products offer the majority of investors the benefits and services they cannot find elsewhere and certainly cannot provide for themselves. Life insurance and investment products can be combined to form a long-term program designed to meet the important long-term objectives of financial planning. It may be difficult to realize that many of your clients are quite able and willing to transfer $5,000, $10,000, or more from savings to a mutual fund or limited partnership program. This means their dollars are working for them.

These are exciting times! Our business is changing and being challenged, almost on a daily basis, with new products, new competition, and a better-informed buying public. The trend developing in the financial planning area serves to blend the life insurance salesperson with the stockbroker.

The common meeting point is now the tailored financial program for the individual. Consumer studies show that the buying public prefers a one-stop approach to purchasing financial services. But where do consumers go to do their one-stop shopping? The news of acquisitions and mergers among banks, retailers, brokers, insurers, and other financial service organizations makes one thing clear: to meet the competition in this revolutionary environment, we must provide broad financial services.

Many life insurance companies have made it possible for you to serve your clients with a broader range of financial services. For the agent, this should mean increased earnings, a share of the investment market, more high-income prospects, and an expanded professional image. But this is only part of the story! The very nature of the financial service products offered to clients requires a review of their existing insurance and financial plans. As you become accustomed to including investment products in concert with life insurance presentations, you will gradually increase your skill in preparing a complete, personalized financial solution for your clients. Experience and skill in uncovering and selling needs, together with the potential of these exciting products, will increase your activity, professionalism, and earnings.

A new generation of insurance/financial professionals is being born, and you can be part of it. The knowledge and skill you gain through reading this book are just the initial step toward a future of enhanced professional standing in the eyes of your clients and peers. Prepare to take your place among the financial professionals of the '80s!

PART I

INVESTMENT PRODUCT SALES

1

Introduction to the Investment Products Sales Process

The success you have already achieved in your selling career is evidence that you already have the skill necessary to follow a sales process and make a sale. The purpose of this chapter is to show you how the same skills can be applied to a set of steps that form the equities sales process. Most of the information in this chapter will be familiar to you—fact finding, explaining features and benefits of products, and closing on minor points as you move toward the sale.

INVESTMENTS VERSUS LIFE INSURANCE

Before getting into the sales process itself, however, let's look at how selling investment products compares with selling life insurance.

1. Prospects for insurance are people who have a need and the ability to pay. Equities prospects are also people who have needs. Often these needs stem from the very fact that they have money to invest.
2. People with insurance needs often have difficulty recognizing those needs and deciding what to do about them. The important role of the life insurance agent is to help them make the right decision now. Making decisions on saving and investment is similar. People need someone to educate and advise them on how they might manage their money wisely.
3. While people may not want to talk about insurance, most

people do like to talk about money, especially those who have it.

To illustrate how your insurance career can be expanded into the investment area, let's look at a couple of kinds of sales opportunities for investment products.

The Lump Sum Purchase

Some of the best opportunities to provide a valuable service and make equities sales are found among people who have already accumulated money in other investment vehicles. Many people have money in savings accounts, CDs, stocks, bonds, etc., and they have financial objectives. The service you can offer is to review those objectives and make sure the investment vehicles match the objectives and provide the best plan for reaching them.

An objective review of the situation may show that one of the products your company offers would be a more appropriate solution to a particular money management problem than the client's current investments. For example, suppose someone is keeping a large amount of money in savings accounts and CDs, but he or she is more interested in long-term growth with tax advantages. You could recommend the purchase of shares in a growth fund, where much of the appreciation is taxed as long-term capital gains. The transfer of $15,000 from savings to such a fund could produce a better match for your client and a sales opportunity for you—namely, a commission based on a sales charge of $1,125 (7.5 percent on a $15,000 purchase)!

The Systematic Investor

Whenever a client has at least the minimum investment to start a particular program, and a long-term investment objective that can be reached by putting money aside on a regular basis, you have a good prospect to form a firm client base.

A prospect is someone who has:

- definite financial objectives;
- an adequate insurance plan; and
- liquid assets to invest.

The continuing flow of deposits will enable your client to reach specific objectives, while you build a base of continuing commissions. If you build a large clientele of systematic investors, the result will be a base of ongoing commissions similar to the renewal commissions from life and health sales.

IRA purchasers of mutual funds are one example. If you set up *one* $2,000 IRA mutual fund per week for the next 52 weeks, you could earn $4,862 in one year, and in five years you could have a base of $24,310 per year on the continuing IRA purchases (based on an $8^1/_2$ percent sales charge and a typical commission scale).

TELEPHONE SELLING

Account executives who sell stocks, bonds, mutual funds, and other similar products do a great deal of selling by phone. This is common to the securities business. Telephone selling is possible because the account executive has developed a good trust relationship with the clients and usually has a pretty good understanding of their financial circumstances. This is very similar to the relationship built by professional field underwriters with their clients.

When an account executive sells over the phone, it usually involves the handling of orders for buying or selling stocks and bonds for existing clients. When it comes to financial planning and selling mutual funds, however, the account executive operates more like a professional insurance agent. The selling is done face to face in the client's office or home. This is true of most kinds of interactive selling. Even products of proven need and value must be sold. They are rarely bought without a knowledgeable, persuasive salesperson on the scene.

This is where life insurance representatives have an edge. You are experts in face-to-face selling, and your company's reputation for personal service gives you a marketing advantage that the public has come to expect and appreciate.

Most of your selling interviews will allow you to complete part of your sales presentation over the phone. If you already know a good deal about your client's financial objectives and attitudes toward investing, you are already well into the sales process. What you say on the phone and the steps to follow are exactly the same as for selling insurance, with one important exception:

> *No discussion or sales presentation of a particular investment can be made unless your prospect has received a copy of the appropriate prospectus.*

This may cause you to wonder how account executives are able to sell by phone. It's really quite simple: much of the selling done by account executives involves the purchase and sale of stocks and bonds that do not require a prospectus. All mutual funds and limited partnerships require a prospectus, and anyone who sells these products must comply with the same rules.

Just how far can you go on the phone?

1. You can establish contact.
2. You can introduce the subject of investments.

3. You can obtain financial questionnaire information when only limited information is necessary.
4. When interest is aroused, you can indicate that you offer the products provided through your company and *identify* one or more of them.
5. You can offer to send a prospectus for a specific investment and indicate that you will call again in several days, after the client has received and had a chance to review the prospectus, in order to discuss the products further and answer any questions. *Or*
6. You can ask for an appointment to deliver a prospectus and discuss the equity program in detail.

You *CANNOT* use the first call to sell or even discuss a specific investment.

The objective of your first call—and, for that matter, of every call you make—is to get some kind of commitment. It may be a commitment to accept another call or an agreement from your client to accept and read a prospectus and sales literature that you will mail. When this has been done, you can call again and attempt to make a sale by phone. You will still need to get an application and a check for the initial purchase. Most representatives prefer to take care of this final step in person, but it is possible to have your clients take care of the details themselves, especially with money market funds.

The key points of telephone selling are listed below.

- Ask for permission to talk with the client for a definite length of time.
- Respect your client's time.
- Get a commitment from the client to do something in the future (think, read, accept another call).
- Make another call after you have sent the prospectus.

The important thing to remember is that you can neither *sell* an investment product without an accompanying prospectus nor *discuss* a specific mutual fund or limited partnership without a prospectus.

Here are some examples of telephone selling situations.

INITIAL CALL

"Hello, (client's name), this is (your name), your (company) agent. How are you?"

[Listen to response.]

"Is everything OK with your insurance program?"

[Listen to response.]

"That's fine, (client's name), just remember that I'm as near as the phone if you need me."

[Listen to response.]

"The reason I'm calling today is that I am offering a broad range of financial services that can supplement your insurance and investment program. This includes products like mutual funds and tax-sheltered plans. May I take a few minutes to give you a general overview of what we have to offer?"

[Follow with generic explanations only.]

If clients cannot give you the time you ask for, respect their wishes and follow with

"When could we get ______ minutes of privacy to talk on the phone?"

Asking for Financial Questionnaire Information After you have introduced the subject of investments, you should move to the next step in the sales process and do some fact finding to determine which product prospectus you should send the prospect.

"(Client's name), I'd like to send you a prospectus and some literature on investment products, but first I really need to know a little more about your investment and savings objectives. I'd like to take five or ten minutes to ask you some questions that will help me obtain what I call 'financial facts.' Could we do that now, or would you prefer that I call back at a more convenient time?"

[If the client agrees to discuss the financial facts now, proceed to the financial questionnaire dialogue later in this chapter. However, an in-depth fact-finding session usually will be handled face to face.]

Sending a Prospectus

"(Client's name), based on your objectives and feelings about investing, I think you'd find our (product) very interesting. I'm going to send you a prospectus and some information about this investment. I'll call you again after you've had a chance to read it over. May I call back about this time next (day)? Or would (day) be better?

[Listen to response.]

In telephone selling, it is important to be sensitive to your client's time. It is vital that you have uninterrupted time to communicate your ideas by phone. Always tell your client how much time you will need and get permission to use that time.

The preceding examples illustrate that an effective approach to selling equity products includes two important elements:

- a broad financial service statement, intended to sell yourself in this role; and
- mention of some of the general features of your investment products.

THE FINANCIAL QUESTIONNAIRE

Using a comprehensive financial questionnaire is an integral part of the financial planning process. Most companies that offer "advanced" life insurance and investment products make some form of questionnaire available to their agents. Though differences among them exist, the types of questions asked and the information gathered are essentially the same. If only some of this information is required, you may be able to take it over the phone. For an in-depth financial plan, however, you will need to take this information in person.

It is crucial during the fact-gathering interview to put your client at ease and to encourage him or her to be as candid as possible. The interview should be conducted in an atmosphere in which your client feels secure, free of annoyances and interruptions or any other distractions that will vie for his or her attention.

After some casual, introductory remarks, begin the interview with some basic, unthreatening questions.

Introductory Questions

"Mr./Ms. (client's name), to begin, please give me the full name, birth date, and social security number of each of your family members."

[Listen to reply.]

"Is this your first marriage?"

[If not, find out details concerning child support, alimony, etc. Then listen to reply.]

"Were all of your children born during this marriage?"

[Listen to reply.]

"Are all of your children living at home?"

[Listen to reply.]

Occupational Information

"Now I would like to ask you some questions concerning your employment. What is your occupation, and where are you currently employed?"

[Listen to reply.]

"How long have you been with your current employer?"

[Listen to reply.]

"What is your current base salary?"

[Listen to reply.]

"Do you receive any bonuses? If so, in what form are they paid?"

[Listen to reply.]

"Is your spouse currently employed?"

[If spouse is employed, obtain the same type of occupational information. Then, listen to reply.]

"Do you anticipate a raise within the next 12 months? If so, what amount?"

[Listen to reply.]

Information Concerning Additional Income

"It is important that I get a complete picture of your total income. With this in mind, are you currently receiving or do you anticipate receiving income from sources such as rental property, royalties, commissions, income from a trust, or other business income?"

[Listen to reply.]

"Before we leave the area of your family's income, are there any other sources we have not discussed?"

[Listen to reply.]

Identifying Assets

"In addition to income, those assets that you have accumulated add to your complete financial profile. Please identify those assets that are liquid; by this, I mean those that are readily available to you in a time of emergency. This would include savings accounts, money market funds, checking accounts, and money accumulated in a credit union. Let's begin with your savings accounts. In what bank do you have your savings account, and what is its current balance?"

[Listen to reply.]

"Do you currently have cash in a money market fund?"

[Listen to reply.]

"What fund have you invested in, and what is the current value of this account?"

[Listen to reply.]

"Where do you currently have your checking account, and what is the balance?"

[Listen to reply.]

"Are you currently saving money at a credit union?"

[Listen to reply.]

Illiquid Assets

"In addition to liquid assets, your financial profile is made up of assets that are considered illiquid. These would include funds deposited in a retirement program such as an IRA or a self-employed plan or possibly a pension plan through your employer. Do you currently have an Individual Retirement Account?"

[Listen to reply.]

"Where do you have your IRA funds invested, and what is the value of this account?"

[Listen to reply.]

"Do you have a self-employed retirement plan? Where are these funds invested, and what is the value of this account?"

[Listen to reply.]

"Do you have a pension plan at work?"

[Listen to reply.]

"What is the value of your pension plan, and are you vested in this program?"

[Listen to reply.]

Investment Portfolio

"Another element of your financial profile is your investment portfolio. To understand your investment objectives, the performance you seek, and the purpose of your investments, I need some information. So let's begin. What stocks do you own?"

[Listen to reply.]

"What is the current value of these shares?"

[Listen to reply.]

"Do you own any bonds?"

[Listen to reply.]

"Who issued the bonds, and what is their current value?"

[Listen to reply.]

"Do you own any mutual fund shares? If so, what is their current value?"

[Listen to reply.]

"Do you own any limited partnership interests? If so, please briefly describe the programs and their tax benefits."

[Listen to reply.]

"Do you have any other investments?"

[Listen to reply.]

Individually Owned Real Estate

"A significant investment for most people is individually owned real estate. I need the location of the property, its value, and any outstanding mortgages. Let's begin with your home. What is the value of your property, and is there a mortgage balance?"

[Listen to reply.]

"Do you own any other real estate?"

[Listen to reply.]

"Are there any outstanding mortgages on these properties?"

[Listen to reply.]

"What are the individual values of these properties?"

[Listen to reply.]

Other Personal Assets

"To complete a profile of your assets, please consider other items such as art, antiques, jewelry, automobiles, recreational vehicles, collections, and so forth. Please describe those items and give me their value."

[Listen to reply.]

Debt Information

"Assets are certainly only one side of the coin. To complete your financial profile, I will need information concerning any outstanding debts you may have. We have already discussed mortgages on your real estate holdings. Other than this, what debts do you currently have?"

[Listen to reply.]

"Please describe what these loans are for and their current balance?"

[Listen to reply.]

Life Insurance Program

"Life insurance plays an important part in any financial plan. To get a better understanding of your current program, I will need some rather specific information. Please begin by telling me what life insurance programs you currently have in force."

[Ask for specific information concerning the name of the company, death benefit, current cash value, type of policy, reason for purchasing the contract, premium amounts, and whether the contract is individually owned or part of a group insurance program. Then, listen to reply.]

Disability Income Insurance Program

"Statistically, the likelihood of disability is far greater than that of death. Do you currently have disability income protection?"

[Listen to reply.]

"Is this an individually owned program, or is it provided by your employer?"

[Listen to reply.]

"What are the total benefits paid by your program, what company do you have this program with, and what are the premiums you pay?"

[Listen to reply.]

Short-term Financial Goals

"Now that I have a complete picture of your financial situation, I would like to get a complete understanding of your short- and long-term goals. Short-term goals are generally considered those that are to be accomplished in one to three years. What short-term goals do you have?"

[Listen to reply and list your client's goals on a sheet of paper.]

"Now that you have listed your short-term goals, let's consider each individually and prioritize them."

[Have your client number the goals in their order of priority.]

Long-term Goals

"Now that we have listed and prioritized your short-term goals, let's consider your long-term objectives. These include objectives that would be accomplished beyond a three-year time period. What goals would fall into this area?"

[Listen to reply.]

"Now that your long-term goals have been listed, let's prioritize those as we did your short-term goals."

[Listen to reply.]

The preceding fact-finding discussion is only a suggested approach. Your individual areas of expertise, the products offered by the company or companies you represent, and the extent of the financial planning process you wish to pursue with your client will all determine just how comprehensive the fact-gathering process will be in each individual case.

As mentioned earlier, a telephone sales situation requires rather limited information, whereas an in-depth financial plan requires information approximating that gathered during an in-depth fact-finding session. You are the best judge as to which approach to take. It is recommended, however, that any in-depth interview be conducted separately from the selling interview. This will give you the opportunity to evaluate the disclosed information and make appropriate recommendations during the selling interview.

THE SELLING INTERVIEW

Your initial telephone call (or approach) sets the stage for the all-important selling interview. In the selling interview you will need to listen hard and probe to uncover all the additional facts you can about your client's financial objectives and plans. Just as in selling life insurance, you should gather the facts, interpret the needs, and make suitable recommendations at the close. The need may be for additional insurance, a mutual fund, a tax shelter, or perhaps a combination. Though you will depend more on logic than on emotion with investments, the sales process will be very similar to that for life insurance.

Here's how the selling interview looks on paper:

- overview of investment products;
- financial objectives and attitudes;
- specific investment product recommendation;
- close.

After you begin the interview with your normal breaking-the-ice introduction, you should say something to sell yourself as the provider of broad financial services, then add a few words about what investments and financial planning are all about. Before getting into any specifics, you should quickly move to the second step, determining the client's financial objectives and attitudes. This is a key step in selling equity products. It is much like needs analysis in insurance selling.

Your company's financial fact finder will guide you through this important step. The answers to the questions on this worksheet will help you determine the client's financial objectives and attitudes.

Sometimes you will already have much of the needed information from your previous dealings with your client. In such cases, you should enter the information you have *before* making your call. Then, in the interview, you can verify the data you have and obtain what you do not have. This will show your clients that you are interested in them and have taken the trouble to maintain an active file.

SPECIFIC EQUITY PRODUCT RECOMMENDATION

This step begins with the product's investment objective, which is stated in the prospectus. Next, the features and benefits of that particular product are explained. As you highlight the benefits for your prospect, you will be referring back to the objectives and attitudes uncovered earlier.

Finally, you will recommend *not only a product, but a specific transfer or allocation of money.* Here is one of the dramatic differences between insurance and securities selling. In the life insurance sales process, you sell the need, then negotiate a premium commitment. In investments, selling the solution is a composite of the product you recommend and the suggested amount of the investment. From your fact finding, you should know both the source(s) and the amount(s) of money you are going to recommend that your prospect invest and the investment product(s) most suitable for meeting the client's objectives.

To be successful as a salesperson, you must be able to build trust, determine objectives, and uncover liquid assets to invest *before* deciding on an investment recommendation. In making the recommendation, first explain why you believe that the investment you are suggesting will meet the prospect's needs and objectives.

THE CLOSE

Get agreement on minor points throughout the presentation and close along the way so that you are able to approach the buying decision from a position of strength.

None of this is new. Studies of the most successful life insurance salespeople have shown that a closing is not something that takes place at the end of a sales interview; rather, it is something that starts happening from the very beginning of the sales process and continues throughout the presentation itself. In the sale of investments, this is an absolute must. So how do you wrap up the sale? There are three steps you should follow as you make the final close:

1. Ask if there are any questions.
2. Highlight the product's objectives and benefits.
3. Make your recommendation.

SUMMARY

The sales process is really quite similar to everything you know and do already. The most important initial step in selling investment products is recognizing prospects. When clients have a sizable amount of money, they should do something with it. You will find many opportunities among people who do not know what to do with that money or who have simply not gotten around to doing something more appropriate with their money.

You can identify those prospects through your initial call, which will help you and the client decide how comprehensive a financial plan to pursue. The information yielded by the financial questionnaire will then allow you to come up with the best possible solution for your client's needs.

2

Investment Products Prospecting

Your first step in selling investment products, just as in life insurance selling, is to find people who need your services and who are willing to listen to your sales presentation. They are people who are concerned about their futures, who believe in and may already have a well-balanced program of insurance protection, and who are also financially able to carry out a program of investing or saving. Inflation and greater awareness of the long-term consequences of inflation have caused an explosion in the number of prospects who are looking for a wider range of financial services.

Public interest in and awareness of the need to accumulate and manage money are at an all-time high. Many people no longer think of saving and investing as being available only to the wealthy. Average citizens are becoming aware that such investments are within their reach. Most of your insurance clients and prospects are also investment prospects. Your grocer, doctor, service station owner, the dry cleaner down the street, teachers, members of clubs to which you belong, and a host of others are all prospects who want to hear about how they too may improve their financial situation.

Prospecting for investment products has the same objectives as everything you are doing now—to open doors, to provide services, to make sales, and to fill other needs from your complete life and nonlife insurance portfolio. The investments product line will complement and supplement the life insurance contracts you already have in force. Among those people who know and respect you and the work you have done, you will now find additional opportunities to sell insurance products. For the people you have not been able to see before, you now have a new and exciting reason to call—a reason that could lead to discussion and sale of the most appropriate product in your multiline portfolio.

What makes a person a prospect for investments? Ideal prospects are those with definite savings goals. This group includes people who are accumulating money to buy a house, send their children to college, provide a comfortable retirement—the same objectives you work with when you sell them life insurance. They may be working couples or single individuals who are simply interested in accumulating funds to improve their future standard of living.

From the wide variety of products offered in our industry, you can select an investment for these prospects, designed to meet their short, medium, and long-range savings goals. Qualifying and selecting your prospect is just as important as in selling life insurance and other lines. An investment prospect is someone who has:

- definite financial objectives;
- an adequate insurance program;
- liquid assets to invest;
- plus an emergency fund.

It's important to realize that a prospect should have both an emergency fund *and* liquid assets. Without an emergency fund, those liquid assets are not truly free for investment. *Liquid assets* here means money to put to work in savings accounts, mutual funds, real estate investments, stocks, bonds, etc. The good news is that these funds are often not the same ones used to pay life insurance premiums. Inflation has brought with it increased insurance needs, increased incomes, and more financial decisions to be made. As a life insurance professional, you are already dealing with some of your best investment products prospects. Also, as a financial services professional, you will generally be discussing investments *after* you and your client have considered all needs.

One advantage of having investment products available is that you can open doors that may have been difficult to open using your life insurance approach. Agents of other life insurance companies who have started selling mutual funds and limited partnerships report that investment products open doors to ideas like money market funds and create new opportunities to clients. You probably know people who like to invest but do not have the time or experience to manage a securities portfolio properly. Undoubtedly, you already have clients who are keeping their savings in low-interest passbook savings accounts.

The list of potential prospects is extensive. People you know, as well as people you have yet to meet, will be interested in hearing about the broad range of financial services you now have to offer. Your next step is to bring this information directly to them. Because investment products selling, like life insurance selling, is highly dependent on a trust relationship, you will find present clients and policyholders to be the best place to begin your prospecting activity. When it comes to money matters, people prefer to deal with companies and individuals they have come to know and trust.

The balance of this chapter will show you how to sell investment products through these familiar prospecting sources and methods:

- clients and policyholders
- other prospects
- referred leads
- direct mail

PRESENT POLICYHOLDERS AND CLIENTS

Policyholders and clients who have bought from you before will be some of your best prospects for sales. People who know and trust you as their agent and are familiar with the strength of your company form a natural market for you. You already know a great deal about the needs, objectives, and financial condition of these people, and getting an appointment to present an interesting new idea should be fairly easy.

When you call your clients, there are three steps you should follow:

1. Reinforce your agent/client relationship.
2. Tell your client about the financial services you have to offer.
3. Ask for the appointment.

CALLING PROSPECTS

Here is an example of what you might say in a call to a prospect.

"Hello, (client's name). This is (your name), your (company) agent. How are you?"

[Listen to response.]

"I'm calling you today to tell you that (company) is now a provider of broad financial services. But first, do you have any questions or problems with your life insurance program?"

[Listen to response.]

"That's fine, (client's name). Just remember that I'm as near as the phone, if you need me. I'm quite excited about the financial services I mentioned. They include money market funds, other mutual funds, and tax-sheltered plans. They're all designed to supplement and complement your present insurance program. I'd really like to stop by and show you what this means for you. Would (day) at (time) be good, or would (day) at (time) be better?"

[Listen to response.]

Here is another way you could approach someone who has bought from you before:

"Hello, (client's name). This is (your name), your (company) agent. I'm sure you know that I appreciate the confidence you have placed in me before, and I'm anxious to continue giving you efficient personalized service, to keep that confidence and help you maintain a well-balanced financial program. Do you have any questions about your insurance today?"

[Listen to response.]

"That's fine, (client's name). Just remember that I'm as close as the phone if you need me. (Client), another reason for my call is to make you aware of a broad range of services that may supplement your insurance program, such as money markets, other mutual funds, and tax-sheltered plans. Some of the investment plans I'd like to show you might tie in nicely with the financial objectives you talked about when we developed your insurance program last (approximate date). I'd like to stop by and tell you all about them. Would (day) at (time) be good, or would (day) at (time) be better?"

[Listen to response.]

When making prospecting and approach calls, you must remember that you are indeed selling an idea and the appointment you want to make, but most of all, you are trying to sell *yourself* as the one who can offer a broad range of financial services. Of course, whatever your approach, you cannot expect to get every appointment the first time you ask for it. When a prospect hesitates to make an appointment with you, you will need to tie your reason for calling to what you already know about each individual, based on the fact-finding questions you asked as you helped develop each person's insurance program. Some additional ideas that will help get your prospect's attention and help them see the value of your meeting follow.

"Some of the investment plans I'd like to show you would tie in nicely with the financial objectives you talked about when we developed your insurance program last (approximate date)."

[Give examples, which may include the following.]

"Whether you're interested in growth, income, or tax savings, you can select a program tailored to your objectives. . . .

"The investment opportunities we have available enable you to spread your risk and provide the benefit of experienced investment specialists. . . .

"As I recall, you were not too happy about all the taxes you have to pay. Some of the ideas I want to share with you are designed to provide real tax relief. . . ."

Resistant Policyholders The first prospects you approach should be all of your current policyholders and transfer clients, and you should use your most effective method to generate additional sales of life insurance and non–life insurance products. There are, however, times when these potential clients just don't respond to your attempts to set up an appointment. Some policyholders may resist your attempts to set a life-oriented appointment or resist making a transition from a non–life product sale. We know from experience that these prospects are not rejecting you or your reason for calling; they simply must be approached differently.

What it comes down to is that these prospects just do not want to be exposed to someone who probably wants to sell life insurance. Now you can talk about saving, investing, and money management plans from the variety of programs offered through your company. This gives another reason to call, another reason for the prospects to grant you an appointment. Your approach might be as follows.

"Hello, Mr./Ms. (client's name). This is (your name), from (company). How are you?"

[Listen to reply.]

"We issued a policy for (insureds) some time ago, and your records have been assigned to me for service. I'd like you to know who I am, and I need to review your contracts and bring my records up to date."

[Discuss those contracts and listen to comments from client.]

"We also have some new information available to all of our clients concerning a broad range of financial services, including money market funds with check-writing privileges. I'd like to make that information available to you. Would next (day) at (time) be convenient, or would (day) at (time) be better?"

[Listen to reply.]

Since you may not have had an opportunity to learn a great deal about the financial needs and personal objectives of these policyholders, you could also try to set up an appointment on the strength of a particular idea like a money market fund or an IRA.

Once into an interview, you can probe for a dominant insurance need before you make an investment presentation. Stress the idea that mutual funds, IRAs, tax shelters, and savings should be considered only after establishing a basic foundation of life insurance protection.

OTHER PROSPECTS

Prospecting has always been an effective method in life insurance selling, whether the strategy was to address single needs, to address total needs, or to build clients. The news of a new home, a new job, a new baby, a promotion, or a new business has always signaled a possible change in a person's insurance protection needs. With investment products, the situations are a little different—the signal here will be the news of new money to be managed and invested.

Remember, your prospect is someone with definite financial objectives and money to invest. Whenever one of your policyholders, friends, clients, or prospects has a lump sum of cash on hand, he or she will need the kind of advice and service you can deliver with either a traditional insurance product or a variety of your company's investment products.

The following situations typically produce these sums of money:

- maturing endowments
- inheritances
- home sales
- IRA rollovers
- certificates of deposit
- income-tax refunds
- bonuses, salary increases
- death claims
- liability claims

The effective salesperson is always fact-finding to be in touch when these situations arise. Your group of investment products will include features, objectives, and the professional management needed to maximize the use of the assets involved. You will learn more about how to uncover these situations later, but now let's look at how you might approach a person that you know has the cash to invest.

"Hello, (client's name). This is (your name), from (company). How are you?"

[Listen to response.]

"According to my record (*or* The last time we spoke, you told me that), you will be receiving (X dollars) from (source) around (date). I promised at that time that I would get back to you with some ideas as to how I might offer you a good return on your money with a high degree of safety. I have that information available now. I'd like to stop by and go over it with you on (day) at (time), or would (day) at (time) be better?"

[Listen to response.]

If your prospect agrees to the appointment, fine! If the prospect raises an objection, bring the conversation back to the investment objective you discussed when you spoke last or probe for interest in inflation, tax savings, or additional income to stimulate interest in the benefits your portfolio provides. The same skills and techniques you have used so successfully in the past are the ones that you will use as a financial services professional now. The sales process is the same; your expanded service and product lines are the exciting differences.

CASH-DATING

You guessed it; this is the investment products' version of X-dating used by the multiline professionals. Cash-dating is the method that uncovers records and manages prospecting activity around policy expiration dates. For the investment products salesperson, the best time to sell a new program or add to an old one is when liquid assets are in the hands of the client.

When you cash-date, you find out when your prospect/client will have additional amounts of money coming in and record the information on your calendar. Start calling back 30 days before that date and determine which product would be most appropriate for your client's objectives.

Here is the way it works. As you meet with prospects and fact-find for financial planning, pay particular attention to where your prospects invest their money and *when* it will be available again for reinvestment. That is your cash date.

When you find that you have uncovered a cash date, do three things in your call to the client:

1. Tell the client the news.
   "I am now a provider of broad financial services, including money market and other mutual funds, as well as investment opportunities that provide tax relief. . . ."

2. Probe for general investment objective or interest.
   "When the time comes for (re)investing that money, will you be looking for income? Growth?"

   [Listen to response.]

3. Get agreement for call-back.
   "I'd like to get back to you a few weeks before you make a decision and show you what I could do for you. Would that be all right"

   [Listen to response.]

To continue the sales process, make sure you record all the information you obtain and follow up 30 days before the money is available. You will be anxious to make the call, knowing the prospect has already agreed to listen and has shared an investment attitude with you. That's trust!

Here are some specific examples of situations or events that produce $-dates:

Certificates of Deposit, Treasury Notes, etc. Your prospect/client tells you that he or she will have, say, $10,000 in a 30-month CD that will come due four months from now. Cash-date and call again in three months with a better idea.

Income-Tax Refunds Many people receive a tax refund every year. In fact, some people actually view this as a forced savings plan. Probe to find out if your prospect pays additional taxes or gets a refund. Either way, you have a potential investment sale. For the person with a refund, you have a cash date. For people who pay more taxes when they file, you can suggest a tax-saving idea like a municipal bond fund or an IRA.

Inheritances When a small policy is submitted for claim, keep in mind that other assets in the estate may also pass to the person with whom you are dealing. Those assets are going to be used or invested somewhere by the beneficiaries. Find out how and when and follow up with an investment idea.

Note: If you have worked with trust officers, attorneys, and accountants in the past, don't forget to schedule a meeting and make them aware of your broad range of financial services.

Bonuses and Salary Increases Anytime you fact-find for assets and income, be sure to probe for bonus payments and ask your prospects when their salary is likely to change. Most people can tell you when their salary will change and give some idea of how much it will be increased. Some even have the option of taking increases in the form of lump sum payments. Effective fact finding may uncover a need for more objective management of these increases in the future. Cash-date the increase or bonus if your client wants to put the money to work.

The more you talk about the fact that you provide a broad range of financial services and money management ideas, the more chances you will have to find people with assets. You can suggest an investment product to these people as the place to put money to work for higher yields, safety, and full-time professional management. Some additional situations or events that may come to your attention are:

- home sales, resulting in investment capital;
- pension rollovers, and
- liability claim settlements.

Awareness is the key word here. Your prospects and clients need to be *aware* of the fact that you now have the products to meet many of their investment needs. You need to be *aware* of what your clients are doing with their money. This is where client building and staying in touch will really pay off in additional sales earnings.

REFERRED LEADS

Long recognized as one of the best and most productive prospecting methods of the insurance professional, referred leads will prove to be equally effective for financial services. The use of referred leads is, of course, based on some valuable service or idea you provide for one person who is impressed enough to recommend you to others. In the case of equities selling, you have the added advantage of asking for referrals to other people who are in a financial position to be interested in things like extra income, money market funds, growth opportunities, and tax shelters. The use of referred leads helps you qualify as you prospect.

Even though you may get a referral from an investment buyer and get an appointment with your newest prospect based on an equities idea, you are still a multi-line professional. You know how to move back to insurance needs whenever there is a need for additional insurance. Here are some models you can use for getting and contacting referred leads.

Asking for Referred Leads

"(Client's name), as you can see, this is a great service we are offering, and there are many people who do not know about it. With something as personal and important as money management, people usually prefer to deal with a reputable company, so what I need to do is get them to know me. I'd like to share some of these ideas with people you know, people with similar interests and concerns about finances. May I ask you some questions?"

[Listen to response.]

With whom do you socialize?"

[Listen to response.]

"Who works with you?"

[Listen to response.]

"Whom do you talk to about money matters?"

[Listen to response.]

"Who asks your opinion or advice?"

[Listen to response.]

"(Client's name), when I see these people, is it OK to mention that I know you?"

Contacting Referred Leads

"Hello, (prospect's name). This is (your name), from (company). How are you?"

[Listen to response.]

"Recently, I had the opportunity of being of service to a (some) friend(s) of yours: (friend's names). Nice people, aren't they?"

[Listen to response.]

"They were very interested to hear that I am able to offer broad financial services, including money market funds and other investment products, as well as tax relief ideas. When I told them I wanted to share these services with a few people they know, you (and spouse's name) were the first people (person) they mentioned. I'd really like to stop by and discuss the subject with you and show you what this is all about. Would (day) at (time) be good, or would (day) at (time) be more convenient?"

[Listen to response.]

If you run into objections, tell the prospect more about the financial services you have to offer and talk about the growing problems of inflation, money management, taxes, etc.

Policy Proceeds

The payment of policy proceeds represents an ideal opportunity for financial review that might lead to an investment recommendation. Beneficiaries of claimants, suddenly presented with a large amount of cash from a maturing endowment or death proceeds from a life policy for a personal injury claim settlement are going to need a safe place to put those funds. What would be better for your client than a vehicle that offers professional money management, the benefits of diversification, a hedge against inflation, and the wide variety of services offered through your company?

The period following the death of a loved one is often hectic and very emotional. During this time rational decisions, particularly about the final disposition of policy proceeds, are difficult to make. Your role, as an advisor and a counselor to your client, is to recommend a product that will preserve the capital and possibly produce gains in the process. Investment products, particularly money market funds, could achieve those goals. A suggested approach when called upon to service a death claim could be as follows.

Death Claim (Agent Completing Claim Forms)

"Mr./Mrs. (client's name), I would like to extend my sympathies to you and your family. I know this is a difficult time for you, but part of our claim process is to complete these forms. I'd like to help you with them, if you can spare a few moments at this time."

[Listen to response.]

During the completion of the claim forms, at the point at which you have explained the settlement options, pick up with this statement:

"Mr./Ms. (client's name), other options are available to you. You may have heard that I am able to offer a broad range of financial services; for example, mutual funds, including money market funds and tax shelter products. I think it would be helpful if I explained them to you."

You must remember that this particular time is very difficult for beneficiaries. They will need your help, the service you can provide, more now than ever. But this approach requires much sensitivity and empathy on your part. One of the suggestions you can make is to have the proceeds placed, for example, in a money market fund, which would be advantageous to your client. With the money market fund there will be no sales charges to decrease the proceeds. When the beneficiaries are better able to make rational financial decisions, such as to purchase additional insurance or to transfer proceeds to a load fund with specific investment objectives, you will have an opportunity to provide the proper insurance or investment services.

On some occasions claim checks are mailed directly to the insured if the claim is submitted directly to the home office. You would certainly still be able to call the beneficiary and express your sympathy for the family's loss and offer to be of service in advising them on the use of the policy proceeds. Your telephone call might sound like this:

Death Claim (Claim Check Mailed by Home Office)

"Mr./Ms. (client's name), this is (your name), from (company). I would like to extend my sympathies to you and your family on your recent loss. You have received (will be receiving) a check representing the proceeds of the life insurance claim you filed. At this time, you may not be ready to make a decision as to what you want to do with those funds, but I would like to recommend that you handle them very carefully.

"You may be interested to know that I am able to offer broad financial services, including money market funds with high yields and no sales charges. This might be a good place for a safe, temporary investment of that money at a competitive rate of return. I would like to stop by on (day) at (time) for a few moments to discuss these services. If that's not convenient, would (day) at (time) be better?"

[Listen to response.]

DIRECT MAIL

Many agents find that mailing a pre-approach letter improves their chances of getting an appointment when they make their initial call. Any time you send out mail, be sure to follow up with a phone call. Remember that the effectiveness of any mail program is improved significantly by a prompt follow-up telephone call. Any direct mail letter you use *must* be approved by your company *before* it is mailed to a potential client!

Another important rule of direct mail programs: *Qualify your mailing list!* Your results really depend on the quality of your mailing list. Since one of the necessary ingredients of investment selling is available liquid assets to invest, you will want to make certain that your direct mail reaches the person most likely to have assets to invest. Mailing lists should be targeted to middle- or upper-income prospects. Do not waste time and money sending investment-type mailings to everyone in town. When following up direct mail, you could say:

> "Mr./Ms. (prospect's name), this is (your name), from (company). Did you receive the letter I sent you a couple of days ago?"
>
> *[Listen to response.]*
>
> "That's why I'm calling. As you may know, I am able to offer a broad range of financial services, including money market and other mutual funds, as well as various tax relief ideas. With interest rates and taxes what they are, I'm sure you'll find these services both interesting and valuable. I'd like to stop by on (day) at (time) for a few moments to discuss these new services, or would (day) at (time) be more convenient?"
>
> *[Listen to response.]*

SUMMARY

There you have it! The prospecting skills you are currently using for life insurance sales can easily be adapted and modified to apply to investment product sales. Prospecting among policyholders, with referred leads, and by direct mail has worked for you before and will work now in equities selling. Finding someone to talk to is still the lifeblood of selling, but now you need to find the investment assets too. You are going to get some surprises as you move into this new dimension of our business. You are going to discover money where you did not expect to find it.

Most of your investments prospects are going to be among the higher-income segment of your clientele, perhaps with two incomes, but do not overlook the possibility that some folks of apparently modest means may have some very large nest eggs that could be earning more for them.

As you are selling equities products, try all of the prospecting methods and seek opportunities to expand the financial services you provide for your clients.

3

Determining a Client's Suitability for Mutual Fund Investments

The various types of mutual funds available offer good investment opportunities for many of your clients. Before you begin the mutual fund sales process, however, you must be sure that your prospects are qualified for this type of investment and that mutual funds are suitable for their needs.

STABILITY

Before investing in a mutual fund, clients should have an adequate emergency fund, sufficient to provide for the unexpected. Funds recently invested should not be liquidated for this purpose. An ideal "parking place" for these contingency funds would be a money market fund. This type of investment offers the liquidity as well as the stability or safety necessary for funds that may be needed on very short notice.

It is equally important that investors have an adequate insurance program. This program should be designed to provide the protection that is emphasized in any comprehensive financial planning procedure. By utilizing a financial questionnaire, you will be able to determine easily if the clients are protected adequately.

Your financial questionnaire will also allow you to identify the position of your clients' current assets. The clients' primary concern should be whether or not the assets are being utilized for maximum productivity.

SUITABILITY

Many investors' first step into the stock market is an investment in mutual funds or unit investment trusts. The reasons are many. The open-end investment company provides diversification and professional management of the investors' fund in a single vehicle. Furthermore, mutual funds stand ready to redeem outstanding shares at any time investors choose to present them for redemption and will issue new shares whenever the investors make a purchase.

The first consideration in choosing a mutual fund should be whether or not the fund's objective matches your client's goals. Mutual funds fall into four broad categories based on investment goal:

- income
- growth-income
- growth
- aggressive growth (maximum capital growth)

Some of the features of each type of mutual fund are discussed below:

INCOME FUND

An income fund invests in bonds or other fixed income securities that pay dividends. Expenses are subtracted from the dividends, and the resulting net dividends are distributed to the shareholder. The managers of these funds usually follow a flexible investment policy that permits an income-oriented combination of bonds and preferred and common stock. These funds are more appropriate for investors seeking a potential for above-average return. The underlying investments range from direct obligations of the United States government to lower-rated corporate bonds.

For investors seeking tax-exempt income, a number of tax-exempt funds have been organized. These fully managed funds, made possible by the Tax Reform Act of 1976, invest mainly in a diversified portfolio of municipal bonds and can best provide shareholders with income exempt from federal income taxes. Depending on the portfolio, all or part of the income may be exempt from state as well as federal income tax.

Furthermore, investors who do not need the income provided by such funds can automatically reinvest all distributions and achieve a cumulative effect of tax-exempt features without additional sales charges.

GROWTH-INCOME FUND

The objective of a growth-income fund is to achieve long-term growth of capital while providing some income. Growth-income funds usually invest in common stock, which pay dividends. This is in contrast to growth funds that invest in growth-type stocks paying little or no dividends. In addition to common stocks, many growth-income funds invest in preferred stocks and bonds. Due to the investment restrictions in the prospectus, portfolio managers will hold the investment for longer periods of time. This results in a higher degree of price stability than with funds whose major objective is strictly growth.

GROWTH FUND

The objective of growth funds is capital appreciation. Some growth funds are more volatile than others, but growth funds generally keep most of their assets and common stock at all times. Growth funds are suitable for investors who want to build capital and who do not seek current income. Distribution may be reinvested or realized automatically.

The portfolio managers of growth funds will acquire high-quality and undervalued common stocks. As a result, these funds will tend to perform conservatively, offering a good potential for growth with a minimal amount of risk. The major objective of most growth-oriented investors is the conversion of ordinary income to long-term capital gains. This should provide the investor with an opportunity for the maximum capital gain by minimizing the effect of taxation.

AGGRESSIVE GROWTH (MAXIMUM CAPITAL GAIN) FUNDS

Aggressive growth funds offer a very speculative and volatile investment opportunity for investors who have the risk tolerance and cash flow to handle the situation. Most investors will not be willing to accept this risk and those who do should be aware of the fact that the speculative aggressive growth investment should constitute only a small portion of their total investment program.

Aggressive growth funds are divided into three types:

- emerging growth
- developing growth
- specialized emerging growth

Emerging Growth Funds These funds invest in smaller and usually poorly capitalized businesses. Because of their young age, these businesses do not have a long history to be analyzed. The fund managers must be confident that they have very strong potential for success. The emerging growth fund is very speculative and volatile.

Developing Growth Funds These funds offer a slightly less speculative alternative then emerging growth funds. They invest in financially sound businesses and reinvest profits in the business. These businesses have financial histories and records of success.

Specialized Emerging Growth Funds Many of these funds are reinvested in various penny stocks and other specialized investments. Specialized emerging growth funds, like emerging growth funds, are very speculative and highly volatile.

The speculative nature and volatility of these funds offer investors maximum advantage of dollar cost averaging. Aggressive investors will see a drop in the market as a golden opportunity to invest in more shares. Rather than a time to sell, a reduction in the market is the time to buy. Buying shares regularly, even in a very low market, will result in a lower cost to investors.

When recommending an aggressive growth fund, you should carefully consider the effect of taxation. As mentioned earlier, the maximum capital gain can be achieved when ordinary income is converted to long-term capital gain. If the turnover ratio of a fund is more than 2:1, or two complete turnovers in a year, then the gains will be short-term instead of long-term. Registered representatives should be very careful to examine the prospectus to determine the turnover ratio. This ratio can be found in the *Per Share Income and Capital Changes* section of the prospectus. The following example will illustrate the difference between receiving a long-term gain and receiving a short-term gain.

Mr. Prospect invests in a very aggressive growth fund that does well and receives a profit of $1,000, which represents 29 percent growth. Mr. Prospect's aggressive fund has a turnover ratio of 4:1, which means the gain will be short-term and treated as ordinary income. Mr. Suspect invests in a growth fund with a very low turnover ratio because most investments are held for a long term. Mr. Suspect also receives a $1,000 profit, which reflects 20 percent growth. Mr. Prospect's rate of growth is much higher than Mr. Suspect's, but does Mr. Prospect really make more money (assuming a 50 percent tax bracket)?

Mr. Prospect		Mr. Suspect	
$1,000	short-term gain	$1,000	long-term gain
–$ 500	tax in 50% bracket	–$ 600	tax exclusion
$ 500	profit	$ 400	taxable income
			($200 tax in 50% bracket)
		$1,000	gain
		–$ 200	tax
		$ 800	profit

Even though Mr. Prospect had 9 percent more growth than Mr. Suspect, who really was the wiser investor?

USE OF MUTUAL FUNDS IN RETIREMENT PLANS

One of the most exciting and untapped markets for mutual funds could very well be in the retirement planning area. Although mutual funds have been used for years to fund individual programs such as IRAs, TSAs, self-employed pension plans, and Qualified Corporate Pension Plans, a large percentage of pension funds are still deposited with banks. The Employment Retirement Income Security Act (ERISA) requirement that the "prudent man rule" must be observed by fiduciaries has opened the door to many opportunities. In short, plan administrators now must monitor the performance of the plan to ensure that it is achieving a reasonable return when compared to other investment indexes. In many cases, the bank will not be competitive. This means the plan is not being maintained solely for the benefit of the participants, as required by ERISA. The plan administrator may be liable for the losses that may result from failure to manage the funds properly.

This, along with the desire to increase productivity, will motivate the plan holder to move the funds from the bank. These and many other sales ideas, as well as additional technical information, are discussed at greater length in Chapters 1 and 2.

CASE STUDIES

The following are case studies that depict real-life situations. You will find that reading these carefully will give you not only a feel for what financial planning entails, but also insights into the creative sales opportunities that exist in this area. You will find that expanding your horizons will allow you to serve your client better.

Each case study that follows begins with a summary of the information collected during a fact-finding interview. Then a recommended solution for the clients' financial needs is presented.

EXTRA INSURANCE WITHOUT REDUCED INCOME

Your clients are Mark and Sharon Wood, who live in a midsize western city. Mark owns and operates his own business, which he established 18 years ago. The business is involved in warehousing special metal and then retailing it to the aerospace industry. Mark's business does a large dollar volume but has relatively few employees. He currently draws a salary of $80,000 a year and is quite proud of the fact that he founded the business with nothing but an idea and subsequently developed it into one of the highest-sales small businesses in the area. Mark has been able to establish a rather substantial pension program through his business and uses the corporation to provide many other perks that, in addition to his income, permit Sharon and him to enjoy a very comfortable lifestyle. Mark's salary is all he considers necessary to take out of the business, although the cash flow and profits of the business could provide a considerably larger amount if he so desired.

Mark and Sharon have two children. One is 18 years old and will go to college this year; the other is a 14-year-old who is just starting high school. After their children began school, Sharon decided she would like to take an active role in the business and now works as the company's bookkeeper. She takes a token salary from the business of $18,000 per year, which she uses to support her hobbies and other activities. Both Mark and Sharon are in their late 40s and have reached a point in life where they are enjoying the rewards of their labor. Both are looking forward to the time when their children are out of college and they can retire. As part of their financial and estate planning programs they have provided adequate amounts of life insurance on each other. Business life insurance plans covering a buy-sell arrangement, and key people in the business have been established.

Mark and Sharon developed a financial plan several years ago and have been conscientious about updating their plan, which will ensure the passage of their estate assets in a way they consider appropriate for their heirs. During the fact-finding phase, you have identified the need for additional life insurance to meet estate liquidity needs. Your analysis indicates that $250,000 of additional life insurance is needed because of increased assets in the estate since their last review.

Mark and Sharon have developed a broad-based investment program as part of their financial plan, which includes a sizable number of stocks, bonds, money market funds, bank savings account, and growth-oriented mutual funds, as well as a number of real estate investments. As mentioned earlier, Mark has established a qualified corporate pension plan with the business and has funded that plan with a portfolio of investments that mirror his personal program. In addition to the company's pension plan, Mark and Sharon have each established IRA's and are making substantial annual purchases of tax-exempt unit investment trusts that invest in municipal bonds. Their current objective is to purchase the additional life insurance, but they would like to do so in a way that would not require the premium to come from their current income.

A Recommended Approach As determined from the fact-finding interview, Mark and Sharon would like to purchase the additional life insurance, but they do not wish to reduce their current income to do so. They feel that they have committed enough of their funds to insurance premiums. The solution in this case would be to direct a portion of their investment program to the purchase of a good growth-income fund. The growth-income fund would generate substantial dividend income that could be used to provide the premium dollars necessary for the purchase of the additional life insurance. Since the growth-income fund offers income coupled with growth, all or a portion of the capital gains distributions could be used for premiums, if necessary. It would make good tax sense for Mark and Sharon to purchase the fund and then gift the fund to one of their children in a Uniform Gifts Minors Act account. The child would also own the insurance. The dividends from the fund would now be taxable to the child. This would reduce the tax liability for Mark and Sharon, providing an additional tax benefit.

RETIRE IN STYLE

Your clients are John and Sarah Williams, who live in a comfortable neighborhood located just outside a major metropolitan area in Florida. John was an engineer for Tennessee Valley Authority (TVA) and is quite proud of the fact that he began at a low level in the company and worked his way up. John went to college while he was working for TVA and graduated with an engineering degree. After receiving his degree, he was able to climb the management ladder, ultimately earning well in excess of $50,000 a year. Last year John retired, and he and Sarah moved to Florida. John receives a pension of $1,857 a month from his retirement program at the TVA, plus social security in the amount of $1,254 per month.

When John and Sarah decided to retire and move to Florida, they sold their home in Tennessee, where they had lived for 27 years. Both are very proud of the fact they they were able to buy their home in Florida without having to take out a mortgage. They are very comfortable with the fact that their home is paid for and that they do not have to worry about mortgage payments during their retirement. Ten years ago John and Sarah's oldest daughter and her husband were killed in an automobile accident. Their grandaughter Jane, who is now 11 years old, moved in with John and Sarah, and they have been financially responsible for her since. John and Sarah want to be sure that funds are available for Jane's college education in eight years.

Over the years, John and Sarah have made several good investments. Among these are several pieces of real estate, some rental property, a rather substantial portfolio of stocks and bonds, and several mutual funds. The major emphasis of their investment program over the years has been growth. John and Sarah have also been conscientious about their estate planning program. They have provided adequate amounts of life insurance and have taken steps necessary to ensure that there will be adequate liquidity from the assets in their estate to pass to their beneficiaries, regardless of who dies first. Since most of their investments have been directed toward capital growth, their primary objective at this point in time is to establish an investment program that will supplement their retirement income. John and Sarah also wish to set aside funds for Jane's college education. These funds should be available in eight years.

A Recommended Approach Since the Williamses' primary objective is to produce income that will supplement their retirement income, you must first look at their tax situation to see if investments in tax-exempt securities might be adequate. Upon examination, you see that John and Sarah have a relatively low taxable income. Thus, it becomes apparent that tax-exempt programs are not appropriate and that the Williamses need investments that will provide the highest possible return. The first recommendation, in this case, would be for John and Sarah to sell their stocks. Since their objective has changed from growth to income, the stocks are no longer appropriate. The proceeds of the stock sale should be invested in a GNMA unit investment trust, which will provide high income, stability, and safety. The problem of educating their granddaughter could then be solved by investing the income from the GNMAs in a high-quality, nine-year-maturity corporate zero unit investment trust. The zero would be given to the minor in a Uniform Gifts to Minors Act account. This shifts the tax liability from John and Sarah to the child. This process should be repeated for four years, thereby providing maturity of a zero each year Jane is in college. After the initial four purchases, the income from the GNMA will be at John and Sarah's disposal to supplement their retirement income.

Smart Tax Business

Your clients are Al and Jan Wilder, who live in a small town outside a major East Coast city. Al is a salesman for one of the leading manufacturing companies in town, where he has been employed for the past 12 years. He entered the sales department as a trainee and has subsequently become one of the top sales people in the company. Al enjoys job security and feels that he has unlimited career potential. He has continuously increased his income over the years and will earn approximately $42,000 with bonuses this year. Next year, it is reasonable to expect that his earnings will exceed $50,000.

Al and Jan have two children, one 14 and the other 12. After the youngest child started school, Jan decided she wanted work, so they invested in a small shop that specializes in selling and servicing sewing machines. She and All started the shop with a small cash outlay and have subsequently developed it into a rather substantial business. Jan calculates her income to be $40,000 per year.

Both are in their early 40s and are enjoying the rewards of their collective success. Al and Jan could take more from the business if needed, since the business is very cash-heavy at this time. Profits are increasing constantly, and Jan and Al are becoming very concerned about their additional income from a tax standpoint.

Several years ago, Al and Jan began a life insurance program that has been reviewed annually; in fact, they have been conscientious about keeping their life insurance programs up to date. They have also begun implementing a total financial plan by building the foundation of their existing investment. Their investment program consists of an ample amount of money in a savings account to handle emergencies, cash value in a universal life insurance policy, mutual funds that stress conservative growth, and two small pieces of real estate, which they hope will appreciate substantially between now and their retirement. Jan and Al have also established IRAs and are considering the possibility of establishing a qualified pension plan for Jan at her shop since it is a corporation.

Al and Jan have two major concerns:

1. They feel that over the years they have been very conservative in their investment program and now it is time to become more aggressive, which would offer them greater opportunities than their current program. This is their major goal.
2. Their second concern is that they need additional tax relief. They feel that by adding a qualified pension plan they would be able to put away more funds for their retirement on a tax-favored basis.

A Recommended Approach As you learned in the fact-finding interview, Al and Jan's concerns lie in two basic areas: (1) more growth and (2) additional tax relief. These goals could be met by implementing a qualified pension plan in Jan's business. You would recommend a defined contribution pension plan, which Jan would fund each year. This plan could also be coupled with a profit-sharing plan that would permit some flexaibility in the amount of funding. In good years, Jan could take advantage of the maximum contribution allowed by law, and in bad years she would not be locked into that higher percentage. You would recommend that the initial investment in a pension plan be made in an aggressive growth mutual fund. Due to the tax-favored nature of the pension investment, this would allow a tremendous expansion in the investment program with no additional tax liability.

Now that you have taken maximum advantage of the pension, you can turn your attention to reducing corporate taxes. Jan's corporation could make additional investments in a tax-managed trust that invests exclusively in domestic corporations. The dividends paid to Jan's corporation would be subject to an 85 percent exclusion from taxes for the corporation. This exclusion of income from taxation would provide additional tax relief that is so vital to Al and Jan at the present time.

LANDLORDS REACH LIMIT

Jerry and Ann Thomas live in a resort city in the mountains of Tennessee. They own and operate two motels in the city. The net income from the motels is approximately $75,000 a year. Jerry and Ann also own several other income properties in the area, which generate an additional $36,000 in net income. Both Jerry and Ann were born in the community and went to high school there. Both their families owned property in the area for generations, and these properties were inherited by Jerry and Ann.

Jerry went to a major university in the area, where he received a degree in business administration. Jerry has been responsible for developing the inherited raw land into the income property he and Ann currently own. Ann makes a very substantial contribution to the business by managing the properties. Both Jerry and Ann are in their late 30s and are happy with their real estate investments.

Several loans that Jerry and Ann took out for the construction of the second motel and one other rental property building will be paid off in the next few months. This will increase their net income by $78,000 a year (the amount currently being paid on the loans). Jerry and Ann feel that they have developed all the real estate that they can manage. From your fact finder you have determined that the objective is to invest in something that will not create additional taxable income. Jerry and Ann also feel that they want to secure the highest possible long-term interest rates. They do not mind sacrificing some liquidity as their cash flow is more than adequate, but they are concerned about safety of principal and are extremely conservative.

A Recomended Approach As you can see from the fact-finding interview and analysis, Jerry and Ann's investment objectives are:

1. tax-free income,
2. highest possible yield, and
3. safety of principal.

An ideal product to meet these objectives would be an insured municipal bond unit investment trust.

The income from the fund will be tax-exempt, due to the tax-free nature of the municipal bonds. The safety factor will be very high, because there is insurance on the timely repayment of interest and principal. This insurance feature will satisfy the conservative attitude of these clients. Finally, because of the fixed portfolio, the trust will lock in favorable rates of return.

SUMMARY

The preceding case studies should give you an idea of the many ways that mutual funds can be combined with other products to allow your clients to make the most of their money. The better you understand your clients' financial needs, qualifications, and attitudes, the more effective will be the financial plans you devise for them.

4

The Mutual Fund Sales Process

This chapter is designed to show you how to use your existing sales skills in the sale of mutual funds. Many of the subjects covered here will already be familiar to you. On the following pages you will find guidelines for presentations integrated with your existing financial planning program for both the middle-income market and the more sophisticated higher-income market for mutual funds. Also, the chapter includes information on prospecting techniques, tips for overcoming prospects' objections, and mutual funds for the qualified plans market.

MUTUAL FUNDS SALES PRESENTATION COORDINATED WITH THE FINANCIAL PLANNING PROCESS

Your initial data gathering via the financial planning process has set the stage for your all-important selling interview. In the selling interview, you will need to listen hard and probe to uncover any additional facts about your client's financial objectives and plans. Just as in selling life insurance, you should gather the facts, interpret the needs, and make suitable recommendations at the close. The need may be for additional insurance, a mutual fund, a tax shelter, or perhaps a combination. Selling mutual funds depends more on logic than on emotion, but the process is very similar to the way you currently sell insurance. Here is how the mutual fund sales process appears on paper:

- review of client financial objectives and attitudes

- generic overview of mutual funds
- specific mutual fund product recommendation
- close

THE MIDDLE-INCOME MARKET

The middle-income market for mutual funds includes individuals with incomes of approximately $25,000–$50,000 per year. Most often, you are familiar with these clients or prospects and their objectives because they comprise a great majority of mainstream America. This is a very large and exciting potential market for the sale of mutual funds.

Answers to the questions on a financial questionnaire will help you determine the client's financial objectives and attitudes. Your first objective in the sales process is to reconfirm your client's financial objectives and attitudes. Then, based on these objectives, you should describe the generic characteristics of the particular type of mutual fund you will be recommending. Third, you should describe the specific mutual fund that you will be recommending. Finally, you will close for a buying decision.

Note that you will be recommending not only a product, but also a specific transfer or allocation of money. Here is one of the dramatic differences between insurance and security selling. In the life insurance process, you "sell need," then negotiate a premium commitment. In investments, selling the solution is a composite of the product you recommend and the suggested amount of the investment. You should know both the source and the amount of money you are going to recommend that your prospect invest in the mutual fund. This process requires that you build trust, determine objectives, and uncover liquid assets to invest before deciding on a specific mutual fund recommendation.

Close Along the Way As mentioned in Chapter 1, you should get agreement on minor points throughout the presentation and close along the way so that you are able to approach the buying decision from a position of strength. None of this is new. Studies of the most successful life insurance salespeople have shown that a closing is not something that takes place at the end of a sales interview; rather, it starts happening from the very beginning of the sales process and continues throughout the presentation. In the sale of mutual funds, this is an absolute must.

As you are closing, there are three steps you should follow:

1. Ask if there are any questions.
2. Highlight the product's objectives and benefits.
3. Make your recommendations and ask for decisive action.

Selling mutual funds to the middle-income market is really quite similar to everything you know and do already. The sales opportunities for mutual funds—particularly in *this* market—lie in the fact that many people either do not know the alternatives available for investment of their money or simply have not gotten around to doing something more appropriate with their money. The following is a model sales track for selling mutual funds to the middle-income market. Work with it until you feel comfortable. You may then modify it to fit your personal selling style.

Mutual Fund Sales Track The objectives of this sales track are to:

1. reconfirm your client's financial objectives and attitudes;
2. describe the generic characteristics of the type of mutual fund you are going to recommend;
3. describe the specific mutual fund you are recommending; and
4. close through a continuous process of "reading" your prospect for agreement or disagreement throughout the entire interview.

"Mr./Ms. (client's name), what I'd like to talk about today are some new investment ideas that would supplement and round out your financial plan. Before we talk about these investment ideas, I would like to review your financial goals and objectives with you, which we discussed in our last meeting. With regard to investments, you indicated that these objectives and criteria were important to you: (professional money management; liquidity; long-term growth; combination of growth and income)."
(This list highlights the primary desires that would suggest the recommendation of a mutual fund. Discuss only *those items applicable to your client's specific situation.*
"Is this correct, Mr./Ms. (client's name)?"

[Listen to response.]

"Mr./Ms. (client's name), before we discuss specifics, let's look at the general characteristics of a mutual fund. A mutual fund is a company that invests its assets in the securities of another company or a government. A mutual fund that continuously offers to buy back or redeem its shares is called an *open-end* mutual fund—the mutual funds we will be discussing today are all of this variety.
"A mutual fund may invest its holdings and securities in companies that are in many different types of business, i.e., a *diver-*

sified mutual fund; or it may concentrate its securities holdings in one type of business or industry, in which case it is called a *special situation* or *nondiversified* mutual fund. All mutual funds provide some diversification in their investments. Most mutual funds have contracts with professional full-time advisors who advise the fund on types of securities in which it should invest. They also have contracts with professional underwriters who sell the shares of the fund.

"The mutual fund concept is not new, in fact, it is over 100 years old. Today, there are more than 800 mutual funds in existence with nearly $250 billion in assets. There are millions of people like you who would like to invest but do not have the time, inclination, knowledge, or experience to select properly and continuously care for their investments. Mutual funds provide the full-time professional management, careful selection, and diversification required to take full advantage of economic fluctuations.

"There are several types of mutual funds, and each general type has a different investment objective, thereby offering investors such as you a variety of options to help them realize their specific investment goals. Let's look at the various types of mutual funds that are available to you.

"The most common type of mutual fund is a common stock fund. Some common stock funds invest exclusively in the blue chip market. These are securities issued by large, stable corporations that are known leaders in their respective industries. Such funds may react slowly or only slightly to day-to-day fluctuations in the market. Other common stock funds may specialize in growth company stocks. These are the securities of emerging companies and industries and may be more volatile in reacting to the market. Common stock income funds invest in common stocks that are known for their high dividend-paying capabilities. Investors requiring current income might seek this type of mutual fund. Other common stock funds invest in specific industries or employ specific management theories.

"Another type of mutual fund is a bond fund, which is designed to generate current income by investing primarily in senior securities of a corporation—those securities having prior claim, over common stock, to the assets and earnings of the company. Senior securities include such things as bonds, debentures, and preferred stock. The yields achieved on these funds vary based on the quality of bonds purchased. The higher the rating, the lower the ultimate yield; likewise, the lower the rating, the higher the ultimate yield or return. Some corporate bond funds invest in the highest-grade bonds, while others, often called *high-income* or *high-yield* funds, invest in lower-grade corporate bonds.

"Municipal bond funds are designed to achieve income by investing in a broad range of tax-exempt bonds issued by the states and municipalities. The interest earned on these bonds is passed to the shareholder free from federal income tax and, in some instances, from state and local income taxes.

"Money market mutual funds are one of the more familiar and more recent types of mutual fund. They invest in short-term money market securities such as treasury bills and notes, bank certificates of deposit, bankers' acceptances, and commercial paper (IOUs of corporations). The return on money market mutual funds is generally about three points below the prime rate. Investors can buy shares in these funds in relatively small amounts, yet earn the high rates of return that big investors receive.

"Tax-exempt money market funds are another form of mutual fund. These funds are also known as *short-term municipal bond funds*. Dividends generated by the portfolio of securities held in this type of fund are free from federal income taxation. While this is true with *any* municipal bond fund, the primary difference is the short-term nature of the bond maturities in tax-exempt money market funds. Typically, the bond maturities do not exceed two years.

"An option mutual fund is a more speculative investment. Option mutual funds generally seek a high current return or higher-than-average growth by writing options. An option is a contract to buy (or sell) a stated number of shares of a security at a specified price during a limited period of time. Option fund earnings consist of dividends, premiums from expired call options, net short-term gains from sales of portfolio securities due to the exercise of the options, and any profits from closing purchase transactions.

"Last is a unit investment trust. A unit investment trust holds a fixed portfolio of specified assets, such as tax-exempt bonds, Ginnie Maes, corporate bonds, or certificates of deposit. The trust issues redeemable securities, each of which represents an undivided interest in the assets held by the trust. Once the trust has purchased a stated portfolio, [they] are not traded; they are monitored. Yields are fixed and predictable due to the underlying fixed nature of the portfolio. When the assets mature, the trust ends.

"Mr./Ms. (client's name), these are the major types of mutual funds. With your specific financial goals and objectives in mind, I have selected a specific mutual fund that may help you achieve those goals. This is a (common stock, bond, municipal, money market, tax-exempt money market, option fund). This particular fund is called (name of fund). Are you familiar with (name of fund)?"

[You must insert specific product information from the mutual fund prospectus and from the mutual fund data sheet, if available. Listen to response.]

"The objective of this mutual fund, as shown right here on the first page of the prospectus, is (read from prospectus). That's quite compatible with your own objectives, isn't it?"

[Listen to response.]

"This mutual fund invests in (read from prospectus). With its full-time professional management, you would have both diversification and liquidity from this fund. Diversification reduces risk because your investment dollars, along with those of other investors, are spread among many different firms and industries. That way, you don't have all of your eggs in one basket if a particular company's stock goes down or a single industry goes sour. The fund provides a high degree of liquidity since all or part of your fund shares can be liquidated at any time. Your money is available to you *if* you need, *when* you need it.

"Professional investment management is provided to you via a staff of full-time professionals who track industry performance and economic trends to make the *best* decisions about what and when to buy and sell. This relieves you of having to spend time following the market on a regular basis."

[Add the following if the automatic reinvestment feature is being sold.]

"The automatic reinvestment feature of this mutual fund allows you to put your dividends and capital gains distributions back to work for you immediately. They are automatically reinvested in additional shares of the fund. Mr./Ms. (client's name), this is an investment I think you should own. Do you have any questions about the fund that I haven't already answered?"

[Listen to reply and answer any questions.]

"Well, Mr./Ms. (client's name), I think you can see why I believe that the investment objectives of the (name of fund) mutual fund match your own financial objectives *very* well. My recommendation is that you take (dollar amount) from (where the money is coming from) and put it into the (name of fund) mutual fund. I've completed some of the information necessary for your application to the (name of fund) mutual fund. Let me double-check to make sure that this is correct."

[At this point, you should verify existing information you have about your client and continue to fill in application information.]

Effective closing comes from experience. Through the use of probes and trial closing statements, you will know when you have given an adequate description of how the features of the fund tie into the client's objectives. All of the words and techniques you have learned in selling life insurance work equally well with mutual funds.

THE HIGHER-INCOME MARKET

The higher-income market is defined generally as those individuals with incomes of $50,000 and up. These individuals share many of the same desires and motivations as people in the middle-income market. In fact, their financial objectives and goals may be just as fuzzy and undefined as those of the less sophisticated or lower-income investor. There are, however, distinctions between the higher-income market and the middle-income market.

Some investment needs and objectives of thc higher-income market may be markedly different from objectives in the middle-income market. For example, mutual funds may be used in the estate planning process to provide liquidity, pay federal estate taxes and state inheritance taxes, and support the descendent's family when the estate owner was uninsurable. Mutual funds are also used by higher-income individuals as a funding medium for trusts. The built-in management diversification and economical and convenient administration of mutual funds can make the trustee's task simple and easy. Mutual fund shares can be used in living trusts, reversionary trusts, charitable trusts, and trusts set up for minors.

Another important sales consideration for the higher-income individual is the need for liquidity. Individuals with higher incomes and greater amounts of accumulated assets tend to become less liquid than other individuals. Often, business owners reflect this trend since the majority of their estate is tied up in illiquid businesses, and they have few investments that can be converted readily into cash.

The impact made by taxes on the incomes of higher-income individuals must be evaluated carefully when recommending investments. Any good investment strategy seeks to maximize income return by minimizing the effect of taxes. Persons in high income tax brackets should consider purchasing tax-exempt mutual fund shares instead of taxable mutual fund shares. For these individuals the tax relief provided by tax-exempt funds may more than compensate for the slightly lower yields of tax-exempt funds.

Higher-income individuals may also buy mutual funds as a vehicle for making gifts and thereby reducing the size of their taxable estate. Gifts may be made in an amount up to $10,000 per year per donee (the person receiving the gift) without incurring gift tax. If a spouse joins with the donor in making the gift, the excludable amount is $20,000 per year donee. Since the person receiving a gift of a mutual fund takes on a basis equal to the fair market value of the mutual fund at the time of the gift, gifting of mutual fund shares that have high potential capital gains has the effect of postponing tax on the capital gains and transferring the tax to the donee.

Another distinctive characteristic of the higher-income market is relationships with other advisors. Higher-income individuals may have existing relationships with attorneys, accountants, bank trust officers, and/or security advisors. For effective selling, you must determine the strength of these relationships since your investment recommendation may need to be coordinated with related planning that has already been performed by other advisors. As a financial planner, you are free to help your prospects structure their investment programs. However, in *no* case should you attempt to draw up a legal document for your client or make legal recommendations of any kind. This is the job of the client's attorney. Even merely offering legal advice puts you in danger of being charged with engaging in the unauthorize practice of law. Suffice it to say that it is imperative that your investment recommendation be coordinated with the advice of other advisors—particularly for higher-income individuals.

The words in your actual mutual fund sales presentation to the higher-income individual will not differ markedly from the presentation that was used for the middle-income market; therefore, we will not repeat the sales talk here. Naturally, your individual mutual fund recommendation must be structured so that it is in full agreement with your client's goals and objectives.

In summary, you will find that this market produces substantially increased sales (and increased earnings) for only a small incremental increase in your prospecting efforts because of the increased asset and income base of the individuals.

MUTUAL FUNDS CREATE MONEY FOR LIFE INSURANCE PREMIUMS

A fundamental principal of investment productivity is that the value of any investment lies not in how much you make but in how much you keep. Outstanding prospecting opportunities exist when you can position after-tax investments that will generate tax-free returns greater than comparable taxable returns. Through the use of the power of tax-free income, you will be able to fulfill additional client needs with no additional out-of-pocket expense. For example, successful life underwriters have created additional premium dollars by recommending the transfer of taxable savings to tax-free investments. Using this approach, you can show your prospects how to modernize their money management system by having most short-term savings and cash flow move through a money market fund. This process produces a windfall of additional dividends and, in turn, helps build a client relationship.

However, not all prospects have sufficient incomes to benefit from tax-free investments. In these situations, the additional yield generated by many money market funds will be very appealing. If your client finds this idea exciting, it will be easier to talk about life insurance. Here is an example:

You have a client, Ms. Brown, who needs additional life insurance coverage. The only problem is that your client does not feel she has the additional dollars necessary to buy the insurance.

You contact Ms. Brown, explain how a money market fund works, and make a specific recommendation. Let's assume that the fund you recommend is currently paying 9 percent and has a check-writing privilege. Your client reviews her financial situation and realizes that she has $12,000 in savings, which is yielding only 5 1/2 percent, or $660 annually. At your suggestion, she puts the entire $12,000 in savings into a money market fund paying 9 percent and earns a return of $1,080 (assuming that the rate for the year averages 9 percent). You have just created $420 of new money that may be used to pay for premiums on the new life insurance that your client needs.

Here is another way that you may create new life insurance premium dollars via mutual fund investment. Both the dividends and capital gains earned from mutual fund investment could be used as additional premium dollars for life insurance. This helps preserve your client's capital and at the same time protects her family from the contingency of death.

OVERCOMING SALES OBJECTIONS

As surely as night follows day, you will encounter objections from mutual fund sales prospects when you secure appointments or discuss investments on the telephone. You have, no doubt, become skillful in overcoming objections to setting up an insurance interview. Now, as an insurance salesperson who also sells mutual funds, you should become familiar with the kinds of objections you can expect to encounter when you begin this kind of prospecting activity and the ways you can overcome them.

Rephrase or restate what the prospect says. This tells your prospect that you are listening, that you care, and you should *always* clarify the prospect's objection before trying to overcome it. For example, in response to an objection about bond funds, you might say something like this:

"Before I answer this, I want to be sure I understand what you are saying. You are concerned about the fact that most corporate bonds take many years to mature, and you will be interested in maximum income for only the next three to five years. Is that correct?"

[Listen to reply. If the prospect agrees, proceed as follows.]

"Well, it's true that many of the bonds in the fund won't mature for many years. But that will *not* affect your personal liquidity. Even though the fund will continue to hold the bonds, you can sell your shares on *any* business day."

COMMON OBJECTIONS TO MUTUAL FUNDS

Here are some examples of other objections that are commonly raised, with possible answers.

Q. "Why should I buy a fund with a sales charge? I read in a financial column that no-load funds are better."

A. "One difference between a no-load and a load fund is service—*personal* service—versus a telephone/mail approach. You should never invest without discussing goals and objectives, so you can select the right kind of investment for *you*. As a full-time salesperson, I look at my relationship with you as an ongoing way to help you do the best job possible of achieving your financial objectives. You don't get that kind of service if you buy a no-load mutual fund through the mail. We feel that personal service is worth the difference. Right now, for example, as I am talking to you *in person,* there are representatives all over the country ready to serve you. On the other hand, the no-load funds have an 800 number and a few salaried clerks. If you have a real problem—a problem beyond the capabilities of a young salaried clerk—you may have to start writing back and forth and do it all by mail and take weeks and weeks to get action on your problem.

"Another difference—a big difference—between load and no-load funds is management fees. For no-load funds, these may be two to three times *higher* than the management fee for a load fund. This means that the cost of "owning" a no-load fund can be far greater than first meets the eye. For example, a load fund might have a management fee of, say, .75 percent, while a no-load fund may have a management fee of 1.5 percent. The difference (.75 percent) over, say, 15 years of ownership is 11.25 percent. The sales charge for load funds is *never* that high.

Q. "Why do I have to pay both a sales charge and a management fee?"

A. "The sales charge really represents the cost of bringing the product to you. Whenever you buy anything—a car, a refrigerator, clothes, food—there is always a sales charge. *Always.* Take clothes, for example. It is a common practice for retailers to markup clothes 50 percent or more.

"In the case of investments—specifically mutual funds—there is usually some kind of sales charge to cover the cost of brokerage, commissions, and marketing expenses. The management fee is generally just a fraction of 1 percent, which is applied to the total assets of the fund. The reason so many people are willing to pay a small management fee is that it is felt that professional managers can do more with .99 cents of your dollar than you or I can do with 100 cents of a dollar."

Q. "I like the liquidity I have at the bank with my CDs. Why should I switch to mutual funds?"

[Yes, this sounds nonsensical, but, you would be surprised at how many times people say this.]

A. "If you have a six-month CD, your funds are 'liquid' only a few days each year. With longer-term certificates, there is *no* liquidity without a penalty. If you withdraw funds before maturity, you lose from three to six months of interest! And in most cases your overall interest rates reverts to $5^1/_4$ percent or $5^1/_2$ percent. With a mutual fund, your money is *always* available because you can redeem your shares at net asset value anytime."

Q. "If I were to do any real investing, I think I would prefer to pick the stocks and bonds myself. Why should I trust someone else to do it?"

A. "You could certainly do that if you wanted to. Many people do. The thing to consider is this: Do you have the time and the expertise to manage your own portfolio? Most of the millions who prefer mutual funds find that the full-time professional management not only handles the buying and selling decisions, but allows them more free time for business and leisure activities—more time for your family, for golf or tennis, for a vacation, or to make money in *your* business."

Q. "I'm really afraid to get involved with investments. What happens if the market goes down?"

A. "That's a very good question. Let me be totally frank with you: the market probably *will*. It never stands still, even for a day. It is a dynamic, always-changing environment. That's where ongoing, highly experienced professional management can help you achieve your objectives and bring you peace of mind. The safest way to make money in the stock market is to buy low and sell high. But most of my clients feel that they would rather rely on the judgment of full-time professional fund managers who pay close attention to improvements in the market *every day* than try to do it themselves."

Q. "I want my money to be safe, and I feel that a savings and loan or a bank is the place to keep my money. Why should I take it out?"

A. "If you are referring to the fact that your deposits are insured up to $100,000 (by the FDIC), you could be right. Unfortunately, there can be some drawbacks to safety. One of the guarantees that they give you at the bank is that your principal *will not grow*. You do, of course, receive interest, but that too is fixed. When you compare those guarantees with our inflation rate, you are probably falling behind. With a mutual fund investment, growth of principal is possible.

"You do have safety with insured savings, but let's look at how much you are paying for it! Your passbook savings account is paying only 5¼–5½ percent, while this mutual fund historically has earned (percentage) percent."

[If you are talking about funds in general, you may want to discuss current money market fund interest rates.]

"Doesn't it make sense to take some of that passbook savings money and put it into a fund that has considerably higher potential?"

[Listen to reply.]

"Is safety the most important factor to you?"

[Listen to reply.]

"In that case, you should consider a very real threat to the purchasing power of your dollar—inflation. Even at a modest rate of, say, 3 percent per year, you can see how this reduces the return on your savings account growth when a bank pays between 5 and 6 percent interest. But inflation has been more than 10 percent in the past and can be again. If you are receiving a return of 6 percent on your savings account deposit and inflation is eroding your money at the rate of 10 percent or more, is this really a good place for your money?"

Q. "I don't want to gamble on the stock market."

A. "I'm relieved to hear you say that. If you did want to *gamble* in the market, I'd have nothing to offer you. The people who do gamble in the stock market are those with little knowledge who pick up one or two stocks on tips or hunches and then watch the quotations in the paper from day to day, hoping for a profit instead of a loss.

"Investment in the shares of a mutual fund is the direct *opposite.* It is a method of capital accumulation for people like you—solid, thoughtful, conservative people. When you invest in the shares of a mutual fund, you are putting your money in the hands of professional managers—these full-time analysts then invest your money for you in dozens of thoughtfully chosen securities. From then on, the same professionals supervise your investments on a day-to-day basis. That's quite different from *gambling* in the stock market, isn't it?"

Q. "I just don't understand why I would be better off going with load funds."

A. "A one-time sales charge is small when averaged over the years of a long-term investment. Dividends and capital gains may be reinvested without a sales charge. This effectively reduces the percentage of the sales charge in relation to total investment.

"Numerous studies indicate there is no discernible difference between long-term performance of load versus no-load mutual funds.

"The no-load funds, as a class, appear to have an expense ratio each year as much as two to three times higher than the loads! The small no-loads definitely have higher ratios than their counterparts."

The preceding question-and-answer dialogue covers most of the common objections that you will encounter in selling mutual funds. As indicated, some objections will be product-specific—they will relate to the specific mutual funds you are recommending. For this reason it is imperative that you have as much information as possible about your recommended fund and that you be prepared to present this information in a favorable manner. As with insurance selling, the better prepared and rehearsed you are prior to your presentation, the higher your closing ratio (and earnings) will be. Know how to use your sales literature in your presentation; it is available to help you sell.

MUTUAL FUND SALES IN QUALIFIED PLANS

INDIVIDUAL RETIREMENT ACCOUNTS (IRAS)

Individual retirement accounts (IRAs) allow for tax-deductible contributions to an individual retirement program whether an individual is or is not covered by a qualified pension or profit-sharing plan at work. In addition to being tax-deductible, contributions accumulate on a nontaxable basis; that is, the investment income is not taxed until it is distributed to the individual.

Mutual funds are an ideal funding medium for IRAs because of their professional management diversification and the fact that the Revenue Act of 1978 prohibited the use of life insurance as a funding medium for IRAs.

Contributions to an individual retirement account must be in cash and may not exceed $2,000 in a tax year (except for rollover contributions from qualified pension or profit-sharing plans). The account must be nonforfeitable, and the commingling of funds with any personal property is not allowed. The account must be a written trust or custodial account, the trustee or custodian must be a bank, credit union, savings and loan, or other institution that satisfies the Secretary of the Treasury. Most mutual funds satisfy this requirement.

It is important to remember that long-term growth is the common objective in retirement planning. This means that some mutual funds are more important than others as funding vehicles. The data that you secure during the financial planning process should help you make the appropriate fund recommendation.

An IRA participant may contribute up to 100 percent of earned income before taxes or $2,000, whichever is less, to the IRA. In addition, a participant with a legally married spouse may elect the spousal option and contribute a maximum of $2,250. In a spousal IRA, the amount of the contribution credited to each party can be designed in any manner desired, but the amount to be credited to one spouse cannot be less than $250.

Part of the Revenue Act of 1978 provided for simplified employee pension plans (SEPs). These allow an employer to contribute up to the lesser of $30,000 or 25 percent to an IRA for each employee. Contributions to this program must be a uniform percentage of salary with no discrimination. Limited integration with social security is permitted. Vesting in this program is full and immediate, and employer contributions must be made for each employee who is at least 25 years old and has performed services for the employer during the calendar year for which the contributions were made *and* was employed at least three of the immediately preceding five calendar years. Employees covered by collective bargaining agreements (subject to good-faith bargaining) may be excluded from participation.

Contributions to an IRA in excess of deductible limits are subject to a 6 percent penalty tax for the year in which they are made and each year thereafter until the excess is removed. If not withdrawn, excess IRA contributions may be deducted in a subsequent year when an individual's deductible contribution is less than the maximum allowable deduction. In the event of excess contributions, the excess may be withdrawn at any time, without being included in gross income, if no tax deduction was previously allowed (that is, participant deposited more than the allowable limit but did not try to deduct the excess amount on his or her income tax return).

The deadline for establishing a new IRA or contributing to an in-force IRA is the due date for filing your income tax return for the taxable year. Thus, an IRA may be established as late as April 15 for the preceding taxable year. Any allowable contributions made within this period would be fully tax-deductible for the filing year.

A rollover into an IRA is a means of investing certain lump sum distributions from corporate retirement plans. The purpose of the rollover is to defer taxation on such distributions and/or to avoid tax penalities resulting from any premature plan distributions before age 59½. To qualify as a tax-deferred rollover, money or property that has been distributed must be reinvested within 60 days. Distribution from an IRA may be partially rolled over within 60 days of receipt. The amounts rolled over will not be taxed, but any amount retained will be taxed when received.

Planned distributions that are not received as a rollover into an IRA are "frozen" until age 59½. No part of the distribution can be withdrawn, borrowed, pledged, or hypothecated in any way. Any such premature distribution would be subject to a 10 percent penalty tax and, in the case of a loan, the disqualification of the plan. A tax-deferred rollover may be made only once each year. Also, such transfers must be made into a separate IRA and cannot be commingled with the assets of another IRA to which an individual is currently making annual contributions.

One of the primary tax advantages provided by an IRA is the deferment of taxation on contributions made to the program from earned income. Contributions and interest earnings will accumulate tax-free throughout the accumulation period. Any investment income that normally would be subject to capital gains taxation would also receive this tax deferment advantage.

Distributions from an individual retirement account must begin after age 59½ but before 70½. These distributions are taxed as ordinary income. If an individual plan participant chooses to receive a lump sum distribution, special ten-year averaging, as available for qualified corporate plans, is not available. However, regular income averaging for IRA lump sum distributions is permitted.

Except in the case of death or disability, a premature distribution from an IRA (prior to age 59½) subjects the distribution to a 10 percent penalty tax. This is in addition to any increase in an individual's regular income tax that might result from including the distribution in gross income. The Internal Revenue Code states that besides being imposed on the actual amount of the distribution, the penalty tax is imposed on any "constructive distribution resulting from a disqualification of an IRA." For example, if an individual *borrows* money from the IRA, the plan will be disqualified as of the first day of the taxable year in which the loan was made, and the individual will be treated as if the entire assets of the plan had been distributed. However, if an individual borrows money, using a portion of the IRA as security, only the portion used as security is treated as a distribution.

Mutual Funds for IRAs Now let's look at the selling of mutual funds via individual retirement accounts. One of the truly exciting aspects of selling an investment vehicle such as a mutual fund via IRAs is the "miracle" of compound interest. That is, a consistent deposit over long periods of time into an IRA can generate hundreds of thousands and sometimes millions of dollars of accumulation—depending upon interest rates and earnings. To assist you in selling the IRA concept in the use of mutual funds as a vehicle, compound interest tables, which will help you excite your prospects about the potential accumulation that they may enjoy by consistently depositing into your mutual fund, are included at the end of this book.

The first table, "Compound Interest One Dollar per Annum in Advance," shows the amount to which $1 deposited in the beginning of each year will accumulate at compound interest. It shows this amount as a factor for a stated number of years at a given interest rate. For example, if you wanted to know how much an annual deposit of $1,000 per year would accumulate to over 30 years at 10 percent, you would look down the year column on the left side of the table to 30, run your finger across the factors to the column that is at 10 percent, and see a factor of 180.9434. Multiply this factor by the annual amount deposited, in this case $1,000. The result is $180,943. Here's how you could integrate this concept into a simple sales talk to a prospect:

> "Mr./Ms. (client's name), at your age, 35, consistent deposits into an individual retirement account can contribute substantially to a retirement fund, which will help you accomplish many of your financial objectives. Let's illustrate the potential of consistent periodic deposits into a mutual fund sheltered in an IRA.
>
> "Assuming that you retire at age 65 (30 years from now) and that the mutual fund in which you invest earns 10 percent over that period, let's determine what lump sum of money would be available to you at age 65.
>
> "We multiply your $2,000 annual deposit by the compound interest factor for 10 percent in 30 years (180.9434). The result tells us that, based on these assumptions, you would have a lump sum available for retirement at age 65 of $361,886. Not bad!
>
> "This could create an ongoing stream of retirement income for you, or, alternatively, you could take a one-time distribution of the money. Many clients choose to receive funds over a number of years in order to spread the tax liability and because they do not need all of the money in one lump sum. Of course, if your spouse chooses to start an individual IRA for the same amount (and assuming your spouse is the same age as you), this potential accumulation should be twice as much. The important aspect of your planning is that you begin to make IRA deposits as soon as possible. Let's take a look at the specifics of the (name of fund you are recommending) mutual fund to see how it can be used in your IRA."
>
> *[Discuss fund specifics here.]*
>
> "Now I have shown you a theoretical accumulation rate of 10 percent. This should not be construed as the rate you will receive on your investment; your interest rate may be more or less than 10 percent."

As you discuss mutual funds with clients or other prospects, you will be pleasantly surprised to find many people who have not begun an IRA program. In addition to younger individuals, do not overlook the potential for large lump sum rollovers from older individuals. These could come from people who are leaving an employer (for whatever reason) and receiving a lump sum distribution from a qualified pension or profit-sharing plan that needs a desirable investment for lump sum distribution. For this eventuality, another compound interest table, "Compound Interest—One Dollar Principal," to be used when you want to determine the amount of accumulation of a one-time contribution, IRA rollover, is included. For example, assume that your client, Mr. Greene, age 50, is leaving his current employer and receiving a qualified and profit-sharing distribution of $100,000. Also assume that his anticipated retirement age is 65 and that you want to show him the results of accumulating the $100,000 at 10 percent until age 65 (15 years). You turn to your new compound interest table, which shows the accumulation of a one-dollar principal at compound interest rates, and look down the left-hand year column to 15 and across the page to the 10 percent column until you see the factor, 4.1772. You multiply this factor by the single sum deposited: $10,000 times 4.1772 equals $417,772. *That* should get Mr. Greene's attention! Your sales talk in most other respects would be the same as the previous sales talk for mutual funds.

One last idea for IRAs is the use of corporate zero-coupon unit investment trusts. As you recall, these are unit investment trusts that invest in zero-coupon bonds. For more conservative IRA investors, this investment offers:

1. a known rate of return typically higher than the return on other bonds; and
2. a fixed portfolio of securities with a stated maturity.

Self-Employed Plans

The Keogh or HR-10 legislation was designed to give the same tax benefits to self-employed individuals as to corporate stockholders/employees. Subsequent amendments since its enactment in 1962 have removed practically all of the original restrictions on the amount and deductibility of contributions that self-employed individuals can make on their own behalf. Today, plans for the self-employed are almost identical to corporate pension and profit-sharing plans.

As with the individual retirement accounts, various funding media are available to potential self-employed plan participants—insurance companies, banks, and most mutual funds make investments available. In choosing a suitable mutual fund, you should again bear in mind that some will be more appropriate than others due to the long-term growth objective of retirement planning. Your data-gathering process should help you determine whether a self-employed plan is appropriate for your particular client.

Contributions made to a self-employed plan by an owner/employee are fully tax-deductible up to the lesser of 25 percent of earned income or $30,000. As with all qualified plans, contributions to a self-employed plan are tax-deductible, and taxation on earnings is deferred during the accumulation period. Also, any taxation on investment gains received during this period is deferred.

An owner/employee who owns a 5 percent or greater interest in the firm is subject to a penalty tax of 10 percent if benefits are received prior to age 59½ except in the case of complete disability or death. If an owner/employee takes a premature distribution from a self-employed plan, then the full amount of the distribution is included in gross income and is taxable. In addition, an income tax penalty of 10 percent of the amount distributed is imposed. On the other hand, employees or self-employed individuals *other than* owners/employees may receive their retirement benefits at any age at which they terminate employment.

The payment of retirement benefits to an owner/employer must commence no later than age 70½, even if the owner/employee has not actually retired. Technically speaking, as long as the owner/employee is still working, contributions to the plan can be continued despite the fact that the owner/employee will be concurrently drawing retirement benefits. Employees and self-employed individuals, other than owner/employees, are not required to accept distribution of retirement benefits until they actually retire. This is true even if they commence retirement after age 70½.

Lump sum payments to self-employed individuals and employees are taxed in the same manner as annuity payments. However, a taxpayer may elect to have a lump sum distribution from a self-employed plan taxed under the special 10-year averaging method available to corporate pension and profit-sharing plans (discussed in more detail later).

Your actual sales talk for self-employed plans would be almost identical to the one used for individual retirement accounts. Most mutual fund vendors provide the necessary documentation to establish a self-employed plan (or an individual retirement plan), which facilitates your sale. To help your prospect visualize the exciting accumulation possibilities of a self-employed plan, you would use the same compound interest tables that were discussed in the IRA section.

As an example, consider your client, Ms. Sherman, who is 45, plans to retire at age 65, and wants to put $10,000 a year into a self-employed plan. You could show her some very exciting potential results. Assuming an interest rate of 10 percent and a time period of 20 years, use the compound interest table that shows the amount to which $1 deposited at the beginning of each year will accumulate at compound interest. Multiply this factor by the annual deposit: $10,000 times 63.002 equals $630,020! This means that, for a $200,000 investment, your client may have $630,000 of accumulation upon retirement. Changes in her contribution amount, the interest rate, or the number of years accumulated may cause that amount to go up or down. The important point here, however, is that Ms. Sherman should *initiate* the self-employed plan as soon as possible to take advantage of as much accumulation time as possible.

The following case analysis will provide some insight into how the investment vehicles discussed in this section of the book can be used to fund an individual retirement program as part of a total financial plan.

Case Analysis: A Rising Star

Your clients are Jim and Sue Whitlock, who live in a comfortable neighborhood located in a small town outside a major East Coast city. Jim has been an executive with the Ford Motor Company for the past 13 years. He began in the lower echelon of his company's marketing department and has worked up to his present position of vice president. Last year, Jim's income was $72,500, and he anticipates that his earnings will exceed $80,000 this year. In addition, he expects to receive a substantial bonus based on his company's recent production gains.

Sue has a PhD in clinical psychology, which she earned after years of study at a local university. She is a partner in a professional corporation located in the city. Last year, Sue's income was $51,400, which she indicates will most certainly increase in the future due to the success of her company.

Both Jim and Sue are in their mid-30s and are enjoying the rewards of their success. In addition to establishing a life insurance program for them as part of a complete financial plan, you are in the process of recommending the establishment of retirement and investment programs designed to meet their future needs for capital. They hastily point out that liberal pension benefits and stock purchase plans are provided by their companies. However, once you have explained the concept of mutual fund investing, from which they can gain benefits such as diversification, professional money management, and flexibility, Jim and Sue agree that this might be an excellent way to accumulate additional capital and possibly reduce their annual tax liability.

During the interview, Jim and Sue explained that their primary financial goals include accumulating the capital necessary to enjoy a comfortable retirement, reducing their income tax burden, and providing a nest egg for future opportunities. Considering the age of your clients, their income position, and their overall financial goals, what categories of mutual fund products would you recommend as vehicles to help them realize their objectives?

A Recommended Approach During your fact-gathering interview, Jim and Sue expressed the opinion that their pension benefits would indeed be "liberal." Though they were not specific about the actual dollar amounts anticipated at retirement, discussing the fact that an IRA would help them achieve two of their objectives, additional cash at retirement and reducing their tax burden, would be most appropriate. The objective of this program would be long-term growth; current income would not be a concern. Both Jim and Sue could establish separate IRAs, each contributing the maximum of $2,000. A growth-type mutual fund would be most appropriate as the funding vehicles because they are viewed as suitable for investors who want to build capital and who do not seek current income. You should recommend that dividends and capital gains distributions be reinvested automatically in extra shares to maximize the growth potential of their account. Also, be certain to point out that these funds will grow on a tax-deferred basis, being sheltered in their IRA accounts. Though distributions are taxable at retirement, it is anticipated that their marginal tax bracket will be lower when they reach age 65.

You could recommend a wide variety of tax-saving strategies to the Whitlocks. One you might consider would be to establish an investment program for them based on a unit investment trust concentrated in tax-exempt municipal bonds. Should Jim and Sue decide to invest in common stocks and corporate bonds, the interest and dividends generated by these investments would be taxable at ordinary income rates. The interest generated from municipal bonds would be free from federal income taxation. If the bond is issued by a municipality from the state in which they reside, the interest would also be exempt from state income taxation. Though this may not be the only tax-saving strategy you would wish to employ, it does lessen their current burden.

The final goal that Jim and Sue indicated as being a priority was to establish a fund for future opportunities. An appropriate recommendation would be to have them transfer funds from a low interest-earning account, such as a bank passbook savings account, to a balanced mutual fund.

This would permit the Whitlocks to maximize the growth potential for the future while maintaining a conservative stance in their investment portfolio. The balanced aspect would provide the necessary liquidity if an opportunity came along. Jim and Sue could capitalize on the growth realized in their portfolio in the future to make additional, more diversified investments.

Corporate Defined-Contribution Pension Plans

In a corporate defined-contribution pension plan, the employer's contribution is fixed and is usually expressed as a percentage of the compensation of covered employees. Contributions to this type of plan are sometimes contributory, requiring the employee to put in funds.

In a defined-contribution plan, retirement benefits can only be estimated and depend on the performance of the funding medium. As a result, uniform benefit levels are impossible to design into this program. Defined-contribution plans favor younger individuals since younger individuals have a longer time period in which to accumulate. Most specialists in this area would define *younger* as those individuals below age 40–45.

Defined-Benefit Plans

In contrast, a defined-benefit plan defines the amount of ultimate benefit that will be received by a participant. A contribution amount is calculated (by an actuary) so that it is sufficient to assure that the proper amount of funds will be available to provide the preretirement benefits. For example, the benefit may be defined as a percentage of salary (e.g., 50 percent of salary upon retirement at age 65). The amount of contribution will vary depending on the earnings of the funding medium and other factors. Nonvested allocated portions of the funding medium for terminated employees serve to reduce subsequent contributions to the plan. Thus, when the retirement benefit is predetermined (usually as a percentage of salary), uniform benefit levels can be designed into this program. They can also be designed to benefit business owners and highly compensated employees. Here are some of the common formulas that are used in defined-benefit plans:

- Flat amount formulas—With a flat amount formula, each participant receives the same benefit, regardless of earnings (for example, $300 a month at age 65). This type of formula was typical of collectively bargained agreements of the past but is not used very frequently anymore.
- Flat percentage of earnings—With this formula, benefits reflect the actual earnings levels of different employees. For

example, the percentage might be based on the three highest-earnings years.

- Flat amount per year of service—The phrase *years of service* is defined as meaning the years during which employee has worked for the corporation since the plan itself went into effect. With this type of formula, the employee receives, at retirement, a flat dollar amount that is paid for each year of service (for example, $10 a month of benefit for every year of service).

There is no maximum contribution that is allowable for a defined-benefit plan, but there is a maximum imposed on the amount of benefit. This maximum is currently the lesser of 100 percent of salary or $90,000.

CORPORATE PROFIT-SHARING PLANS

The Internal Revenue Code defines a profit-sharing plan as a plan established by an employer to provide for the participation in the profits by the employees or their beneficiaries. The plan must define a definite predetermined formula for allocating the contribution among the participants and distributing to them the funds accumulated under the plan.

Distributions from the profit-sharing plan may be made after a fixed number of years, at the attainment of a stated age, or upon the prior occurrence of some event such as a layoff, illness, disability, death, or severance of employment.

There is *no* requirement that a definite predetermined contribution be made; however, there is a requirement for *substantial and recurring contributions* to be made from profits to meet the IRS requirements that the plan be permanent. A corporation's board of directors may use a discretionary formula that allows for flexibility and payments that do not exceed the amount currently deductible for a corporation by the Internal Revenue Service. Discretionary formulas usually impose maximums and minimums that shall be contributed from profits. Definite predetermined formulas promote increased morale among the employees and improve planned security.

Plan Formulas When contribution allocation formulas are used by the employer, they must indicate the basis upon which contributions are divided among planned participants. The two types of contribution allocation formula are described in the following paragraphs.

Compensation Formula This formula uses a proportion of the participant's compensation as compared to total eligible compensation (e.g., uses a discretionary formula that allows for an employee to receive 10 percent of the allowable contribution where his or her earnings are $10,000 per year and the total eligible compensation is predetermined as $100,000).

Compensation and Service Formula This formula allows for unit credits to be given for each year of service and for each unit of compensation. For example, say each unit for compensation equals $100 and each unit for service is one year. An employee who has 30 years of service and earns $15,000 per year would have accumulated 30 units for service and 150 units for compensation, for a total of 180 units. The employee's percentage would be 180 divided by the grand total of units credited in the company.

A profit-sharing plan, like all corporate plans, must be in writing and communicated to the employees. A trust must be used, and voluntary employee contributions may not exceed 10 percent.

A profit-sharing plan provides for a maximum deduction of 15 percent of covered payroll. If 15 percent is not contributed in one year, a credit carryover of up to 25 percent may be contributed to the program during the following year or years. A contribution carryover provides that contributions in excess of the allowable amount are not deductible. However, these contributions can be carried forward and deducted in future years.

Combination plans limit the total contribution for a combined defined-contribution pension plan and profit-sharing plan to 25 percent. The profit-sharing portion cannot exceed 15 percent.

Plan Distributions On lump sum distributions, no income tax is due on any amount employees include in their basis. The amount over the cost basis qualifies for favorable 10-year averaging when the employees are terminating service or retiring, they are over 59½ years old, and the distribution is complete (i.e., the total amount of the account will be received in a single taxable year). The ten-year income-averaging rule can be used for employees who did not participate in the plan prior to 1974. If an employee did participate before 1974, part of the distribution qualifies for capital gains treatment, which is even better than ten-year averaging. The primary advantage of ten-year averaging, if available, is that the tax computed via ten-year averaging is determined *separately and apart from the employee's other taxable income* without deductions and without regard to community property laws at the rate used by single persons.

Only one election for ten-year averaging may be made with respect to an employee who has attained age 59½. A widow may elect to average a distribution she received on the death of her husband (her husband's benefit) and later make an election for her own retirement distribution even though she and her husband were both past 59½ at the time of the distributions. However, any recipient who elects ten-year averaging, must elect it for all lump sum distributions received in the year. Furthermore, the taxable amounts for all lump sum distributions made with respect to the recipient in the five previous tax years (for which the ten-year averaging was elected) must be aggregated for the purpose of figuring the tax.

Favorable tax treatment can be lost if employees continue to work for the same employer, even though they are not being compensated, since there is a requirement for total severance of employment.

In addition to the qualification requirements that apply to qualified plans in general, special requirements have been imposed by the Internal Revenue Code for "top-heavy plans" for plan years beginning after December 31, 1983. "Top-heavy plans" are plans in which owner employees have more than 60 percent of the benefits (technically, the present value of the accumulative accrued benefits under the plan). Top-heavy plans must meet fast vesting requirements as well as certain minimum benefit and contribution limits. If you have any doubt as to whether your prospect would have a top-heavy plan, you should consult with your mass mutual pension specialist or other pension expert.

CORPORATE PLANS PROSPECTING

A powerful prospecting technique for corporate plans is a performance evaluation.

What is performance evaluation? To answer that question, review the responsibilities of the person who makes the investment decisions for a corporate plan—the plan fiduciary. The pension reform act (ERISA) requires that fiduciaries discharge their duties *solely in the interest of plan participants and in a prudent manner.* In addition, ERISA imposed the *ongoing* duty of monitoring the performance of the plan to make sure that it continues to meet participant needs and that the investment return is satisfactory. One way to do the latter is to compare the plan's investment performance with benchmarks such as the S&P 500 and the Dow Jones Industrial Average. An evaluation will compare a plan's actual investment results with a bond, an aggressive growth fund, or an equity fund. In many cases, these funds will show historical returns greater than the corporate plan has achieved. You are then in a position to recommend an investment change to the plan trustee or investment manager.

After showing a plan fiduciary that the current corporate plan is not performing as well as it could be, try this approach:

"Isn't this sufficient cause for you to make an investment decision?"

[Listen to response.]

"Mr. (plan fiduciary's name), very small differences in performance can make a *big* difference in the final value of a plan participant's account. For example, a *1 percent* difference—9 percent versus 10 percent—on a $100,000 investment over 15 years is: $417,725 at 10 percent versus $364,248 at 9 percent, or *over $50,000.*"

[Be sure to show the figures to make your point.]

"Why not consider a fund that historically has had that extra edge? Let's look at the performance of the (name of fund you are recommending), mutual fund."

This technique has placed other investment representatives into very lucrative sales situations.

501 (C)(3) AND 403 (B) PLANS—TAX-SHELTERED ANNUITY PLANS

Since 1942, under Section 501(c)(3), employees of nonprofit organizations have been able to take advantage of tax-sheltered annuity programs. Also, Section 403(b) was amended to include employees of public school systems. To participate, an employee must be a bona fide employee, a contract must be purchased by the employer, employee rights must be nonforfeitable, and the maximum exclusion allowance must be honored. Any employee of qualified organizations may participate, even seasonal and part-time employees; however, the person must be an actual employee, not an independent contractor.

The plan allows for participants to reduce their salary and purchase an annuity or mutual fund with before-tax dollars (tax-deductibly). The exclusion allowance (maximum amount available for a contribution and reduction of pay) is 20 percent of the adjusted pay after the reduction. This actually amounts to one-sixth of gross pay prior to the reduction (16.667 percent). Any contribution by the employer to a qualified pension plan reduces the exclusion amounts. The exclusion amount can be increased by credit for past service.

As long as the participants are living and not receiving benefits, they are subject to no adverse income taxes. If there are excess contributions to a plan, the excess only is taxed as ordinary income.

Proceeds at retirement are taxed as ordinary income. Taxes

after death are generally the same to the beneficiary as they would have been to the decedent.

SUMMARY

In conclusion, mutual funds may be utilized in any of the qualified plans discussed. When presenting mutual funds as a funding medium, you should emphasize their basic benefits. At times, you may be involved *only* with the investment aspect of a corporate plan while another party does plan administration. For IRAs and Keogh Plans, each individual fund normally provides you with necessary documentation.

5

Determining a Client's Suitability for Limited Partnership Investments

The value of any limited partnership offering is based on the underlying economic viability of the investment, not merely the tax benefits generated. Obviously, one combination of benefits will not be suitable for all investors. During an analysis of the financial questionnaire you will identify the location of your prospect's assets. While you are evaluating the productivity of those assets, opportunities to allocate them more effectively will arise. Selecting the appropriate balance between tax benefits and investment performance will ultimately influence tax productivity of your client's entire financial plan.

SUITABILITY

The first step is to decide whether your particular client should consider tax-advantaged investments, by carefully evaluating the client's income. Obviously, those who must spend every after-tax dollar to maintain their lifestyle are not candidates for tax-advantaged investing. For these people, the first goal must be to restructure spending habits and to start a regular savings program.

PREDICTABILITY OF INCOME

The predictability of a potential investor's income is also an important consideration. All investors should have a good idea of what their income will be for the next several years because many tax-advantaged investments, particularly privately placed real estate limited partnerships, require payments over a multiyear period. Investors who are unsure of future income should not commit themselves to a several-year investment. Also, getting out of a tax-advantaged investment may entail certain costs. Investors must be prepared to meet these possible future costs before getting into tax-advantaged investments.

Predictability of income is important in another regard. Since tax-advantaged investments are, after all, just another form of investment, investors must expect both good and bad results. This problem is handled by stock market investors through diversification, and the same strategy can work for tax-advantaged investments. Investors who maintain a carefully planned tax-advantaged investment program over a period of several years, are less likely to suffer a major loss than those who invest in a single deal. To embark upon such a program, investors must be reasonably sure of future income so that, once started, they can continue.

Liquidity

In addition to income level, the potential investors' liquidity must be addressed before embarking on a tax-advantaged investment program. Liquid assets, such as cash and marketable securities, should not be diverted to tax-advantaged investments if the investors may have need for the funds in an emergency.

Tax-advantaged investments, as a rule, are highly illiquid. In the first place, many limited partnerships restrict the right of partners to freely transfer their partnership interests, in order to preserve their partnerships tax status. In the second place, securities laws restrict the transfer of unregistered securities, and most tax-advantaged investment interests obtained through private placements are unregistered securities. Finally, unlike the stock market, there is no formal secondary market for limited partnerships. Even if there were no legal restrictions on their sale, most investors would be hard put to find willing buyers for interests in a limited partnership investment.

Adding to the illiquidity problem are the possible adverse tax consequences from a premature disposal of a tax-advantaged investment. Leverage and phantom income could cause a sale of a limited partnership investment to product no real return to the investor. Even a tax-advantaged investment that makes both tax sense and economic sense may not be the right investment for individuals who might need liquid assets for an emergency or other purposes.

Attitude Toward Risk

Tax-advantaged investments are, as a general rule, more risky than other forms of investment. If this were not so, there would be no need for the tax advantage. Investors who embark on a tax-advantaged investment must be prepared for the possible loss of their investments. This possibility exists no matter how carefully the type of investment and specific program are examined and evaluated. After all, evaluations of all tax-advantaged investments must be made on the basis of certain assumptions and projections that are subject to a wide margin of error. Investors who cannot afford to lose money invested in a tax-advantaged investment, simply should not invest. In cases in which total loss would be a financial hardship, investors should pay their taxes and invest what is left in an alternative medium.

Just as some potential investors are unsuited to the stock market, some potential investors are psychologically unsuited for tax-advantaged investments. Besides the ever-present risk of losing their investments, there is another threat hanging over certain tax-advantaged investors' heads: a privately placed limited partnership increases the chances for selection by the IRS in an audit lottery. Some investors may simply not want to increase their audit risk through tax-advantaged investment write-offs. Investors who cannot accept this increased risk are not candidates for tax-advantaged investments.

All successful tax-advantaged investments will provide some combination of three forms of investment return: cash flow, tax benefits, and appreciation. Cash flow is, of course, the actual after-tax cash distributed to, or realized by, the investors while they hold their interest and upon the investment's liquidation. Tax benefits are the tax savings generated by the investment. These benefits flow from the initial deductions provided by many tax-advantaged investments, as well as deductions generated over the life of the investment, such as interest costs, depreciation, and depletion. Finally, appreciation is the actual rise in the value of an investment because values increase over time, such as has occurred with real estate; because of growth, such as the increase in the value of a stand of timber; or because of the actual activity of the tax-advantaged investment, such as the discovery of oil in an exploratory oil and gas program.

SELECTING THE APPROPRIATE INVESTMENT

The structure and type of tax-advantaged investment will determine the nature of the return to the investor. Investors can choose a tax-advantaged investment that will yield greater cash flow with reduced tax benefits or one that will yield greater tax benefits with reduced cash flow and appreciation potential. The choice, of course, will depend on the individual investor's investment objectives. Also, investors can select from different types of tax-advantaged investments to provide a balance of cash flow, tax benefits, and appreciation.

To choose among the various types of tax-advantaged investments, investors must know what they want to accomplish with an investment program. Generally, investors embarking on a tax-advantaged program will have one or more objectives in mind; usually these will fall into the general categories of minimizing taxes, deferring a tax liability, providing current funds, and/or building equity for the future.

Given a choice between a limited partnership investment and an alternative tax-advantaged investment that offers a similar after-tax return, investors seeking to minimize taxes will choose the investment that results in a smaller tax liability. It does not matter to such investors that the end result of either investment is the same number of actual dollars in hand. What matters is the number of dollars going to the government. In fact, some investors are willing to accept a degree of risk for the same potential return simply to pay less in taxes.

Obviously, this is a shortsighted investment objective. How much is paid in taxes should not matter as long as investors can keep more than they would from an alternative investment. In any event, investors who are seeking to minimize taxes will choose tax-advantaged investments in which the tax benefits predominate. Such investments might include government-subsidized housing and leveraged equipment-leasing deals.

Investors who are paying taxes at the highest marginal rates may want to defer a portion of their tax liability to lower-income years in the future or convert highly taxed income into more favorably taxed capital gain. Cash flow is obviously a minor consideration. Limited partnerships that defer income tax liability by offering high front-end deductions, such as equipment leasing programs, may help these investors achieve their objective.

Investors who are looking for current spendable income will have cash flow uppermost in their minds. They will want an investment that produces current income that can be distributed to them, which at the same time offers current deductions to shelter this income from taxation. To achieve this objective, investors may choose residential or commercial real estate, possibly a deal involving existing properties in which the income can be projected with a fair degree of accuracy. Highly leveraged real estate investment programs and government projections will not produce significant cash flow. Another possible choice for these investors would be an income and gas program. These oil and gas partnerships offer greater income potential than exploratory drilling, and depletion deductions are available to shelter a small portion of the income from the property.

Investors who have the objective of building equity for the future are not overly concerned with current income or write-offs to reduce taxable income from sources other than the investment itself. These investors will be looking for programs that will prow in value through equity buildup. Again, certain real estate investments may be what these investors want to use to achieve their objective. Cable television programs may also be considered. A successful cable TV program can achieve a significant buildup in value but naturally entails a certain element of risk.

The four possible objectives of a tax-advantaged investment program—minimizing taxes, deferring a tax liability, providing current funds, and building equity for the future—are not mutually exclusive. Investors may have more than one objective, in which case they will look for a mix of investment types that produces the right blend of taxable income, tax deferral, current income, and equity buildup based on their own tax profile.

THE CLIENT'S TAX PROFILE

Once you have clarified an investor's objectives, you must take a careful look at your client's tax profile. Having certain objectives is one thing, but achieving those objectives can be profoundly influenced by the investor's tax picture. Since no two taxpayers are identical, a tax-advantaged investment that can achieve a certain objective for one investor will not necessarily achieve the same objective for another investor. The fact-finding questionnaire will disclose to you the pertinent information relating to your individual client's tax situation.

Individuals currently taxed at the top marginal federal rate, who are also subject to high state and local income taxes, may want to consider tax-advantaged investments that offer the most in the way of tax benefits. Investors who expect to remain in the highest bracket for many years should consider some longer-term investment that offers a high degree of tax benefits in the early years and requires a long-term commitment to the investment.

Investors may be faced with a large amount of income at one time but may not expect future income to remain at such high levels. Although these investors may be subject to the same tax rates as high-income investors, at least for the current year, they are not going to be attracted to the same types of investments as the investors who expect to remain highly taxed for many years to come. These investors will want to avoid the types of investment that are attractive to the long-term, high-income individual. Instead, they will be looking for tax-advantages in short-term deferral investments such as equipment leasing.

On occasion, unusually high earnings may not come all at once but rather may be spread over several years. For example, an individual may spend years building a business and then sell out in some sort of installment sale in which regular payments of principal and interest will be received over a period of years. This type of individual has the advantage of knowing in advance the amount and type of income that will be received in future years. As a result, it is much easier to tailor a tax-advantaged investment program to match the stream of income. Through diversified investments in oil and gas, real estate, or equipment leasing, the investor can not only shelter the income received, but also preserve the capital value built up in the asset when it is sold.

Typically, the peak earning years come just before retirement. Those approaching retirement face the prospect of high taxes for several years, followed by a substantial reduction in their income. The tax-advantaged investment program for such individuals must not only defer current taxes but also provide some appreciation that could be realized in their postretirement years. Equipment-leasing limited partnerships have historically provided early tax benefits combined with above average growth potential. As in the previous example, combinations of tax-advantaged partnerships would also prove suitable.

Private Placements vs. Public Offerings

Private placements generally require larger investments than do public offerings. The investor's search for the right type of tax-advantaged investment may have already eliminated one or the other type of program. An investor with $5,000–10,000 to invest will probably be limited to a public deal.

Public offerings are usually much larger in size than private placements. This has both advantages and disadvantages. The size of public offerings allows investors to reap to rewards of "economies of scale." A large program investing in many properties or prospects may spread much of the management cost, resulting in a lower per-unit cost than a program investing in one or two properties or prospects. The size of public offerings offers another advantage: greater diversity. Investors in a public program are usually investing in several real estate projects or oil and gas wells at one time, thus reducing the risk that an entire investment will be lost, but also reducing the opportunity to make enormous profits.

Private placements, however, are not without advantages. Due to the limited number of properties or wells, this upside potential is far greater than for public programs. The tax benefits available to investors in the private placement can be multiplied through the use of leverage and the staged-in payments for the partnership interest. These staged-in payments provide that the general partner will fulfill certain stipulations of the partnership agreement before additional funds will be allocated to the project. They avoid the cost of public registration, which can be considerable, and to that extent more of the investor's dollars can go into the actual investment. Taking into account the various advantages and disadvantages of public and private deals, investors must invest in a particular program based on the potential return the program offers.

When a private placement is involved, the investor's advisor should study the offering material carefully. These advisors can review what tax benefits are promised and what type of return can be expected. Needless to say, the advisor must be satisfied that the tax benefits and other aspects of the investment will be suitable. Regardless of whether a public or private partnership is involved, the experience of the general partner is critical. Whether a particular program will deliver "as promised" depends, to a great extent, on the capabilities of the program's management. The offering materials are also a good starting point for getting an idea of the management capabilities of those involved in the program.

Promoter's Track Record

The track record of the promoter should be examined in detail. Only completed programs give an accurate indication of the ability to manage from acquisition to disposition. One spectacularly successful program can hide numerous failures or mediocre programs and averages. A "good" track record means good for a number of programs, not just averages. If the promoter's track record is good, are the management people involved in the current program the same ones who managed the previous ventures? A change in management may indicate a change in future results.

Concentrating on your clients' financial information, their objectives for the future, and their willingness to assume risk, examine the information provided during the fact-gathering interview. Directing their assets to the most productive use of both tax and economic opportunities will result in additional discretionary investment income. This income may then be allocated to other needs uncovered throughout the financial plan.

CASE STUDIES

As with life insurance, individual objectives may be accomplished through various methods; the recommendations presented in the following case studies are only suggested approaches. As you evaluate the facts presented, attempt to formulate your own recommendations based on your knowledge of tax-advantaged limited partnerships offerings.

MARVIN AND MARJORIE MIDDLE CLASS

Marvin and Marjorie are a married couple who file joint tax returns. Last year their combined taxable income, after deductions and personal exemptions, was approximately $45,000. Of this amount, $2,000 comes from interest on their nest egg of about $20,000. Neither of their jobs is providing them with spectacular salary increases, but they do expect a series of cost-of-living raises to keep them ahead of inflation. Neither Marvin nor Marjorie plans to have a family in the foreseeable future; nor do they anticipate assuming any other major responsibilities. Last year their federal income-tax liability amounted to $9,354, which placed them in the 35 percent tax bracket.

Marvin and Marjorie are missing out on one tax break that could provide them with $4,000 in deductions per year with minimum risk. This tax break is an individual retirement account for both of them. As explained earlier, an individual can contribute up to $2,000 per year of earned income to an IRA. Since Marvin and Marjorie are both working, each can set up an IRA. In addition to the deferral of taxes on contributed amounts, the taxes on earnings from an IRA are also deferred until withdrawn. Setting up two IRAs and contributing maximum amounts will cut Marvin and Marjorie's federal tax bill by $1,400 per year. This may be all the tax shelter this couple would need or want.

During the fact-gathering interview, you discovered that Marvin and Marjorie require a significant increase in the coverage provided by their disability income insurance programs. Currently, they each have short-term disability income coverage through their employers that provides minimal, 13-week coverage. You have demonstrated the need for additional protection in this area and recommend a program that provides a benefit amounting to 70 percent of their respective incomes with a 90-day elimination period and an age-65 benefit period. Your clients acknowledge that this has been an area of concern and one that requires immediate attention.

Marvin and Marjorie's needs are multidimensional. Based on their goals, retirement planning, tax savings, and disability income protection are their major concerns. Carefully structuring a financial plan to meet their identified needs will involve a combination of interrelated programs.

A Recommended Approach One type of tax-sheltered investment that should be considered seriously is a limited partnership program investing in existing real estate storage facilities. This investment opportunity is already producing rental income. The rental income will be offset by depreciation deductions, thus providing Marvin and Marjorie with a tax-sheltered cash flow. In addition, they would benefit from appreciation that would be realized at the end of the program and subject to favorable capital gains tax treatment. Gains from this real estate limited partnership program could then be reinvested in another offering and continue funding an effective retirement supplement plan.

Their primary retirement program should, however, focus on separate individual retirement accounts for both Marvin and Marjorie. It is recommended that each make the maximum contribution of $2,000 from current income. The tax savings realized from this program will help fund their disability income protection. The tax savings realized from the real estate limited partnership program will make a substantial contribution to the balance of their disability income protection premium.

Using this recommended approach, you will have increased Marvin and Marjorie's net worth and provided a vital protection need. As you can see, through a multidimensional approach to satisfying a client's needs, a combination of products and programs can overlap into several areas of a well-structured financial plan.

THE GOOSE THAT LAID THE GOLDEN EGG

Jack and Jill Gander are relatively well off financially. Jack is an owner of a corporation, and he earns about $175,000 of taxable income per year. In addition, the couple has a sizable investment portfolio consisting of stocks, bonds, and short-term cash investments, which Jill manages. Currently, their investment portfolio produces about $25,000 annually after all expenses. Jill also manages the two vacation homes that they own. One of these homes is located at a ski resort in the mountains, and the other is an attractive estate on the seashore. These homes represent the only tax-advantaged investments Jack and Jill have made. The homes produce an additional $10,000 per year of taxable income having long since outlived their tax-advantaged position.

From the information you gathered during a fact-gathering interview, it became readily apparent that Jack and Jill owe their success and current financial position to Jack's earning ability. Though their income from earnings and investments is substantial, maintaining their current lifestyle requires the total amount of income received. The recommended plan indicates a need for additional life insurance amounting to $750,000. Initially, Jack and Jill resisted allocating the specific funds necessary to implement the life insurance program required to achieve their financial objectives.

Last year, Jack and Jill reached the top tax rate. Unless they pursue a tax-advantaged investment program, they will be liable for $41,502 in federal income tax. After analyzing their financial profile, it becomes apparent that tax preference items should not present any additional complications for this couple, if they are careful. They would have to shelter their income substantially with investments that produce tax preferences before being subjected to the alternative minimum tax. The potential for a minimum tax liability, however should be noted carefully.

Because of their top tax rate, Jack and Jill may find investments structured to emphasize tax benefits to be profitable. Investments that emphasize cash flow do not seem necessary given their current circumstances. Of course, appreciation in any investment would be welcomed for their retirement, which is still many years away. Jack and Jill should be able to enhance their investment return with tax-advantaged investments, with the ultimate selection relying on their evaluation of current market risk.

A Recommended Approach You have determined that a privately placed real estate limited partnership that invests in the resyndication of existing government-subsidized housing will generate significant tax benefits and modest cash flow as well as provide substantial appreciation.

During your review of the program summary prior to your sales interview, it was determined that the tax losses, cash flow, and appreciation in combination would appear to meet your client's needs as determined during the fact-finding session. The program, Wrinkle Village, is a resyndication that has an investment unit size of $203,000. The property is located in a small town within the borders of your client's state of residence. Wrinkle Village is currently 98 percent occupied by senior citizens who qualify for government-subsidized housing.

Recognizing that your clients require income tax relief, you note the substantial tax benefits of this program. The tax loss generated during the pay-in period is estimated to be 1.9:1. This represents tax losses of $393,594 during the pay-in period. The total tax loss ratio for the anticipated 12-year life of the program is 3.2:1 for a total dollar amount of $652,918. At your client's tax bracket of 50 percent, over the 12-year life of the program, this would represent a combined tax savings of $326,458.

The estimated cash flow for the 12-year life of the program

would amount to $18,312. The total benefit of cash flow and tax savings for this program would be $344,770. The tax benefits and cash flow, coupled with the compounded appreciation rate, using a 4 percent growth assumption at the sale of the property in 12 years, will equal $392,150.

It is recommended that the tax savings and cash flow be directed to a permanent insurance contract, thus funding Jack's need for additional life insurance amounting to $750,000. You note during your review of the program summary that at the disposition of the property in 12 years approximately $164,446 will be due in taxes. Using the tax savings and cash flow to fund a permanent life insurance contract will, in all likelihood, provide the necessary funding from cash values when these taxes are due.

The sum effect of this investment will be that your clients will realize a total net after-tax benefits of $396,150 on a capital investment of $203,000. In addition, the performance of this investment will fund the life insurance need, uncovered during the financial planning process.

EFFECTIVE PLANNING: THE DIFFERENCE BETWEEN IVY LEAGUE AND BUSH LEAGUE

Wendall and Wilhelmina Smythe have been married for 14 years and file joint tax returns. Their combined taxable income for last year was $60,000. In addition, they received approximately $10,000 of investment income represented by interest and dividend returns. Wendall and Wilhelmina are the proud parents of Wanda, age ten, and Wilfred, age eight. As concerned parents, they worry about their children's future and would like to provide them with a good college education or at least give them a good start in their adult lives. Unfortunately, doing this without jeopardizing their own security or their current standard of living seems to become a more difficult goal with each passing year. Last year, Wendall and Wilhelmina paid $30,800 in federal income taxes, placing them in the 44 percent tax bracket. Wendall and Wilhelmina can substantially reduce their tax bill while providing a fund for their children's education.

Recommended Approach Since Wendall and Wilhelmina are in a fairly high tax bracket, they should consider investments structured to provide slightly more tax relief than other types of programs. With this objective in mind, their advisor will recommend a two-tiered approach.

The first tier would involve placing $5,000 of their investment income return in a public cable television limited partnership each year for four years. It is recommended that the parents of Wanda and Wilfred own the limited partnership units for three years. After reviewing the program summary, it is noted that this coincides with the estimated life of the partnerships's tax benefits. At the end of this initial three-year period it is further recommended that these units be gifted to the children under the Uniform Gifts to Minors Act. The law influencing this type of ownership permits the establishment of a custodian account for a minor in which property is given irrevocably to the child and placed in a custodial account until the minor reaches the age of majority. Wendall and Wilhelmina, as donors of the gift, may not change their minds about their decisions, although they may be named as the custodians of the account. One of the most important aspects of this arrangement is that income and profits in a Uniform Gifts to Minors Act account are taxable to the minor and not the donor. This usually results in income tax savings.

The program summary indicates that this is a ten-year program. This means that from the time of the gift the value of the program will continue to appreciate for seven more years. When the cable television systems are then sold and the partnership dissolved, Wendall and Wilhelmina will have realized their goal of achieving growth to fund their children's education.

Tier two would involve contributing the additional $5,000 of investment income received each year in a moderately leveraged, new-construction, luxury garden apartment complex. The program you are considering has estimated tax advantages of approximately 80 percent of their investment over the program's life in addition to providing a modest cash flow. As opposed to receiving cash flow, which would be taxable at ordinary income tax rates, the outstanding growth potential of this program offers the opportunity to convert ordinary income to long-term capital gains. The life of the program is estimated to be ten years, positioning the gain available from the sale of the program's property holdings at a time when your clients will need it most to fund their children's education.

Their recommended plan would, therefore, be to invest in the tier-one and tier-two programs the amount received as investment returns from their existing portfolio for a period of four years. This systematic investment plan will allow returns to be generated at times when they are needed most throughout each child's college career. Note that staggering the contributions over a four-year period will mean that the returns will also be staggered to coincide with college tuition costs. In addition, the investment returns being generated by your clients' existing portfolio will receive the tax-advantaged benefits realized from the tier-one and tier-two limited partnership programs.

DEDUCTIONS CONCEALED IN A VELVET GLOVE

Percy Poindexter founded the Amalgamated Glove Company and currently serves as its president and sole shareholder. Amalgamated is a world-renowned manufacturer of high-quality hand wear for fashion-conscious individuals around the world. Amalgamated has provided Percy with a substantial income and a handsome pension plan. The corporation itself, however, has never had much in the way of taxable income because Percy has made sure that he takes as much as he can in salary and tax-free fringe benefits in order to avoid dividend taxation. In fact, Percy has the whole family on the corporate payroll, even his children Penelope and Palmer, during their summer vacations.

Recently, Percy made a shrewd marketing decision by developing a single glove fashioned after the one worn by a prominent rock and roll star. The development of this unique hand garment required little modification of existing machinery and production capabilities. Overnight, Percy's invention became all the rage. Suddenly, the corporation was taking in money faster than Percy could find ways of getting it out. Percy knew his corporation would soon move into the top corporate tax bracket, but as soon as the fad ran its course, Amalgamated would go back to the 15 percent corporate tax bracket. This is one of the few situations in which tax-advantaged investments may make sense for a corporation. Amalgamated Glove will have a couple of years at most in a top corporate tax bracket. If some of that income could be deferred, the net result could be a substantial reduction in the total corporate tax bill.

Recommended Approach It is recommended that Percy follow a two-tiered investment plan. Tier-one will involve a private equipment-leasing limited partnership program investing in hospital equipment. The proceeds of the limited partnership offering will purchase body scanners, which are in considerable demand at health care facilities across the country. The program summary indicates that Percy's investment of $301,000 will be staggered over a series of four installments.

The first installment of $52,170 will provide a tax write-off this year of 4.0:1. The next installment, due six months from now, will be $82,990, providing losses of 3.2:1. Twelve months later, Percy will make another installment payment of $81,850, providing losses amounting to 3.0:1 of his installment contribution. Twelve months later, the final payment of $83,990 will be due, providing a write-off of 2.9:1. In the fifth year of the program, though no payment is required, the tax losses will amount to 3.3:1 of the total investment made to date.

It should be noted that this equipment-leasing program will be utilizing a five-year Accelerated Cost Recovery System (ACRS) depreciation schedule. As a financial planner who conscientiously reviewed this program's offering memorandum, you indicate to Percy that he will be at risk for a total of $1,126,380, which will serve to increase his cost basis in the program. The increased cost basis provides the ability for Percy to utilize fully the extensive tax write-offs featured by this limited partnership.

Your tier-two recommendation would be for Percy to invest the considerable tax benefits from the private equipment-leasing limited partnership in a mutual fund that takes advantage of the 85 percent dividend exclusion available to corporations. In this way, Percy will be able to fund the eventual tax liability generated by phantom income due in years six, seven, eight, and nine of the limited partnership offering.

This combination of programs will provide the immediate tax benefits that Percy's corporation will desperately require and will fund the future tax liability that will be due from the phantom income produced by the equipment-leasing program.

SUMMARY

As for mutual funds, it is crucial to determine whether your prospects are suited to investing in limited partnerships. This is especially important in selling this type of investment product because of the high risk typically involved. In general, prospects should be able to predict their incomes over several years to come and must be able to live with the illiquidity of most limited partnerships. It is your job, as a registered representative, to determine exactly what the clients' objectives are in order to recommend the most suitable limited partnership investment.

6

The Limited Partnership Sales Process

The technical discussion of limited partnerships in Part III will give you an overview of the nuts and bolts of limited partnerships. In this chapter we are going to look at the sales specifics for limited partnerships. Because the sale is more complex than for mutual funds, the sales track will identify and define more terms for the prospect, and you will continuously be advised to look for feedback from the prospects to make sure that they understand the concepts. Throughout the sales presentation, it is important that the prospects understand *results;* often the precise mathematics that went into arriving at the projections are less crucial than to the basic concepts that must be understood by prospects.

This is not to suggest that your presentation need not be accurate; it *must* accurately explain all relevant aspects of the specific limited partnership investment you are recommending. But for purpose of conceptualizing, view the process as one in which the prospects must first understand the risks and potential costs of their investment and second the potential benefits to them.

SALES PRESENTATION COORDINATED WITH THE FINANCIAL PLANNING PROCESS

As for mutual funds, we will first address the sales process coordinated with the total financial planning process, for both the middle- and higher-income markets.

THE MIDDLE-INCOME MARKET

As you may have surmised, because of the higher risk involved in limited partnership investing, your sales efforts in the middle-income market will be targeted primarily at those individuals with moderately higher incomes. This limits the *number* of prospects that you may deal with, but your earnings per case should be substantially greater in the higher level of the middle-income market than with many other products that you sell.

The information that you have collected from your client on the financial questionnaire will help you determine the client's objectives and attitudes and let you determine if your client is a candidate for a limited partnership interest. The sales process will include four steps:

1. Reconfirm your client's financial objectives and goals.
2. Describe the generic characteristics of the particular limited partnership investments you will be recommending (real estate, oil and gas, leasing, etc.).
3. Describe the specific limited partnership you are recommending.
4. Close for a buying decision.

Because limited partnerships are far more complex than other investments, it is vital that you explain all concepts to your client in a simple, straightforward manner. In addition, throughout the sales process, you should elicit feedback from your prospect so that you are certain that there are no misunderstandings. Lack of understanding is evidenced by a glazed look on your prospect's face, a frown, or another body language sign. We are emphasizing the understanding aspect of your sale because, with limited partnerships, chances are your prospects will not buy if they do not feel comfortable with all of the concepts you are describing.

In addition, prospects *must* feel confident that *you* are confident and that you understand all of the concepts that you are discussing as well as the specific investment you are selling. Because of this, the section in this chapter on answering objections for limited partnerships includes numerous questions and answers concerning complex concepts that often confuse prospects. These answers are meant to be *sales* answers to these concepts; i.e., they are not complete technical answers to questions but rather provide your prospects with a general understanding of concepts.

Model Track Sales The following is a model sales track for selling limited partnerships to higher-income individuals within the broad-based middle-income market. Note that there is a "generic" section for three separate categories of limited partnerships: real estate, oil and gas, and equipment leasing. Naturally, you will want to use that particular generic description to match the particular kind of limited partnership you will be selling.

"Mr./Ms. (prospect's name), what I'd like to talk about today are some new and unique investment ideas that can supplement your financial plan and potentially provide substantial tax benefits for you. Before we talk about these investment ideas, I'd like to review your financial goals and objectives with you, which we discussed at our last meeting. You indicated that these objectives and criteria were important to you:

- Immediate income-tax savings. You have indicated that it is very important to reduce the taxation of your existing income.
- Long-term capital growth. Capital growth that results from long term appreciation is important to you.

"Is this correct, Mr./Ms. (prospect's name)?"

[Listen to reply.]

"In return for these benefits, you have also indicated a willingness to assume greater risk as well as a degree of investment illiquidity. Liquidity is the ability to convert an investment quickly into cash, and, as we discussed, limited partnerships are *not* liquid. This is because there is no formal secondary market for your limited partnership investment and because partnership agreements normally provide for substantial limitations on your liability to sell or transfer units. Is that correct, Mr./Ms. (prospect's name)?"

[Listen to reply.]

"Mr./Ms. (prospect's name), a tax-advantaged limited partnerships investment may very well meet your objectives. First, let's look at the general characteristics of a tax-advantaged limited partnership investment. A tax-advantaged limited partnership investment is a direct investment in a business enterprise. It is different from other investments that you make because it provides you with tax benefits *when you make the investment*. You, the investor, report profits and losses of the partnership directly on your individual tax return. One primary benefit of the partnership is that tax deductions available are then used to offset taxable income from your salary or other separate sources.

"Many people mistakenly believe that a limited partnership is only good to create tax deductions. This is totally incorrect. The primary rule, the rule that I always use in advising my clients, is that a limited partnership must *first* make economic sense before it can be considered for investment. This means that, disregarding the tax benefits, the investment must have the potential to earn a profit. If it does not have the potential to earn a profit, the consequences to you range all the way from bad to terrible. This is because the investment may wind up creating income tax that you must pay at some date without creating the *cash* to pay for the tax. Therefore, uppermost in our minds should be a thorough analysis of any particular tax-advantaged investment to determine its *business merit*.

"How does a tax-advantaged limited partnership save you taxes? It's really very simple. The basic equation that Uncle Sam applies to your investment is this: business income minus deductions equals profit (or loss).

"If you purchase a real estate limited partnership, the IRS treats you as though you are in the real estate business. Your limited partnership will give you a loss whenever deductions exceed income. Tax-advantaged investors generally invest in those businesses that generate *more deductions* than income in the early years in order to report losses for taxes in those years. Normally, Uncle Sam has given these tax-advantaged businesses additional tax incentives for capital investment—incentives such as depreciation deductions, which further increase the reportable tax loss.

"You don't actually have to be losing money to report a tax loss. You may have an excellent investment and at the same time be reporting a loss on your tax return. Oil field development is an example. Between the time that an oil well is drilled and the time it actually begins to gush oil, there is a time lag. In the first year of operation, substantial drilling expenses are incurred and no income realized. Your deductible expenses would exceed your income in that time period. This is tax 'shelter.'

"What is the big deal about receiving tax deductions in the first year? A deduction today is worth *more* than the same deduction next year because you have the use of the money in the meantime. Also, the ability to delay reporting profits is another tax advantage enjoyed by some businesses. If the tax on profits can be put off, you are ahead because delaying the tax payment frees up money that otherwise would have to be paid currently to Uncle Sam. Real estate investment is a good example of the ability to delay the recognition of income. Appreciation—the increase in property value—is not taxed until the property is sold or disposed of. This amount is not currently taxed.

"I said that the tax shelter loss has the effect of reducing your total income tax. The basic equation for this is:

> Personal income minus tax shelter loss equals your personal income subject to tax.

"The more tax shelter losses you have, the more personal income you shelter. However, being an astute investor, you have probably surmised that there is another side to this coin. When your investment starts to make money, you will have an *increased* tax liability. When the tax shelter loss becomes a profit, the profit is added to your personal income, thereby increasing your taxable income. Remember our primary rule: *Your tax shelter must be a sound business investment.* Chances are that you will have cash from the investment with which to pay the income tax. In some shelters, however, the tax liability may exceed the cash available from the shelter.

"Tax-advantaged limited partnerships are not for everyone. You should not buy one unless you are in a tax bracket that maximizes the deductions generated. The higher your tax bracket, the greater the benefit you will receive from the deductions. Also, tax shelters are risky investments. However, in almost all cases, your potential economic loss is limited to the amount of your investment.

"Mr./Ms. <u>(prospect's name)</u>, now that we have gone over the many general concepts of tax shelters, let's look at the specific type of shelter that I will be recommending to you today."

[You should now proceed to the appropriate section that deals with the "generic" aspects of the type of shelter you are selling.]

Real Estate Limited Partnerships "Real estate tax shelters are by far the most popular kind of tax-advantaged limited partnership because they are tangible and easy to understand. Real estate investment has many economic advantages:

1. The investment appreciates in value during inflationary times.
2. Leverage (You may use other people's money—you borrow money—to make your investment.)
3. Cost and revenues in conservative real estate investments tend to be more predictable than in other shelters.

4. Government subsidies/guarantees to low-income housing projects make these economically feasible shelters.

"Real estate tax shelters also offer many important tax advantages:

1. The at-risk rules do not apply. This means that Uncle Sam allows you to take tax deduction for amounts that are greater than the amount you invested.
2. Ordinary income may be converted into capital gains. This happens because, going into the shelter, deductions offset ordinary income generated by the shelter and, upon sale, much of the income is capital gains income.
3. The 18-year write-off period for cost recovery gives you depreciation deductions. (The 1984 Tax Act increased the minimum number of years for write-off from 15 to 18 years.)
4. Investment tax credits are available for rehabilitation of old buildings.

"These are the economic and tax advantages of real estate partnerships in general. Now let's look at the specific investment I will be recommending. In this regard we will be looking at many different concepts. Some of the primary items that we will cover include the following:

1. Potential appreciation in value.
2. *Leverage*—Does the investment make productive use of borrowed money? Leverage can multiply the economic benefits of your investment and multiply the tax benefits as well because depreciation deductions are based not just on your equity investment but on the full purchase price of the property.
3. *Stability*—For the conservative investor, real estate has a relatively high economic stability. If stability is an objective, then it may be wise to stay away from speculative real estate investments such as the purchase of raw land.
4. *Government Subsidies*—These are typically applicable to low- and moderate-income housing programs.
5. *The Promoter/General Partner*—What is the quality of the promoter or developer who is acting as the general partner of the partnership? This is a very important factor. The deal cannot succeed unless the promoter is honest and knows what he or she is doing and does the job well. In this regard, my company carefully evaluates each shelter it offers to ensure that the promoter and general partner are reputable."

The items above may merely scratch the surface of what you will discuss with your prospects. Naturally, you must insert specific information from the offering memorandum in order to sell the partnership properly. Remember, your prospects don't care how much you know until they knows how much *you care*—about their dreams, goals, and objectives. You must win their confidence through your ability to understand them. And you must show complete technical understanding of the investment you are selling. You will want to coordinate your specific sales talk with the information found in the Objections to Limited Partnership Sales' section. In that section you will find very simple, conceptual sales answers to most technical concepts you must explain to your clients.

Oil and Gas Limited Partnerships

"Oil and gas limited partnerships, Mr./Ms. (prospect's name), offer the unique and appealing combination of tax savings *plus* the potential for above-average profits. Here's the good news: It is theoretically possible for an oil well to pay back 10 to 20 times what it costs. The bad news is that you must select oil and gas programs *very* carefully in order to find the potential good deal, i.e., the one with reasonable opportunity for profit.

"Some people think that the tax benefits in oil and gas are so good that they don't have to worry about finding oil. They are wrong! If your partnership does not find oil, you will lose money. This is true regardless of your income tax bracket. This is why I place *primary* emphasis on the *economic* soundness of a deal.

"Oil and gas partnerships are easy to understand. You, the passive investor, put up money to finance the drilling of wells. In return, you receive tax deductions in the year of investment plus a share of any oil or gas produced. In the year the well is drilled, currently deductible costs of drilling are allocated to investors who receive a tax deduction normally equal to approximately 75–90 percent of their investment.

"If the well is dry (there is no oil), you lose your money—all you have gotten out of the well is a tax deduction. But, if commercial quantities of oil and gas are found, steps are taken to complete the well and tie into pipelines. It usually takes a year or two to do this. Therefore, you will realize a tax loss in the first year when there are expenses but no income. Remember, what you want is a big gusher that gives you deductions right now and cash later on. Always think of oil and gas partnerships as an *investment* with potential for making a favorable return with the added feature of tax benefits.

"In oil and gas, we can define the amount of risk involved by choosing a partnership involved in wildcat drilling *or* developmental drilling, a mixture of the two, or proven reserves.

"Drilling wells close to proven reserves to expand on an existing site is called *developmental drilling*. On the other hand, *exploratory* or *wildcat wells* are wells drilled in new territory. Wildcat wells, as you may surmise, are much riskier because the chance of discovering oil decreases as our available information decreases. In fact, the industry average for wildcats is only about one out of nine! Developmental wells will be productive as much as half the time. Keep in mind now, Mr./Ms. (prospect's name), that *any* oil and gas venture has high risk. Also, like most partnerships, oil and gas programs are highly illiquid.

"In oil and gas, your big upfront tax deductions come from what are called *intangible drilling costs*—such things as labor, fuel, repairs, hauling, and supplies. These items are all currently deductible.

What should you look for in an oil and gas tax shelter? In a nutshell, you should thoroughly review all of the information provided in the offering memorandum. Of primary importance is always the question: Is this a sound business investment? The objective of the partnership, the structure of the deal, and the track record of the general partner are just a few of the items that are important in an oil and gas partnership. At this point, Mr./Ms. (prospect's name), let's take a look at the (name of specific product) oil and gas partnership in order to understand fully how the numbers work and how it may apply to your particular situation. We will be covering the offering memorandum in detail. Do you have any questions up to this point?"

[Listen to reply.]

Chances are your prospect will have lots of questions at this point. Make sure that they understand the *concepts;* your discussion of the specific partnership and the specific numbers should help clear up any confusion. You should continuously strive to drive home the idea that oil and gas, as well as all partnerships, must be good *investments* in order to be good deals. Review your offering memorandum thoroughly and insert specific product information in this section.

Capital Equipment Leasing

"Equipment leasing partnerships, Mr./Ms. (prospect's name), involve buying equipment—boxcars, barges, computers, automobiles, medical lab equipment, etc.—and renting it to someone else. The deal combines the opportunity for substantial profits with attractive tax incentives. The economic benefits come from the rents you collect and the ownership of the equipment you ultimately sell.

"The tax benefits, on the other hand, come from depreciation deductions and the investment credit. Depreciation deductions are a method of recovering the cost of property over its useful life. It works in exactly the same manner for equipment leasing as it does for real estate except that write-offs come more quickly. This is because equipment has a much shorter useful life than real estate because accelerated depreciation typically is used.

"The investment tax credit is the other tax benefit. Tax credits are very beneficial items because a *credit* is a *dollar-for-dollar* reduction of your tax as opposed to a tax *deduction*, which gives you less than a dollar in reduction of the tax. The credit was provided by Uncle Sam as an inducement to invest in equipment; it's equal to 6 percent for property depreciated three years and 10 percent for property depreciated for five years or ten years. It is taken only in the first year and is an addition to any tax benefits provided by the shelter.

"You may be asking yourself at this point why a business would rent its equipment if owning the equipment has so many tax benefits. There may be several reasons:

1. The business can't benefit from the deductions because it is in a low tax bracket.
2. The business doesn't have the capital necessary to buy the equipment.
3. The business doesn't want the risk of ownership in the event the equipment becomes obsolete.

"As always, the most important evaluation factor is the economic quality of your investment—you must find equipment that produces enough rent to meet the carrying charges and retains a large part of its original value. The ideal equipment to buy might be something that is in great demand, will not wear out quickly, and will not become obsolete quickly because of changes in technology. Typical types of equipment that are sold as tax shelters to individuals include barges, boxcars, containers, yachts, medical equipment, and, occasionally, aircraft. This type of equipment may be leased on a short-term basis and is easily transferred to a new user.

"Many equipment-leasing programs are structured as limited partnerships. (Others involve direct ownership of the equipment.) Often, recourse notes are used to finance your investment. This means that you pay in a portion of your investment and borrow a portion of your investment. They are called *recourse notes* because you have liability for the notes and, if the deal fails and losses are incurred, you will be responsible for them. The good news here is that you are *leveraging*, which means that the potential benefits of the deal can also be amplified. The important thing to remember about equipment leasing is that the quality of the equipment itself is crucial to your sheltering success.

Mr./Ms. (prospect's name), I am recommending the (specific product name) equipment-leasing partnership. Let's take a look at the specifics of this program by first reviewing the offering memorandum."

At this point you must insert specific information from the offering memorandum of the particular shelter you are selling.

The Close The close of a limited partnership sale will begin when you first open your mouth to discuss limited partnerships and will depend totally on the degree of understanding that you convey to your prospect. Understanding means the understanding of your client's desires and objectives as well as a thorough understanding of general tax shelter concepts and the specific partnership you are offering. You are selling your expertise—most prospects for limited partnership interests will put total trust and confidence in your judgment. This is a big responsibility. Your closing technique should continuously involve questions to your prospects and "reading" of their understanding. Your sales talk should be punctuated with comments such as:

"Does that make sense to you, Mr./Ms. (prospect's name)?"

"What do you think of that, Mr./Ms. (prospect's name)?"

"Would you like me to go over that again, Mr./Ms. (prospect's name)?"

"I know this material is sometimes confusing. Which concepts would you like me to go over again?"

If you continuously use phrases such as this, your prospect's understanding level will remain high, which will generate trust and understanding. Assuming that the shelter you are recommending is suitable, you then have the sale.

The Higher-Income Market

Sales objectives in the higher-income market are precisely the same as they are in the broad-based middle-income market:

1. Reconfirm your client's goals and objectives.
2. Describe the characteristics of shelters *in general* and the specific type of shelter you are recommending.
3. Review and describe the specific shelter you are recommending.
4. Close.

You should be concentrating your efforts for sales of limited partnership interests in the higher-income market. These are the people who are concerned about tax savings and become quite disturbed about the level of income tax that they are required to pay. Their motivation may be more tax-savings-oriented than an individual who is not in the 50 percent income tax bracket. However, you should never lose sight of the concept that a limited partnership must first be a good investment before you advise a client to invest.

The words used in your actual sales presentation of limited partnership interests to higher-income individuals will not differ substantially from the presentation just reviewed for the middle-income market. Therefore, the sales talk is not repeated here. You should understand, however, that the selling of limited partnership interests is one of the higher forms of salesmanship and that you must convince your prospects of your fiduciary desire to recommend a course of action in their best interests. You must also do so with complex investments while interfacing with other advisors.

SINGLE-NEED PRESENTATION

When you are marketing limited partnership interests, invariably your focus will be on individuals in high income tax brackets who should be willing and able to accept the higher risk of tax-advantaged limited partnership investing. In the single-need situation, you will merely be focusing on the need to cap or reduce income taxes and invest in a venture with high potential rewards *without* the coordination of total financial planning.

An additional aspect of sales presentations not previously discussed is how to go about conceptualizing your detailed discussion of the offering memorandum. One way to do this is to concentrate on the following topics—even prepare a complete summary of each subject prior to the sales presentation:

1. Summary of the offering. This is usually at the beginning of the memorandum and outlines the deal.

2. The accounting projections and footnotes. It is these projections that really sell the deal; they are prepared using optimistic assumptions. Remember that they are not cast in stone and that, if the assumptions are not valid, projections will not be realized.
3. The section describing use of the proceeds of the offering. This is the section describing fees and how much goes into the actual investment.
4. Compensation paid to the general partners and affiliates.
5. Track record of the promoter from prior programs.
6. Description of the experience of the general partner, its employees, and other key persons.
7. Discussion of the tax considerations.

You will find with experience that tax-advantaged investments of all kinds are easier to sell than life insurance. This is probably because of the natural desire of most people to dwell on the living aspects of planning opposed to death planning. Thus, it is your professional responsibility always to provide full and complete information about the investment you are selling. Chances are that not only will you maintain a long list of satisfied clients, but you will also receive a substantial number of referrals from those satisfied clients.

LIFE INSURANCE NEEDS AND LIMITED PARTNERSHIP INTERESTS

Coordination of your prospect's tax planning needs and basic life insurance needs is critical and should not be overlooked. In the course of the excitement over a limited partnership, it is very easy to disregard or forget the more basic life insurance needs of your client, which may not create the same level of excitement in your prospect's eyes. Nevertheless, because of the high risk involved in limited partnership interests, basic insurance needs should always be addressed *first*.

While this may not occur all the time, it may be possible to tie in the purchase of a limited partnership investment with a desirable purchase of life insurance. For example, if your client invested $10,000 in a real estate limited partnership and received $20,000 in income tax deductions the first year, this would reduce the client's taxes by $10,000, assuming a 50 percent income tax bracket. Part or all of that $10,000 saving could be used as life insurance premiums; naturally, you must look at the tax benefits beyond the first year in order to recommend an intelligent method of using the deductions to purchase life insurance.

One possible solution would be to tie in the amount of tax savings, which will change each year; with the purchase of universal life insurance because universal life offers premium payment flexibility. Even if you do not recommend the specific use of the tax savings to purchase insurance, you should point out to the prospect the concept that potential tax savings *offset* premiums paid for insurance. If your prospect understands the "low-cost or no cost" effect of having a tax benefit via a limited partnership offsetting insurance premiums, you will develop improved understanding and a stronger trust relationship.

OVERCOMING SALES OBJECTIONS

So far we have intimated that objections to limited partnership interests will result for the most part from lack of understanding on the part of the clients or from the fact that you may not have recommended the most suitable investment for your prospect's financial goals and objectives. Consequently, much of the following discussion of objections will focus on specific answers—*sales* answers—to questions about generic limited partnership concepts. An example of such questions might be: In 25 words or less, just what is a limited partnership tax-advantaged investment? Regardless of what the particular question might be, your technique should involve rephrasing or restating what the prospect says. You may visualize the concept of paraphrasing (rephrasing) in the following manner:

1. *Listen* to the objection.
2. Restate or paraphrase what your prospect is telling you.
3. Show understanding of your client and his needs. For example, you might say, "I can understand how you might feel that way. . ."
4. Answer the objection.

Let's look at an example of this technique. You have been merrily discussing the benefits of tax-advantaged investment to your prospect, when he or she begins to frown and asks this question:

Q."I just can't seem to understand why I shouldn't buy a mutual fund (or stock) instead of a real estate limited partnership."

A."That is an *excellent* question, Mr./Ms. (prospect's name). Let me see if I understand you correctly. You do not see the tax and investment differences between real estate limited partnership and mutual funds. Is that correct?"

[*Listen to answer.]*

"Well, I can understand how you feel. Tax-advantaged investing can be a very confusing subject. Limited partnerships have tax benefits that mutual funds do not. With mutual funds (or stocks), you receive no tax *incentive* when you make the investment. In the future, you receive a deduction if there is a loss of your investment.

"On the other hand, with a tax-advantaged limited partnership, you receive a deduction right up front—initially—as though you lost your money. A tax deduction up front in the first year is good for you because money has a time value; that is, it's better to get the deduction the first year than in some later year. With a tax shelter you then pay a tax in the future if it turns out that you make money. You pay for the tax benefits of a tax shelter in the form of higher risk than most mutual funds or stocks. Does that make sense, Mr./Ms. (prospect's name)?"

[Listen to answer.]

Let's look at another example of how you would structure your response to an objection using the planned paraphrasing technique. Let's assume that the deal you are presenting is a real estate limited partnership.

Q. "Everything you said so far sounds terrific, but I am still uneasy about what happens if the property goes under. For example, what if the rents and occupancy rates do not work out as planned? What happens to my investment? What are the effects?"

A. "That is an excellent question, Mr./Ms. (prospect's name). If I understand you correctly, you are concerned about the possible economic and tax consequences—favorable or unfavorable—should the program *not* make money. Is that correct?"

[Listen to answer.]

"Well, I can understand why you would feel that way. You should be thoroughly comfortable in your understanding of the investment, and certainly one on the most important aspects is the degree of risk involved and the potential for unfavorable consequences as well as benefits. First, let's look at the potential economic loss. The only potential amount of money that you can lose is the amount of your investment. This is because the investment is structured as a limited partnership, and therefore you have only limited liability. No one can come after any of your other property. Does that make sense?"

[Listen to answer.]

"Let's now look at the income-tax consequences. Let's assume that you are in a real estate program that is in default (a housing project). Let's also assume, for ease of illustration, that the project cost $10,000, with a $2,000 down payment and the balance financed by a mortgage of $8,000. Depreciation of $4,500 has already been taken. Your basis is therefore $10,000 minus $4,500, or $5,500. Also, at the time of default the mortgage is $7,500. Your basis is *below* the mortgage. We call this a *negative basis.* This means it is negative in relation to the mortgage. When the property is foreclosed, you will have taxable income of $2,000 ($7,500 minus $5,500 equals $2,000). Unfortunately, you will not receive any cash with which to pay the tax. This is the bad news. In any event, you should always understand and accept the possibility of 100 percent economic loss of your investment. Does that make sense Mr./Ms. (prospect's name)?"

[Listen to answer.]

Here is another common objective to limited partnerships:

Q."I've been told that the fees in a limited partnership investment are high. Is that right?"

A."To answer that, Mr./Ms. (prospect's name), you must consider the cost of owning and managing this particular form of business *on your own,* without the benefit of the limited partnership form. You would have initial purchase expenses *plus* ongoing management fees. Furthermore, you would *lose* the economies of scales available to limited partnership investors. Finally, my company has a legal *duty*--called *due diligence*—to make sure that fees are *not out of line.*"

These are just examples of techniques to answer objections and explain highly technical information in a simple manner.

LIMITED PARTNERSHIP INTERESTS IN QUALIFIED PLANS

You have just come to one of the most exciting and largely untapped areas in the sale of limited partnership interests: qualified plans. As you may recall from Chapter 4, on mutual funds, qualified plans include the following.

- individual retirement accounts (IRAs)
- self-employed individuals' retirement plans
- corporate pension and profit sharing plans
- 401 (K) plans
- Tax-sheltered annuity plans (section 501(C)(3) plans); limited partnership investments are not typically used in TSA plans.

We learned that mutual funds are an ideal investment vehicle for any of these plans; in many cases, certain limited partnership interests will also be an ideal *investment* for a qualified plan.

At this point you may be wondering how the tax-sheltering benefits of limited partnership interests fit into qualified plans since a qualified plan has tax benefits itself. Aren't amounts contributed to qualified plans tax-deductible, *and* aren't the earnings that accrue within a qualified plan tax-free?

The answer to these questions is that you must focus entirely upon the good-investment aspects of limited partnership interests in qualified plans. This is because the qualified plan tax rules will govern the tax results for any particular investment that is purchased by the plan. The tax attributes of a limited partnership interest will be lost when it is purchased within a qualified plan. Thus, we return to our basic simple rule for limited partnership investing: The investment *must* make good economic and business sense.

Typically, a certain amount of liquidity should be maintained within plan investments. This is particularly true in corporate plans in which terminations will occur and distributions from plan assets must be made at random times. The concept of diversification should also be one of the factors considered in qualified plan investments. How does this impact limited partnerships? Because limited partnerships are typically not liquid investments, the plan should be balanced with respect to investments. For example, you may recommend that, say, 40 percent or 50 percent of plan assets be invested in limited partnership interests with the balance of plan assets in more liquid funds such as mutual funds (primarily corporate plans). A balanced portfolio will also tend to reduce risk via diversifications.

Let's now look at each separate type of qualified plan and the possible use of limited partnership interests as an investment vehicle. First, consider individual retirement accounts (IRAs). Your broker/dealer probably has a number of limited partnership interests available and suited for investment within an IRA; these limited partnership interests are suitable for qualified plans. Your prospects would want to consider these interests on the basis of the business merits. As an equity representative, you must sell the potential earnings of the investment. And, since an IRA involves only one individual, liquidity may not be as critical a factor as it would be in a corporate pension or profit-sharing plan. After all, the stated intent of the plan is long-term growth; therefore, liquidity would probably be a secondary consideration.

Limited partnership interests are also a sound investment for self-employed (Keogh) plans. Again, economic benefits must be sold to the prospect. Because contribution maximums are considerably higher than IRA maximums ($30,000 vs. $2,000) *and* more than one participant may be in the plan, liquidity should also be provided in these plans. This may be accomplished with a balance of limited partnership investment and mutual funds.

For corporate pension and profit-sharing plans, limited partnership investments are creating more and more interest. Qualified corporate plans by far constitute the largest segment of all qualified plans. Certain promoters, as previously mentioned, have designed their products to be qualified plan investments. This is done by allowing for purchase in small dollar units, (e.g., $1,000, $2,000, $5,000). Because the corporate qualified plans market is so large, some equity representatives decide to concentrate sales efforts in this market. Ongoing contribution amounts and existing assets are both large; this means considerably larger earnings per case than in other qualified plans. However, it also requires more prospecting in a more sophisticated market than is the case for IRA or HR-10 plans sales.

What about sales techniques in a qualified market for limited partnerships? Your specific sales techniques for limited partnerships will not differ significantly from those you use in selling mutual funds to qualified plans. You must "sell the sizzle." You might use the compound interest tables found at the end of this book to demonstrate the miracle of compounding periodic contributions to an IRA or a self-employed individual's plan.

Answering objections and closing should also be no different from the processes previously discussed in this chapter. In summary, limited partnerships in qualified plans constitute a fast-growing market. If you are prepared to sell the business merit of limited partnership investing, you can look forward to substantially increased earnings.

SUMMARY

Because limited partnerships commonly carry a high risk for investors, and because the concepts involved are more complex than for mutual funds, it is essential that you thoroughly explain those concepts to your prospects. In all sales presentations, you should concentrate on establishing mutual understanding and trust with the clients. Make sure they realize that you are sympathetic when confusion arises and that you are willing and able to explain anything that they do not comprehend. A limited partnership that both makes economic sense and provides the tax benefits and total returns your clients need can be a very desirable product, especially for higher-income prospects.

7

Seminar Selling of Investment Products

The objectives of this chapter are threefold. The first goal is to define the seminar concept and explain the central elements—attendance, the program, and follow-up for the individual interview. The second is to suggest ways to use seminars successfully to prospect for investment products clientele, to educate the clientele, and to motivate them. The final objective is to present pragmatic seminar methods that have been used by both successful life insurance agents *and* successful financial planners as a primary marketing method in selling their respective products.

Seminars are not the only way to market investment products, and the methods and techniques described are not the only methods or the best methods of utilizing seminars. These are merely ideas, but they have been tested in the marketplace and are proven tools if you have the dedication and desire to use the seminar method for selling investment products.

Seminar selling, in the simplest terms, simply involves seeing large numbers of people at one time who are prospective buyers for your investment products and thereby increasing your productivity geometrically. Many agents who begin to use seminars effectively for the sale of investment-type products have more prospects to see than time permits. As you will see as you proceed through this section, seminar presentations take many varied forms; however, the results are usually the same—more good prospects for equities seen per hour, per day, and per year.

Seminars may include meetings with free admission, or they may require a fee. Seminars may also have different objectives.

For the most part, the type of seminar described in this manual will be the seminar that attempts to motivate your prospect to use financial planning and utilize the investment products you have available through your broker/dealer.

Seminars will *not* always be the best way to find prospects; they can be expensive, and not everyone is suited to be a seminar speaker. Nevertheless, this is a marketing technique that may be used by all registered representatives.

Seminar selling involves three distinct and interdependent parts:

1. audience choice and marketing;
2. program content and delivery; and
3. follow-through with the individual interview.

Too many people view the seminar program as the only important element of the seminar. Often this attitude produces little or no attendance. Even if attendance is strong and participants are adequately motivated, all benefits of the seminar can be lost if you fail to follow through promptly with individual interviews. Thus, it is important to understand and accept the fact that all three parts of seminar planning require extensive and equal efforts.

PSYCHOLOGY OF SEMINARS

For a number of important reasons, seminars can be one of the most important prospecting tools you use to sell investment products. This is because our educational backgrounds and experiences have trained us to accept a group environment for educational experiences. Second, we are also tuned into the group environment for motivation, not only in educational areas, but in terms of emotional impact, such as in listening to political speeches, attending mass meetings, etc. The formality, stiffness, and possible embarrassment of one-on-one meetings is certainly reduced and may be eliminated by group meetings. A healthy sharing occurs within a group, and exchange of ideas and experiences is generally the result. Concepts that would otherwise embarrass or anger the listener—neglect of financial planning, lack of awareness, or ignorance of investment options—can be discussed in the group without fear of rejection. The individuals within the group realize that some or all of these concepts are really applicable to their own situation.

A seminar also presents an excellent psychological environment for the agent to motivate an audience to action. The personality, profession, reputation, etc., of the communicator (speaker) certainly help determine the degree of audience motivation and colors the message.

TARGETING THE AUDIENCE

Some general factors that you would want to consider in targeting your seminar audience are age, sex, occupation, marital status, annual income, and net worth. You may consider concentrating on a specific market. Market concentration permits you to develop an expertise in solving peculiar problems related to a specific industry. You can attend industry meetings and conventions, receive industry periodicals, and otherwise be identified as a person particularly attuned to the specific problems and opportunities faced by professionals in every career. Groups such as farmers/ranchers, physicians, teachers, engineers or architects, young marrieds, two-income families, new homeowners, existing clients, and business owners are some possible groups that you might target. Some representatives target a subset of business owners; for example, a specific manufacturing business or service business. Another specific market could be advisors to business owners such as lawyers, accountants, or bankers.

Specialization may be especially important in working with physicians, farmers, ranchers, widows, public corporations, or certain types of family-owned businesses. These people believe that they have special financial and investment concerns unique to their circumstances. The financial planner who understands the nature of these problems and can provide investment solutions will probably have a ready and eager audience.

Seminar cosponsorship or complete sponsorship by a third party such as an association, an organization, or a college or university is also an effective method of targeting an audience. A most effective technique is to have a trade or professional association serve as the sponsor of your seminar. In conjunction with their other meetings, trade and professional associations hold annual conventions and state and regional meetings at regular intervals. These groups are usually staffed by permanent personnel under the direction of a paid executive officer. Additionally, associations usually have elected officers selected from their members. Officers and staffs of these groups constantly search for important services, information, and speakers that they can make available to their members.

Another vitally important marketing issue is size of audience and method of initial contact. Most financial planners who successfully market via seminars mail out formal invitations or letters in conjunction with newspaper advertisements or possibly third-party brochures. If a letter is used, it should contain a response card or some other method of having the individuals indicate their willingness to attend.

You must set an attendance goal, anticipate a response rate, and plan accordingly. For cold calls (i.e., mailing to a list of strangers), seminar promoters report response rates of 2 to 6 percent. Of those who actually respond, as few as 50 percent of *respondents* have been known to show up. For example, if your goal is to attract 50 attendees from cold-call lists, and you anticipate a 5 percent response, you would need to send out 2,000 invitations: 5 percent of 2,000 equals 100 positive respondents; 50 percent who actually attend equals 50 attendees. The letter or invitation should include an agenda and speaker information if available without taking a hard sell approach to the seminar. Generally, in the long run you should develop your own mailing list. Also, a follow-up call should be made to respondents approximately a week before the seminar.

PROGRAM CONTENT AND DELIVERY

Program considerations that must be made are content and choice of speaker or speakers. Planners should be aware that some professionals are so inundated with seminar and conference announcements that it can be difficult to capture their attention. Here is where you must use your imagination and creativity.

For example, in the investments area you must give your audience a special reason to attend your seminar rather than one sponsored by a competing investment firm. Your strategy might be to try to provide information to your audience in an area in which you feel they are weak or not knowledgeable. Chances are you can do this with almost any group; it just takes a little investigation.

The seminar name itself should be truly intriguing. An example might be "Special Situation Investments in Qualified Retirement Plans," "Financial Planning for Young Professionals," or "How You Can Save Your Business from Federal Tax Destruction." Another idea would be to target attorneys or accountants to inform them in a specific area in which they are not knowledgeable, such as limited partnership interests or real estate tax shelters.

Your choice of speakers and the subject matter are invariably tied together. Seminar speakers should be chosen on the basis of their ability to communicate in a simple, relaxed, understandable manner and to make the program interesting. Speakers should hold an audience's attention and must use special techniques such as using specific illustrations, storytelling, humor, and extensive amounts of audio-visual materials. You should be choosing speakers not so much for technical expertise but for showmanship, ability to motivate, and ability to create a stimulating emotional experience for attendees.

This is not to suggest that the speakers should not be knowledgeable in the investment area; they should never say anything they do not understand and they are not reasonably sure that the audience can understand. However, showmanship and the ability to motivate are probably of more importance than precise technical knowledge. These comments suggest that it is more important for attendees to understand the *results* of equity investments than the calculations needed to arrive at those results. For example, show the ultimate income tax impact in a case study of investment in a limited partnership interest and emphasize *results* rather than mathematical processes needed to arrive at the results. Speakers should also be cautioned not to get bogged down in technical jargon; they should speak the language of the audience involved.

Can *you* be your own seminar speaker? It takes a certain personality, and you must be able to master the presentations and rehearse them yourself. For financial planners beginning their practice, this may be the only practical approach to speakers. Another possibility would be to enter into a joint venture with another registered representative from your agency and share speaking responsibilities. Larger seminars can be cosponsored with other professionals, such as a legal firm, an accounting firm, or a bank trust department. In this way, you may avoid having to pay for an outside speaker.

Your speaker should use humor (in good taste, of course), anecdotes, or other similar techniques to warm up your audience. This also helps relax the registered representative, who may have a mild case of stage fright before the meat of the seminar begins. The presentation should not be too slick, to prevent possible distrust by skeptical members of the audience. It should be rehearsed so that it comes naturally. In your opening remarks, you may cover some basic "housekeeping" issues such as whether or not the audience should interrupt with questions or hold them for later, eating arrangements, etc.

Since you want to project a positive image and be professional at all times, you will also have to control potential problem attendees, such as late arrivals, the "big mouths," the "experts," and the "sidetrackers." In most cases, potential problems such as these can be handled smoothly with a response such as the following:

> "That's a very interesting question. Unfortunately, at this moment we do not have the time to delve into that problem in detail. If you would like to discuss that with me further, let's get together at the next break."

Regardless of your specific speaker or content, communications specialists invariably recommend the use of audiovisual equipment and materials. No one can deny that today's American buyer has been more influenced by television than by any other form of communication. To many, reading and verbal communication have become something that their parents used to do. Some experts contend that television commercials and debates have decided more winners in recent elections than ability, experience, and integrity combined. Experience seems to show that representatives who are equipped with effective audiovisual presentations will make more calls, close more sales, and obtain better referrals than representatives relying solely on written or verbal seminar presentations.

An audio-visual presentation also establishes the representative as the "expert" and permits him or her to control the direction a meeting takes. Furthermore, experts say that the effective use of audiovisuals increases retention by a factor of three to five.

Great care should be taken in planning the audiovisual equipment and its use. A 35-millimeter slide presentation for several hundred people can be a catastrophe with an inadequately sized screen or without an extra projection bulb.

SEMINAR LOGISTICS

Seminar logistics should *all* be geared to making the seminar *convenient* for your attendees. The following is a checklist of the major logistical concerns that you must deal with:

1. *Location.* You may use a hotel meeting room, restaurant, insurance agency meeting room, library, or other public place. Make certain that your location is *convenient* and *quiet.*
2. *Length of meeting.* Seminars can be developed that range in length from one hour to all day; this is a function of your target market. For example, meetings for husbands and wives (general public) will normally be evening meetings and therefore limited to one or two hours. Develop a timetable and stick to it; begin on time and end on time. Nothing irritates potential clients more quickly, or puts them to sleep faster than waiting for a program to begin or end.
3. *Day of the week.* Most seminars are held on Tuesdays, Wednesdays, or Thursdays, because speakers and attendees more commonly take vacation time on Mondays and Fridays.
4. *Time of day.* Again, this will depend on your target market. For business owners, for example, a one- or two-hour breakfast meeting may attract considerable numbers, while a meeting between 5:00 and 6:00 P.M. may be attractive to

dentists or doctors because it is toward the end of their professional day.

5. *Seating arrangements.* Seating arrangements can be classroom style, U-shaped, or circular, depending on the audience and number of attendees.
6. *Supplies.* Make available pads and pencils for note-taking, water pitchers, name tags, tent signs, and handouts. With regard to handouts, always make sure you have a sufficient number of copies to distribute.
7. *Sign-in at hotel/restaurant lobby.* If the sign-in is in the lobby, guests will have an easier time finding the meeting. The person signing them in can direct them to the meeting room.
8. *Check-in table at room entrance.* The check-in table may be merely a point at which to distribute handouts or literature. It may also be a point in which guests register prior to entering the meeting room. However, some authorities consider this approach ineffectual because many people simply won't register. Another way to obtain attendees' names, addresses, and telephone numbers is to do so on your critique form, which should be distributed toward the end of the seminar. To elicit critique information, you may say something like this: "Would you give me some information about what you found interesting about the seminar? Oh, yes, would you also give me your name and telephone number?"
9. *Podium, microphones, screen, audio-visual equipment.* If you are using a hotel or restaurant facility, most of these items can be provided by the facility. In any event, make sure that you are prepared to continue the program even if one of these items should not be available or fails to function.
10. *Lighting and acoustics.* Someone will need to control lights assuming you are using audiovisuals.
11. *A full room.* If you are not certain about attendance, it is better to have a slightly *smaller* room than necessary than a larger room, which does not look like it is full.
12. *Refreshments, breaks, menu selection.* If a meal is provided, attendees will not have to leave the building to find something to eat.
13. *Seminar coordinator.* Ideally, this should be a clerical person who can coordinate the seminar and attend the seminar.
14. *Cost control.* Make sure you have a budget and stick to it. Depending on size and location, your costs may range from

hundreds of dollars to in excess of $10,000 per seminar. Remember, however, that commissions generated via the seminar should be many times anticipated expenses.

15. *Check planning*. Finally, *double-check* and *triple-check* all planning for the seminar.

One final concern is the question of whether or not to charge a fee for the seminar. Fee-structured seminars have some distinct advantages. First, the fee provides a source of income or at least helps to offset costs; and second, it separates the wheat from the chaff. People who pay a fee are more interested and more sincere listeners. Accountants and lawyers are conditioned to paying fees. If the representative intends to charge a fee for the seminar, it is *imperative* that all subject matter be *generic;* the attendee who pays a fee will not expect to be inundated with a specific product hard sell and will appreciate generic, objective information.

Many financial planning and investment seminars, however, are provided on a no-fee basis.

SEMINAR EVALUATION

Seminars should be critiqued by participants and seminar sponsors. You should provide participants with an evaluation or a critique form, which not only gives you some constructive ideas for the next seminar but also helps you qualify attendees for the follow-up telephone call and personal interview. The evaluation form can also be used to obtain referred leads using a question such as: "Do you have friends or associates who could benefit from a seminar such as this?" As the sponsor, you should ask yourself what went wrong and what didn't. Were there enough invitations, and was there enough audience participation?

FOLLOW-THROUGH: THE INDIVIDUAL INTERVIEW

Seminar follow-up is normally done via phone call; usually this can tie in with the participant's evaluation of the seminar. You may also offer attendees a free financial counseling interview. In follow-up interviews, you must use concepts from the seminar to tie into individual needs and your solutions for these needs.

Obviously, to conduct the individual interview, you must possess the knowledge and competency to satisfy the investment needs and objectives of the prospect. In the beginning, you may find yourself in the position of being called upon to provide a service for which you are not 100 percent prepared; in this situation, working jointly with a more experienced agent could be an ideal arrangement. How many clients can you expect from this follow-up? Experienced seminar sponsors report that as many as 50–80 percent of their attendees eventually become clients.

SUMMARY

In summary, seminar selling is challenging and time-consuming, but very exciting, thrilling, and rewarding. Although we have only scratched the surface of the potential of seminar selling in this chapter, the material included here is intended to be informative on a technique that is rapidly gaining in popularity. On the following pages are a few sample invitations, surveys, and possible titles for equity sales seminars.

Figure 7.1 Seminar Checklist

Seminar objective:

____

____

____

Subject:

____

____

Speaker: ____

Prospecting/attendance strategy (lists, type of mailing, etc.):

____

____

____

____

____

____

____

____

____

____

____

____

1. Location:
   Quiet? ☐ Yes ☐ No
   Convenient? ☐ Yes ☐ No
2. Length of meeting: ______________________
3. Day of week: ______________________
4. Time of day: ______________________
5. Seating: ______________________
6. Supplies needed: ______________________
   ____
7. Sign-in: ☐ in the room ☐ on critique form
8. Check-in table: ______________________
9. Podium, microphone, screen, audiovisual equipment needed:
   ____
   ____
10. Lighting/acoustic needs: ______________________
    ____
11. Room size: ______________________
12. Refreshments: ______________________
13. Seminar coordinator: ______________________
    ____
14. Budget amounts: ______________________
    ____
15. Handouts needed: ______________________
    ____
16. Follow-through done by: ______________________
    ____

Figure 7.2 Suggested Invitation Letter

Dear ______________:

You are cordially invited to attend a seminar on:

SPECIAL SITUATION INVESTMENTS FOR QUALIFIED RETIREMENT PLANS

The seminar will be held at the ____________ Hotel on _________, June 1, 19__ beginning at _____ and ending at ______.

This seminar has been planned for business owners and professional advisors, and practical solutions to employee benefits will be offered. ___________ will be conducting the seminar; he is a partner in a financial planning firm specializing in pension, profit sharing, and financial planning.

Space is limited. I'm sure you won't want to miss this exciting session. Kindly complete and return the reply card as soon as possible. If you have any questions in the interim, please contact Mr./Ms.________ at _________.

Very truly yours,

Paula Planner

Paula Planner

The letter should be accompanied by a brief outline of the topics to be covered in the seminar.

Figure 7.3 Follow-up Letter

Dear __________:

I would like to thank you for attending our seminar, "Special Situation Investments for Qualified Retirement Plans."

In a large group we could not, of course, address specific situations that apply to your firm. But we would be pleased to do so in a private counseling interview. I will call you in a few days to discuss this further, or you may call me earlier if you have an urgent problem that needs immediate attention.

Very truly yours,

Paula Planner

Figure 7.4 Seminar Evaluation

We hope that you enjoyed our seminar on

____

To assist us in future planning of seminars of this type, we would be most appreciative if you would respond to the following questions.

1. Did you find the seminar instructive and enjoyable? Please comment.

2. Were the day of the week and time of day convenient for you? Please comment.

3. Would you like to attend similar seminars in the future? What special subjects would be of interest to you?

4. Any other comments:

NAME: ______________________________________

TEL.: ________________________

ADDRESS: ____________________________________

____

Figure 7.5 Suggested Titles for Equity Sales Seminars

1. "Financial Planning for the Physician, [or dentist, attorney, engineer, etc.]"
2. "Dynamic Tax Savings via Limited Partnership Interests"
3. "Family and Education Planning with Tax-Advantaged Investments"
4. "Special Situation Investments for Qualified Retirement Plans"
5. "A Financial Planning Overview for the Corporate Professional (or wage earner, corporate employee, etc.)"
6. "How Can You Save Your Business from Federal Tax Destruction"

PART II

MUTUAL FUNDS

8

What Is a Mutual Fund?

A mutual fund is a company that invests its assets in the securities issued by other corporations or by governments. A mutual fund that continuously offers to buy back or redeem its shares is called an *open-end* mutual fund. A mutual fund may take one of two approaches: it may invest its holdings in securities of companies engaged in many different types of businesses, in which case it is known as a *diversified* mutual fund; or it may concentrate its holdings in securities of one type of business or industry, in which case it is called a *special situation or nondiversified* mutual fund. However, all mutual funds provide some diversification of investments. Most mutual funds have contracts with professional advisors who advise the funds on the types of securities in which they should invest. They also have contracts with professional underwriters who sell the shares of the fund.

The mutual fund investment idea is more than 100 years old, but it really took off in the early 1930s. Today there are more than 800 mutual funds in existence with nearly $250 billion in assets. The mutual fund industry grew by 70 percent in 1981, faster than ever before. While the phenomenal popularity of money market funds powered this expansion, sales of common stock mutual funds matched those of the record year, 1969. Shareholder accounts now total 17.5 million compared to 12 million a year ago.

A release issued at the end of 1983 by the Investment Company Institute stated:

> Mutual funds have advanced on almost every front in the last 12 months. Over the years in all sorts of economic conditions, they

have shown that they are capable of meeting whatever needs investors have. Despite their remarkable expansion to 162.5 billion dollars from 77 billion in 1980, money market funds continue to grow in popularity among those who want the highest short-term interest rates available, combined with the ability to get their money back at any time.

During 1983 money market funds paid dividends of approximately 13 billion dollars to shareholders, almost triple the amount they would have earned had their money been held in $5^1/_2$ percent saving accounts.

Sales of mutual funds which invest in common stocks were just about the highest ever. They were 42 billion dollars, running at 7 times the record level set in the boom year 1969.

The record of mutual funds in the past is impressive but should be exceeded in the future as investors seek the unique advantages offered by a wide variety of mutual funds. Millions of people would like to invest but do not have the time, inclination, knowledge, or experience to select and care for their investments properly. Mutual funds provide the full-time professional management, careful selection, and diversification required to take full advantage of economic fluctuations.

A large sum of money is not required to start an investment program through the use of mutual funds. As you will see, the funds you will be offering your clients have varying minimum initial investment requirements, and subsequent investments can be made at any time in much smaller amounts.

TYPES OF MUTUAL FUNDS

The investment objectives of individual mutual funds differ, thereby offering investors a variety of options to help them realize their specific investment goals. Let's examine the various generic types of funds that are available throughout the industry:

- common stock funds
- bond funds
- municipal bond funds
- money market funds
- tax-exempt money market funds
- option funds

COMMON STOCK FUNDS

Most mutual funds are common stock funds. Some common stock funds concentrate exclusively on the blue chip market. These are securities issued by large, stable corporations that are known leaders in their respective industries. Such funds may react slowly or only slightly to day-to-day fluctuations in the market. Other common stock funds may specialize in growth company stocks. These are the securities of emerging companies and industries and may be more volatile in reaction to the market. Common stock income funds invest in common stocks that are known for their high dividend-paying capabilities. Investors requiring current income might seek this type of mutual fund. Other common stock funds invest in specific industries or employ specific management theories.

Bond Funds

Bond funds are designed to generate current income by investing primarily in senior securities—those having prior claim, ahead of common stock, to assets and earnings. Senior securities include bonds, debentures, and preferred stock. The yields achieved on these funds vary based on the quality of bonds purchased. The higher the rating, the lower the ultimate yield, and vice versa.

Some corporate bond funds invest in the highest-grade bonds, while others, often called *high-income* or *high-yield* funds, invest in lower-grade corporate bonds.

Municipal Bond Funds

Municipal bond funds are designed to generate income by investing in a broad range of tax-exempt bonds issued by states and municipalities. The interest earned by these funds is passed to the shareholder free from federal income tax and, in some instances, from state and local income taxes.

Money Market Funds

Money market funds invest in short-term market securities such as Treasury bills and notes, bank certificates of deposit, banker's acceptances, and commercial paper. The return on money market funds is generally about three points below the prime rate. Investors can buy shares in these funds in relatively small amounts, yet earn the high rates that big investors receive.

Tax-Exempt Money Market Funds

Short-term municipal bond funds are also known as *tax-exempt money market funds.* Dividends generated by the portfolio of securities held are free from federal income taxation. While this is true with any municipal bond fund, the primary difference is the short-term nature of bond maturities. Typically, maturities do not exceed two years.

Option Funds

An option fund is a more speculative investment. Option funds generally seek a high current return or higher-than-average growth by writing options or from dividend-paying common stock in which call options are traded actively. (A few funds buy options as well.) Option fund earnings consist of dividends, premiums from expired call options, net short-term gains from sales of portfolio securities due to the exercise of options, and any profits from closing purchase transactions. Such funds may also write put options, but that is usually a minor activity for option funds.

DETERMINING CLIENT SUITABILITY

Many investors' first step into the stock market is an investment in a mutual fund, or an open-end investment company. The reason is simple. The open-end investment company provides diversification and professional management of investors' funds in a single vehicle. Furthermore, mutual funds stand ready to redeem outstanding shares anytime an investor chooses to present them for redemption and will issue new shares whenever an investor makes a purchase.

Your first consideration in choosing a mutual fund should be whether or not the fund's objective matches your client's goals. Mutual funds fall into four broad categories based on investment goal:

- growth
- growth-income
- balanced
- income

Some of the features of each are described in the following paragraphs.

GROWTH FUNDS

The objective of growth funds is capital appreciation. Some growth funds are more risk-oriented than others, but in general growth funds keep most of their assets in common stock at all times. They offer investors a greater potential for growth than any other types of funds, but with higher risk. Thus, growth funds are more suitable for investors who want to build capital and who do not seek current income, although some growth funds pay dividends. The dividends and capital gains distributions can be reinvested automatically in extra shares, if desired.

Growth fund investments are appropriate for individuals seeking long-term capital appreciation. Growth funds tend to be somewhat more aggressive than other types of mutual fund products; however, they do offer the security of professional management and diversification. Growth funds are suitable for investors who require long-term growth but do not have a need for current income.

GROWTH-INCOME FUNDS

The objective of growth-income funds is to achieve long-term growth of capital while providing some income. These funds have a stated objective of providing investors with reasonable dividends and generally have past records of relatively stable income. In contrast to growth funds, which invest in growth-type stocks paying little or no dividends, growth-income funds usually emphasize common stock but favor stocks that pay dividends. Growth-income funds may also hold bonds or preferred issues. The distinction between growth funds and growth-income funds is that the latter provide the investor with some income. Also, in declining markets, growth-income funds can be expected to show a somewhat higher degree of price stability than capital gain-oriented funds.

Growth-income funds are designed to achieve long-term capital appreciation in addition to providing current income. This would be the ideal funding vehicle for individuals who wish to achieve a long-term savings objective as well as receive current income to satisfy an existing need. One hypothetical situation in which this would be the preferred recommendation involves parents who are planning to supplement their retirement income while providing current funds to assist their children with college.

BALANCED FUNDS

The objective of balanced funds is to minimize risk without sacrificing possibilities for long-term growth. Such funds invest specified proportions of their assets in fixed-income securities and common stocks. As a result, balanced funds do not show as large a gain during rising markets as do most common stock funds, but they usually suffer less setback in declining markets. The investment income dividends from balanced funds are less likely to fluctuate widely than those of growth-income funds. The chief difference between balanced funds and growth-income funds is that balanced funds specifically state what proportion of their assets will be invested in fixed-income securities and what proportion in equities. Growth-income funds do not.

Clients who exhibit a low risk tolerance but whose investment objective is long-term capital growth would find balanced funds an ideal investment vehicle. The potential for capital appreciation with this type of fund is somewhat lower than with an aggressive growth fund. Therefore, balanced funds are less likely to fluctuate in value in either up or down markets. Such an investment is ideal for conservative individuals who have long-term investment goals but require the security of a low-risk portfolio.

INCOME FUNDS

The objective of an income fund is to produce dividend or interest income and provide as much income as possible for its shareholders. The managers of these funds usually follow a flexible investment policy that permits an income-oriented combination of bonds, preferred stock, and common stock. These funds are more attractive to persons seeking a liberal current return, such as retired people, and less attractive to individuals who, because of tax considerations, seek capital gains rather than income.

Income funds invest in securities that provide a steady flow of current income, such as bonds and high dividend-paying stocks. Income funds are attractive to individuals such as retired people, who seek a relatively high current return from their investment dollars. Note that this type of investment is ideal for clients who require income to fund current needs, but it would be inappropriate for individuals with long-term goals.

TAX-EXEMPT FUNDS

For investors seeking tax-exempt income, a number of tax-exempt funds have been organized. These fully managed funds, made possible by the Tax Reform Act of 1976, invest mainly in a diversified portfolio of municipal bonds and can thus provide shareholders with income exempt from federal income taxes.

Furthermore, investors who do not need the income provided by such funds can automatically reinvest all distributions and achieve a cumulative effect of the tax-exempt feature without additional sales charges.

A tax-exempt fund is an appropriate recommendation for client's who want to lessen their tax burden while meeting a need for current income. The income generated is exempt from federal income taxation because investments are made primarily in a diversified portfolio of municipal securities. State income taxes may also be avoided when funds direct their investment portfolio to securities issued by municipalities within an investor's state of residence. Tax-exempt funds should be recommended to high-income individuals who require current income without increasing their tax liability.

MONEY MARKET FUNDS

As a registered representative, you have an obligation to make certain that investment recommendations are suited to your client's circumstances and investment objectives. In a broader sense, however, suitability cannot be limited simply to an investment recommendation. It must be viewed in the context of the whole financial plan and the security of the purchaser.

Money market funds are ideal for individuals who require liquidity, since investments are made in short-term money market instruments. This type of fund is an ideal receptacle for dollars earmarked to satisfy short-term needs. Money market funds offer a competitive return in excess of bank passbook savings accounts, and most offer check-writing capabilities as well.

Before investing, any client should have an adequate emergency fund, defined by many financial planners as equalizing three to six months of income, sufficient to provide for the unexpected. Funds recently invested should not be liquidated for this purpose. It is equally important that a prospective investor have an insurance program that adequately covers existing needs. As a licensed life insurance agent, you have the products to fill these and other financial planning needs.

You know that, as a financial planner, many doors are open to you—life, health, pension, IRAs, etc. Having mutual funds and other investment products available not only opens another door, but also opens doors that may have been closed in the past. These greatly enhanced opportunities were covered fully in Part I.

SHAREHOLDER SERVICES PROVIDED TO YOUR CLIENT

A significant consideration for mutual fund investors is the variety of shareholder services available. When the category of fund that best serves your client's needs has been identified, consider which funds offer the combination of services that is most compatible with your client's investment goals. The following is a listing of services offered by most mutual funds.

Purchase of Shares

An investor is generally required to make an initial investment of a specific amount, usually from $100 to $5,000. Additional amounts can then be systematically or periodically invested at a low minimum, generally $25, with no maximum stipulated.

Right of Accumulation

A right of accumulation refers to the shareholder's opportunity to count the current total dollar value of all shares owned in funds under the same management toward the purchase of additional shares to gain breakpoint savings.

The initial breakpoint varies with different funds; i.e., they may start at $5,000, $10,000, or $25,000. As a general rule, breakpoints are structured as shown in Table 8.1.

Table 8.1 Typical Breakpoints

Amount of Purchase	Sales Charge*	Usual Dealer Reallowance
Less than $10,000	8.50%	7.50%
$10,000–24,999	7.50	6.50
$25,000–49,999	5.75	5.20
$50,000–99,999	4.00	3.60
$100,000–249,999	3.00	2.70
$250,000–499,999	2.50	2.25
$500,000–999,999	2.00	1.80
$1,000,000 and over	1.00	.90

*Sales charges may vary with different fund groups.

LETTER OF INTENTION

Purchasers who anticipate making an investment that might place them in a breakpoint position to take advantage of a lesser sales charge should execute a letter of intention on the form provided by the fund. The anticipated purchase must take place within 13 months of the initial investment.

CONCURRENT PURCHASES

When the distributor of a particular fund is also the principal underwriter for shares in other funds, reduction in the sales charges and offering prices will generally be applicable to concurrent purchases of shares in two or more of the funds.

CUSTODIAL SERVICES

Customarily, a bank or trust company acts as a custodian of a fund's securities and cash, receiving all income and making all disbursements. Shares purchased may be left with the transfer agent, or certificates will be issued, whichever the investor prefers. The transfer agent will automatically reinvest distributions if so specified on the investor's application.

REINVESTMENT OF DIVIDENDS AND CAPITAL GAINS

By so indicating on the application or by written notification to the fund, a shareholder may elect to have dividends or both dividends and capital gains reinvested. If a shareholder elects to receive distributions in cash, payment will automatically be issued on the payment date of such distribution.

Exchange Privilege

In most instances, shareholders of a fund within a family of funds under the same management and sponsorship may exchange shares of one fund for those of another at a nominal charge (typically $5) or at no cost. For tax purposes, an exchange of shares of one fund for those of another is regarded as a sale and a new purchase. Such is not the case with funds utilized in conjunction with a tax-advantaged retirement plan.

Systematic Withdrawal Plan

A shareholder may elect to make systematic withdrawals on a monthly or quarterly basis. Generally, such withdrawals may not exceed 6 percent annually. In some instances, a shareholder must have a specified minimum balance before this plan can be initiated. Any withdrawal plan is a voluntary and flexible arrangement.

Self-Employed Individual Retirement (Keogh) Plan

Most funds make available a prototype retirement plan and trust agreement for those self-employed individuals who wish to purchase shares in conjunction with the Self-Employed Individuals Tax Retirement Act of 1962. In some instances, split-funded plans that combine the purchase of mutual fund shares and life insurance may be arranged.

Individual Retirement Account

Under the Employee Retirement Security Act of 1974, an individual under age 70½, with earned income, may set up an IRA. Lump sum distributions from tax-qualified retirement, pension, and profit-sharing plans can be rolled over into an IRA to defer taxation on the distributions.

Simplified Employee Pension Plan

Most funds now make available the contribution forms required to establish an employer-sponsored individual retirement account. This plan is described in detail in Chapter 3.

Corporate Retirement Plans

Most funds also make available master plans and trust agreements or prototype plans and trust agreements that corporations can adopt without extensive legal processes and with a minimum amount of administrative effort. These master plans and trust agreements or prototype plan and trust agreements enable corporations to purchase fund shares in conjunction with pension, profit-sharing, or thrift savings plans.

Redemption Privilege

Shareholders may liquidate some or all of their shares upon tender of a properly executed certificate(s). If shares are held by a custodian, they may be liquidated upon written request accompanied by a signed, guaranteed stock power.

MUTUAL FUND PRICES AND VALUES

As an informed mutual fund representative, you should be able to quote (or have readily available) the offering price and the net asset value of each fund you represent. The question is: Where do you find this information, and how should it be interpreted?

The best source is the daily financial page in the *Wall Street Journal* or almost any other daily newspaper published in a large metropolitan area. To find the price of a fund in the Oppenheimer family of funds, for example, open your paper to the financial pages and look for the heading "Mutual Funds." You will see a wide variety of funds listed under it. Your fund will be listed under the heading "Oppenheimer Funds" (except the money market funds, which will be discussed later in this chapter). The name of the fund will appear in the left-hand column; the net asset value will be listed in the next column; the offering price, which includes the sales charge, is shown in the next column; finally, the change in net asset value from the previous day's close will be listed. (See Figure 8.1.)

Interpreting Prices

Net Asset Value The net asset value of mutual fund shares is determined daily and is based on closing stock market prices. Net asset value is determined by updating the market price of each security in the fund's portfolio and determining a total dollar value for the entire portfolio. *The fund's debt obligations and liabilities are then deducted from the value of the portfolio,* resulting in the fund's net asset value. The net asset value is divided by the total number of fund shares outstanding to give the net asset value per share. Since the fund portfolios are quite large, either the management company or the custodian calculates the net asset value by computer. An increase in the market value of a fund's portfolio is known as *market appreciation*.

For example, if the total assets of a fund's portfolio holdings

Figure 8.1 Sample Mutual Fund Listing

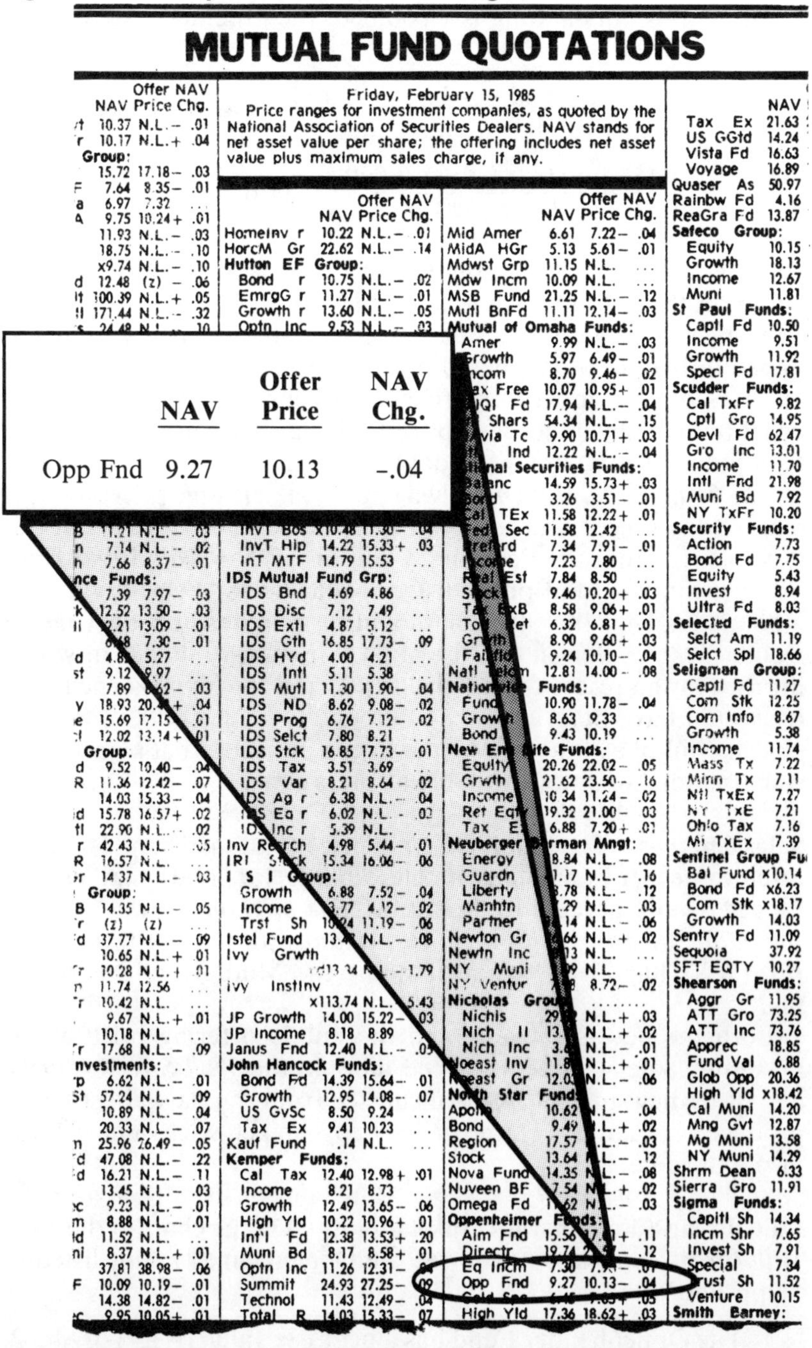

MUTUAL FUND QUOTATIONS

Friday, February 15, 1985

Price ranges for investment companies, as quoted by the National Association of Securities Dealers. NAV stands for net asset value per share; the offering includes net asset value plus maximum sales charge, if any.

	NAV	Offer Price	NAV Chg.
Opp Fnd	9.27	10.13	-.04

Source: *Wall Street Journal,* February 15, 1985. Reprinted by permission of *Wall Street Journal,*

are \$50,000,000 the fund's liabilities are \$5,000,000, and the number of shares outstanding is 9,000,000, then the net asset value is \$5 per share:

$$\frac{\text{Total assets of portfolio} - \text{Fund's liabilities}}{\text{Number of shares outstanding}} = \text{NAV per share}$$

$$\frac{\$50{,}000{,}000 - \$5{,}000{,}000}{9{,}000{,}000} = \$5 \text{ per share}$$

Changes in NAV (Net Asset Value) The sale of fund shares is based on the net asset value next calculated after the order is entered by the dealer. Since the net asset value is ordinarily determined only once a day, based on the closing stock market prices, an investor who makes a purchase on February 3 (day on which order received by issuer) will pay the closing price as of February 3 (computed at 4:30 P.M. each day).

The Wall Street Journal always lists the closing prices for the market day preceding the day of publication. For example, if this excerpt was from the February 3 edition of *The Wall Street Journal,* the mutual fund prices listed would be for February 2. The amount paid by the investor making a purchase on February 3 would not be given in this listing. The February 4 edition would list the closing prices from February 3, and that is what the investor would have paid.

The symbol *z* in the newspaper listing indicates that a quote, for some reason, was not available at press time.

Sales Charges The public offering price for a load fund is the net asset value per share plus a sales charge (or load) that usually ranges from 1 percent to 9 percent. *The method for determining the public offering price must be explained in the fund's prospectus.* (See Chapter 9, "Understanding the Mutual Fund Prospectus.")

Both the net asset value and the public offering price at the maximum sales charge are listed daily in the *Wall Street Journal* and other newspapers. As you can see from the partial listing reproduced in Figure 8.1), the daily change in net asset value is given in the third column.

Calculating Sales Charges (Sales Loads) On the chart in the daily *Wall Street Journal* you can see the Oppenheimer Fund, listed as "Opp Fnd":

1. The Oppenheimer Fund has a net asset value (NAV) of \$8.82.
2. The offering price is \$9.64–. (The – indicates that the offering

price has decreased from the previous day. Conversely, a + indicates that the price has increased.)

3. The NAV ($8.82) subtracted from the offering price ($9.64) determines the amount of sales charge the customer pays per share. In this case it is $.82.

To express the sales charge as a percentage of the offering price, simply divide the sales charge ($.82) by the offering price ($9.64). It is important to remember that the sales charge is a percentage of the offering price, *not* a percentage of the NAV. For example:

$$.82 \div 9.64 = .085, \text{ or } 8.5\%$$
$$\text{Amount of sales charge} \div \text{Offering price} = \text{Sales charge percentage}$$

An investor making a purchase of the Oppenheimer Fund would pay a sales charge of 8.5 percent.

The sales charge is also included in the fund's prospectus. (The sales charge calculation method shown here may produce a slightly different sales charge from what you know to be correct. This results from rounding off in listings of share values. The sales charge rate given in the prospectus is correct.)

The dollar amount of a sales charge can also be calculated from the sales charge percentage and the offering price. Let's use the Oppenheimer Fund as an example again. If you know the fund has a sales charge of 8.5 percent, and the offering price is $9.64, multiply $9.64 by .085 to find the sales charge amount:

$$\$9.64 \times .085 = \$.82$$

Distinguishing between Load and No-Load Funds A load fund includes a sales charge, in addition to the net asset value; a no-load fund does not. Thus, the offering price of a no-load fund may be either above or below the NAV. Also, you can easily identify a no-load fund by the symbol *N.L.* under the heading "Offer Price" in the newspaper listing. Review these examples:

Fund	NAV	Offer Price
A. Oppenheimer Fund	$ 8.82	$9.64
B. Safeco MB	$11.73	N.L.

A. The Oppenheimer Fund is a load fund because the offering price is higher than the NAV, thus reflecting the addition of the sales charge.

B. The Safeco Municipal Bond Fund is a no-load fund, indicated by the *N.L.* in the offering price column. This means that the offering price and the NAV are the same since there is no sales charge.

Money Market Funds As previously mentioned, money market funds are not shown in the same section of the newspaper as other mutual funds. This is because the share values of money market funds do not change from day to day. Instead, once each week, usually on Friday, major newspapers list the large market funds and show average yields for the previous seven, 30, and/or 365 days. They also shown the average maturity duration (in days) for the securities in the fund's portfolio. (See Figure 8.2.)

UNIT INVESTMENT TRUSTS

The unit trust differs from a mutual fund in that the unit trust is an inflexible investment. The trust buys a stated portfolio of securities and deposits it with the trustee. Thereafter, no new securities are added or sold unless it appears that a particular issue in the portfolio could be having a problem and could possibly default.

Because the underlying portfolio does not change, the yield is fixed and predictable. If the portfolio is bought in the open market, the yields are slightly below those of the underlying securities because the sponsor's sales charge is built into the price. The sales charges average between 4 and 4½ percent on most new offerings and can be as high as 5½ percent in the secondary market. The primary advantages of a unit trust, however, are a diversified portfolio and the ability to buy in increments of approximately $1,000 without affecting liquidity. Many sponsors offer to redeem units at net asset value.

Because most unit trusts are composed of debt instruments, they are highly sensitive to interest rates. For example, if an investor buys a corporate bond unit yielding 10 percent, and interest rates go up to around 15 percent, the principal value will be discounted to the current yield. In other words, the $1,000 unit would be worth approximately $650 if sold today. If an investor buys a unit yielding 15 percent, and interest rates go down to 10 percent, the unit might sell for $1,500.

The unit trust offers investors the following features.

Fixed Annual Income Clients are assured of a steady annual income on their investment. (Unit trusts of equities and GNMAs will not have a fixed yield.)

Quality Investment grade debt obligations (A-rated or better) are professionally selected by the sponsor.

Figure 8.2 Sample Money Market Fund Listing

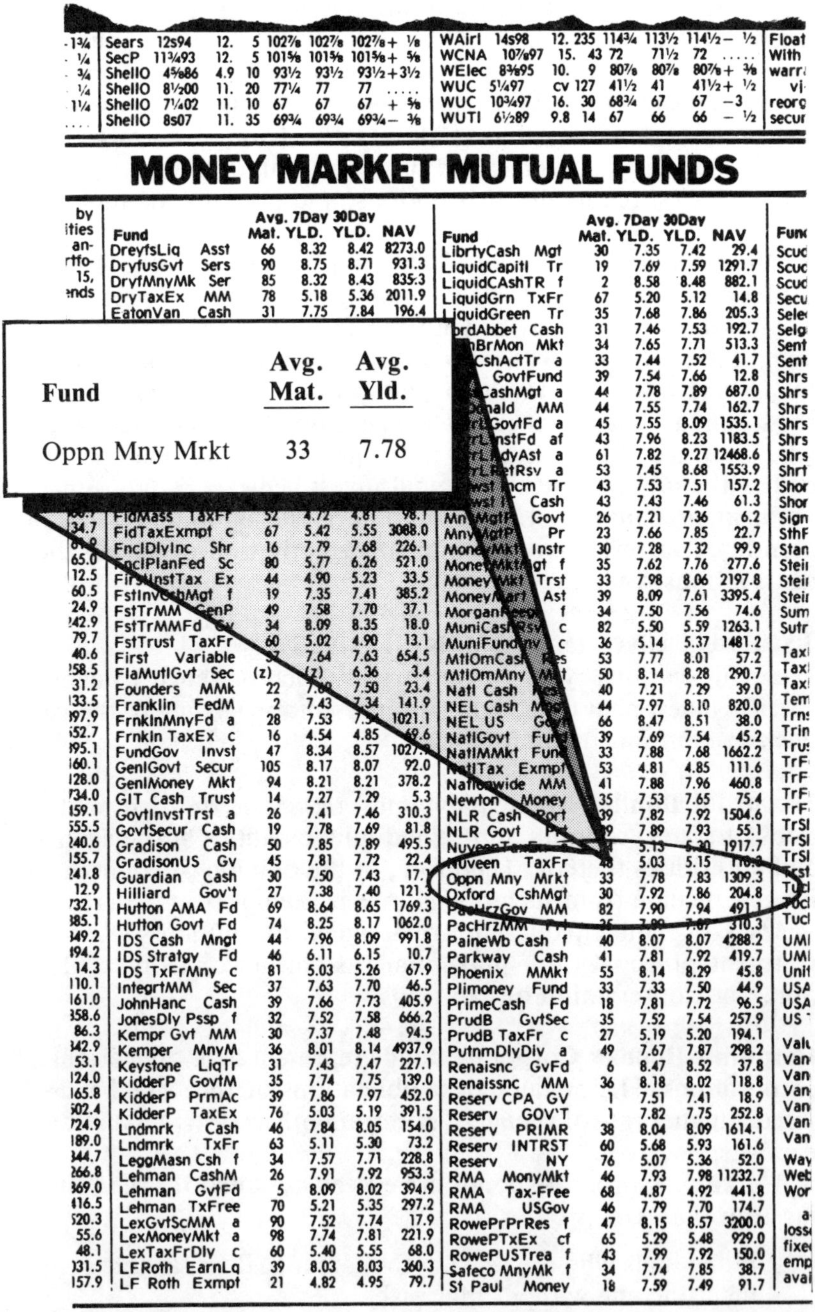

Source: *Wall Street Journal,* February 15, 1985. Reprinted by permission of *Wall Street Journal,* ©Dow Jones & Company, Inc., 1985. All Rights Reserved.

Diversification The broad diversification of issues by type and by maturity provides advantages not readily available to the single investor. Diversification provides more stability to the unitholder than that available through ownership of individual obligations.

Convenience The unit trust is a convenient way to own debt obligations. The trustee administers the trust, processes called bonds, collects the interest and principal from issuers, safeguards the securities, remits the distributions, and provides an annual report.

Professional Monitoring The sponsor's experienced staff of professionals will monitor all the obligations in each portfolio.

Liquidity Units may be tendered directly to the trustee for redemption or offered on the secondary market. The price at which the trustee will redeem units or the sponsor will purchase units in the secondary market is generally based on the then current aggregate bid price of the securities in the portfolio. This may be more or less than a unitholder's original investment.

Payment Options Unitholders have the option of receiving monthly, quarterly, or semiannual distributions or of having these distributions received.

TYPES OF UNIT INVESTMENT TRUSTS

There are various types of unit trusts, each designed to achieve specific investment objectives. A representative listing of the various types of unit trusts follows.

Municipal Bonds Municipal bonds represent the debt obligations of states, counties, cities, and municipalities or the agencies and authorities thereof. Therefore, in the opinion of counsel, the interest income from such obligations is exempt from federal tax.

Market Municipal bonds are designed for investors whose investment objectives are maximum tax-free income, diversification, and conservation of capital.

Corporate Bonds Corporate bonds represent debt obligations of corporations. Historically, debt obligations of this type have offered a higher rate of return than certain other securities and bank deposits.

Markets Corporate bonds are especially suited for the following four markets:

1. individuals who are seeking to maximize their taxable investment income without high risk
2. Keogh accounts, IRAs, IRA rollovers, and pension and profit-sharing plans

3. retired persons, persons investing under the Uniform Gifts to Minors Act, and people in low income tax brackets
4. foundations, universities, other nonprofit organizations

Income Fund—Short-Term Series These trusts are formed for the purpose of providing a high level of current income through investment in a fixed portfolio of securities having maturities of approximately six months. These trusts consist of certificates of deposit of foreign banks, foreign branches of domestic banks, and domestic branches of foreign banks, as well as short-term notes of foreign banks, each having assets in excess of $3 billion.

Market Short-term series income funds are suited for investors seeking high current income.

Government National Mortgage Association The GNMA trust has a portfolio consisting primarily of mortgage-backed securities of the modified pass-through type, fully guaranteed as to principal and interest by the Government National Mortgage Association (GNMA). Statements to unitholders will clearly delineate such principal and interest income paid.

GNMA offers investors a pro rata share of pooled government-guaranteed and -insured mortgages in one negotiable certificate. Each GNMA certificate guarantees a proportionate share of interest and principal collected from the underlying mortgage pools. This guarantee of timely payment of principal and interest has the full faith and credit of the United States government. Unitholders receive their pro rata shares on the subsequent distribution date. Prepayments of principal are also distributed, as collected on a pro rata basis.

Although GNMAs are backed by 30-year mortgages, due to prepayments and mortgage foreclosures, the average life of GNMA securities is 12 years. Also, because of prepayments and foreclosures, GNMA payments of interest and principal are irregular.

Market GNMAs are well suited for conservative investors seeking safety of capital and relatively high return through the purchase of pro rata share in a portfolio of government-guaranteed securities.

Equity Income Trust This trust has a fixed portfolio of publicly traded common stocks issued by domestic public utility companies for the purpose of obtaining current income. The value of units will fluctuate with the value of the underlying securities.

Market Equity income trusts are particularly suited for these two markets:

1. corporations seeking income that qualifies under the 85 percent dividends received exclusion for corporations
2. individuals seeking current income that may continue to increase and who are willing to accept the market risk as well as the special risks involved in the gas and electric public utility industry

SUMMARY

Today's burgeoning mutual funds market may offer an ideal investment vehicle for your clients, especially for those who have never made investments before. As a salesperson, it is your job to determine which type of mutual fund is best for your prospects, and you can do so only by understanding your prospects' goals and matching them with the appropriate growth, growth-income, balanced, or income fund. Make sure that any recommendation you make fits in with the client's overall financial plan and that your client understands the services provided to shareholders of these funds.

Your client's confidence in you will be fortified by your knowledge of the advantages and disadvantages of each type of mutual fund. When it comes to making a specific recommendation, you should be armed with all of the pertinent financial facts concerning the product, including current offering prices and net asset value.

9

Understanding the Mutual Fund Prospectus

The Securities Act of 1933 requires that a corporation making a public offering of new shares of stock present a current prospectus of that offering to any prospect for the purchase of such shares. An open-end mutual fund, one that makes a continuous offering of new shares, fits this description. Therefore, a prospectus must accompany or precede any sales effort with respect to such mutual funds.

A prospectus is actually part of the registration statement. The 1933 act requires that any security being offered for sale be registered with the SEC. The registration statement contains the information required by the SEC to clear the security for public sale. The prospectus, usually the major portion of the registration statement, contains those facts that in the opinion of the SEC, are necessary for a prospect to make an informed decision as to whether or not to invest. Thus, the prospectus provides the necessary full disclosure to the prospect.

The matters covered in the prospectus, the way in which they are presented, the content of financial statements, the location of certain items (fund assets), and even specific wording are all prescribed by the SEC. The prospectus, like other legal documents, contains legal language and terms as well as financial language and terms. Because this terminology may be unfamiliar to many people, some parts of a prospectus may not be easy to read and understand.

The purchase of mutual fund shares is an investment in securities, the results of which cannot be guaranteed. Therefore, full disclosure requires that not only the opportunities, favorable features, and possible advantages of an investment be revealed, but also cautions and possible negative aspects of the investment. For example, if a mutual fund has an investment policy that involves a somewhat greater-than-usual degree of speculation, this must be pointed out clearly.

A mutual fund prospectus usually contains much of the following information, in both summary and detailed form:

- description of the type of fund
- investment objectives and any restrictions on investments
- the types of investments to be made (the intended makeup of the invested portfolio)
- an explanation of the lack of guarantee of results
- a statement, in language prescribed by the SEC, that the securities have not been approved or disapproved by the SEC, nor has the commission passed on the accuracy or adequacy of the prospectus
- a statement about the risks of investment, particularly when the fund engages in more speculative investment techniques
- a brief narrative history of the fund as well as a financial history
- identification and perhaps some description of the fund manager, distributor, investment adviser, transfer agent, and custodian
- information concerning how to purchase shares, including sales charges; purchase minimums; opportunities for obtaining lower sales charges by combining purchases or (considering amounts previously purchased) making larger purchases; and signing a letter of intent
- address of where to send purchase payments
- management fees imposed
- mention of other funds in the same family of funds and a description of a right to transfer shares between funds without further costs
- procedures for redeeming a share totally or partially at regular intervals and the tax implications of doing so
- distributions of investment dividends and capital gains, in cash or reinvestment in fund shares, and the tax implications thereof
- a listing and brief description of fund officers and directors
- method for determining share value
- current financial statements
- a current schedule of fund investments
- a statement by independent auditors

Since the prospectus, including all of the information just listed, constitutes full disclosure, any other material used without the prospectus is not full disclosure. For this reason, the prospectus must accompany or precede any effort you make to sell the fund and must be used with any other literature you give your prospect about the fund. You will find that most funds offer other more attractive, more readable sales literature for your use in discussions with prospects, so the prospectus can be left with your prospect for more careful reading later.

Unlike insurance and annuities, even variable annuities, no contract is given to the owner of mutual fund shares. Therefore, the prospectus is your client's only complete statement of the features, rights, obligations, etc., of fund ownership. For this reason, the prospectus should be retained by the fund owner for ready reference. A statement to this effect is contained in every prospectus.

The mutual fund prospectus is dated, and only the most current prospectus may be used. The prospectus is reissued at least once every year, usually at a time when the financial statements can be updated to be sure they are no more than 16 months old. This is an SEC requirement, so when you receive a new supply of prospectuses, you must throw out the old ones.

A SAMPLE PROSPECTUS

Now let's go through a typical prospectus, briefly reviewing each section. The example used is a current prospectus for a fictional fund called the STT Fund. Of course, prospectuses will vary from fund to fund because each prospectus describes a specific fund. Therefore, features described in one prospectus may not necessarily be described in another. Although the wording used to describe a given feature may also vary somewhat from one prospectus to another, and sometimes a different heading or sequence of information may be used, the next few pages should serve as a good example to make you more comfortable with a prospectus.

COVER PAGE

The highlights of the STT Fund are reviewed briefly at the top of the cover page. This provides the prospect with a general knowledge of the fund, its practices and objectives.

As you can see in Figure 9.1, the cover includes these items:

1. identification of the fund, including location
2. a statement of the fund's investment objectives
3. a statement of the nature of the investments that will be made in an attempt to achieve investment objectives

Figure 9.1 Cover Page

STT Fund, Inc.

22 Middle Road Southborough, MA
(617) 222-4685

The STT Fund (the "Fund") is a common stock growth fund. Its goal is to create capital gains for investors. While current income is not its major goal, it is hoped that growth in income will accompany capital gains. The Fund invests through a professionally managed portfolio consisting primarily of common stock.

THESE SECURITIES HAVE NOT BEEN APPROVED OR DISAPPROVED BY THE SECURITIES AND EXCHANGE COMMISSION NOR HAS THE COMMISSION PASSED UPON THE ACCURACY OR ADEQUACY OF THIS PROSPECTUS. ANY REPRESENTATION TO THE CONTRARY IS A CRIMINAL OFFENSE.

February 20, 1985

Investors are advised to read and retain this Prospectus for future reference.

4. prominently presented SEC disclosure to the effect that the SEC has not approved or disapproved the fund or passed upon the accuracy or adequacy of the prospectus
5. a suggestion that the prospectus be read and retained

The SEC prescribes and limits what is contained on the front cover of a mutual fund prospectus. No material, other than that listed here, is supposed to be on the front cover. However, some companies interpret the requirements in different ways and may include prominent logos; a very few even use pictures.

FUND SYNOPSIS

Figure 9.2 Fund Synopsis

INVESTMENT OBJECTIVE
The Fund's objective is long-term capital growth. While current income is not its major goal, it is hoped that growth in income will accompany capital gains.

PURCHASE OF SHARES
Purchase of shares of the Fund is at offering price, which is net asset value plus sales commission of 8½% of offering price (9.3% of net amount invested).

The minimum initial investment is $500 (other than in plans for intended monthly investments). Subsequent purchases or purchases in monthly plans are $25 minimum. Reduced sales charges are available for larger investments (see "How to Purchase Shares").

Redemption: Fund shares are redeemable at net asset value either in person or by mail on any business day. There is no redemption charge.

Management Fees: The Fund pays an investment management fee to STT Investment Managers, Inc. equivalent to 1/2 of its average daily net assets during the year. STT Investment Managers, Inc. also acts as investment manager to other investment companies.

NOTE FOR INVESTORS
The Fund is not appropriate for investors whose main goal is assured income.

In this section, the type of fund, its main objectives, and other key facts of concern to the prospect are summarized briefly (see Figure 9.2). This summary may be presented as a listing or in narrative paragraphs, but it always precedes the main body of the prospectus. Information concerning shares offered, minimum purchases, sales charges, shareholder redemption, and other pertinent facts are presented.

For a fund that was in existence and being marketed before the date of the prospectus, the fund highlights or synopsis section contains a table of changes in per-share income and value for the past ten years or the life of the fund, whichever is less. The SEC requires that this table appear no farther back in the prospectus than page 5. Other items, such as the index, may be included between the synopsis and the main body of the prospectus.

INVESTMENT POLICIES

Figure 9.3 Investment Policies

INVESTMENT POLICIES
The Fund's objective is long-term capital growth, through investment, for the most part, in common stocks. Many factors will be considered by STT in selecting securities in which to invest. STT Management will consider earnings and profit margins, the management team, the dynamics of the industry in which the company operates, and potential for new product development, as well as general and specific business conditions.

Occasionally, because of the state of the economy or stock market, prudence may indicate that all or part of the Fund's assets be placed in bonds, government securities or cash equivalents. Each shareholder should understand that all investments have a risk factor. Therefore, there is no guarantee that the objectives will be met or that the investment policy will be successful. The Fund's shares may fluctuate in value either more or less than they cost the investor. The Fund is not suitable for investors whose principle objective is conservation of capital.

This section outlines the policies the fund will follow in attempting to achieve its objectives (Figure 9.3). In this particular instance, the fund's objective is capital growth, with emphasis on the importance of flexible management to achieve the stated objective.

INVESTMENT RESTRICTIONS

Figure 9.4 Investment Restrictions

INVESTMENT RESTRICTIONS

The Fund has imposed upon itself certain investment restrictions, which, along with the investment policy, are fundamental policies. Neither the investment restrictions nor investment policies can be changed without shareholder approval.

Under these restrictions, the Fund cannot:

1. Invest more than 5% of its total assets at cost in the securities of companies which have a record of less than three years of continuous operation.
2. Invest in real estate or mortgages on real estate; invest in interests (other than equity stock interests) in oil, gas or other mineral exploration or development.
3. Invest in commodities or commodity contracts.
4. Borrow money for any purpose other than redeeming its shares and purchasing shares for cancellation, and then only as a temporary measure for extraordinary or emergency purposes.
5. Purchase or sell securities on margin.
6. Make short sales.

Any restrictions on investments are also listed in the prospectus (Figure 9.4). These restrictions are designed to safeguard the interests of the shareholders, but do not conflict with the need for flexibility in managing the funds. Some restrictions are self-imposed; some may be required by outside jurisdictions, such as those imposed by state and federal agencies.

DIRECTORS AND OFFICERS

The prospectus lists the names of the fund's officers and directors, together with their occupations for at least the past five years (Figure 9.5). These individuals represent long and varied experience in the economic and investment fields.

It is important to note that a majority of the board of directors of a registered investment company must consist of members who are not considered "interested persons." The names of "interested persons" are identified with an asterisk(*).

Figure 9.5 Directors and Officers

DIRECTORS AND OFFICERS OF THE FUND
The name, address and principal occupation during the last 5 years are as follows. As of February 20, 1985, all of the Directors and Officers of the Fund as a group owned less than 1% of the outstanding shares. The address of each is 22 Middle Road, Southborough, MA, except as noted.

Bret Stanger, Chair of the Board of Directors*
Lion Cay
Nassau, Bahamas

Edward Brown, Director
Partner of Brown, Brown & Brown (a law firm).

Katherine Gibb, Director*
Chief Executive Officer of China Trade Corporation (an import-export firm).

Mort Gally, Director
Professor of Marketing, Graduate School of Business Administration, Southborough University; Chairman of the Board of Stellar Resource Laboratories (manufacturer of space station and satellite components).

Net Asset Value

A description of net asset value per share and information on when and how it is determined are also included in the prospectus (Figure 9.6). The net asset value per share is the net worth of the fund divided by the number of shares outstanding. (Net worth is equal to total assets minus liabilities.)

$$\frac{\text{Net worth of the fund}}{\text{Number of shares outstanding}} = \text{Net asset value per share}$$

Fund assets are the securities in its portfolio. Because their value changes daily, total assets, net worth, and net asset value per share change daily, with or without any change in the number of shares outstanding.

Money market funds are the exception. For these funds, an effort is made to stabilize net asset value at $1 a share from day to day. The method of accomplishing this is described in money market prospectuses in the section entitled "Determination of Net Asset Value." This stabilization is advantageous in that clients can readily determine the value of their holdings by simply multiplying the number of shares held (shown on the clients' statements) by $1.

Figure 9.6 Net Asset Value

NET ASSET VALUE
The net asset value of the Fund's shares is computed as of the close of trading at the New York Stock Exchange on every day it is open by dividing the value of the Fund's securities plus any cash and other assets (including accrued dividends and interest) less all liabilities (including any accrued expenses) by the total number of shares outstanding.

Each listed security for which last sale information is regularly reported is valued at the last reported sale price on that day. All other securities, if there has been no sale on that day, the mean between the last current bid and asked price is used.

Debt securities having a remaining maturity of less than sixty days are valued at cost adjusted for amortization of premiums and accretion of discounts. Accumulated unrealized appreciation or depreciation on the sixty-first day, if any, is amortized to maturity.

The Board of Directors may suspend the determination of net asset value for the whole or any part of any period (1) during which the New York Stock Exchange is closed other than for customary weekend and holiday closings, (2) during which trading on the New York Stock Exchange is restricted, or (3) for such other period as the Securities and Exchange Commission may by order permit for the protection of the holders of common shares.

How to Purchase Shares

This section of the prospectus (Figure 9.7) is one to which the shareholder may often refer. It explains how shares may be purchased and how an application should be submitted. Minimum initial investment and minimum subsequent investment amounts

Figure 9.7 How to Buy

HOW TO PURCHASE SHARES
The minimum initial purchase order is $500—other than in plans for intended monthly investments, such as a pre-authorized check plan, sponsored payroll deduction plan, or similar plans. Subsequent purchases or purchase of monthly plans must be in amounts of $25 or more.

Shares are sold at the offering price, which is net asset value per share plus a sales commission not exceeding 8.5% of the offering price. The commission is reduced on larger sales as shown below:

Amount of Purchase	As a % of Offering Price of Shares Purchased	As a % of Asset Value of Shares Purchased
Less than $10,000	8.5%	9.3%
$10,000 or more but less than $25,000	7.5	8.1
$25,000 or more but less than $50,000	6.3	6.7
$50,000 or more but less than $100,000	4.5	4.8
$100,000 or more but less than $250,000	2.8	2.9
$250,000 or more but less than $1,000,000	1.6	1.7
$1,000,000 or more	.8	.8

are given, along with an explanation of the method used to determine the offering price. The breakpoint table is also covered in this section.

Reduced sales charges, including right of accumulation and letter of intent, are explained in detail.

Figure 9.8 Group Purchases

GROUP PURCHASES
Reduced sales charges are also available to partners and employees of a single employer when they purchase as a group of 25 or more participants. Because of the economies resulting from dealing with a group, a reduced sales charge is possible. The maximum sales charge to such a group will be 6.5% and will be based on the total sales and share holdings of all group members. To be eligible for such reduced sales charges, all purchases must be made in accordance with an employer sponsored plan open to specified partners or employees of the employer and its subsidiaries, if there are any.

The group purchase discount (Figure 9.8), a feature of this fund that may not necessarily be included in other funds, is also covered in the "How to Purchase Shares" section.

Figure 9.9 Tax-Deferred

TAX-DEFERRED RETIREMENT PLANS
The following retirement plans are available to the Fund's shareholders;

- for employees of tax-exempt organizations
- for individuals whether or not covered by other qualified plans
- for corporate employees

RETIREMENT PLANS FOR EMPLOYEES OF TAX-EXEMPT ORGANIZATIONS
(403 (b)) Employees of public school systems and organizations of the type described in 501 (c) (3) of the Internal Revenue Code may enter into a deferred compensation arrangement for the purchase of shares of the Fund without being taxed currently on the investment. Contributions which are made by the employer through salary reduction are excludable from the gross income of the employee.

Finally, this section includes a discussion of the use of this fund for Section 403 (b), Employees of School Systems and Public Educational Organizations, and Section 501(c)(3), Employees of Nonprofit Organizations and Tax-Sheltered Annuity Plans (TSAs). (See Figure 9.9.) The section concludes with an explanation of the distribution agreement.

Exchanges of Shares and Investment Plans

Investors may transfer shares from one fund in the STT family of funds to another if they feel that a change in their investment objectives warrants such an exchange. This exchange privilege is subject to minimum initial and subsequent investment requirements. There is no sales change for making such transfers unless the transfer is from a no-load money market fund to a load fund. In such instances, the regular sales charge will apply. Any exchange of shares between funds is considered a sale, and investors may realize a capital gain or loss for income-tax purposes. (See Figure 9.10.)

Figure 9.10 Exchange Privilege

EXCHANGE PRIVILEGE

Shareholders may exchange Fund shares for shares of the STT World Fund, the STT Reserve Fund, or the STT New England Fund without sales commission, subject to a $5 service charge.

The eligible funds have different investment objectives, policies, and methods of operation. This exchange privilege does not in any way constitute an offering or recommendation on the part of the Fund of an investment in the above mentioned funds. Any shareholder considering acquiring shares in these funds should first secure and review the pertinent prospectus before exercising the exchange privilege.

This section also describes automatic withdrawal, an arrangement by which shareholders whose fund shares have a minimum value of $15,000 may receive regular monthly or quarterly checks of a set amount not less than $40. Each payment represents a surrender of shares subject to capital-gains taxation. (See Figure 9.11.)

Figure 9.11 Automatic Withdrawal Plan

AUTOMATIC WITHDRAWAL PLAN

Any shareholder who owns or purchases shares of the Fund valued at $15,000 or more at current offering price may establish an *Automatic Withdrawal Plan* under which the shareholder will receive a monthly or quarterly check in a stated amount, no less than $40, on a stated date. Dividends and distributions must be reinvested at net asset value and the shares of the fund will be redeemed as necessary to meet the stated withdrawal payments. Shares acquired by reinvested dividends will be redeemed first to provide the withdrawal payments, thereafter other shares will be redeemed when necessary, which means that the investor's principal may be depleted. A withdrawal plan may be terminated at any time by the shareholder or the fund.

It is also important to note that a withdrawal plan is not an annuity and that, if the value of an investor's shares does not grow at least at the rate of withdrawal, an individual may eventually exhaust both the principal and earnings of the account.

How to Redeem Shares

Shareholders always have a market for their shares. Every STT fund will redeem its shares for cash on any business day at the net asset value. Ordinarily, ownership of mutual fund shares is not evidenced by a certificate, as is stock ownership. When there is no certificate, a written request, signed by the shareholder, is required for redemption. In the rare case in which there may be a certificate, it must be submitted, either signed by the shareholder or with an accompanying stock power signed by the shareholder. Whatever the case, the signature must be guaranteed by an officer or a broker who is a member of the New York Stock Exchange or an officer of a commercial bank. Payment is made within seven days after the request is received. However, there are times when such payment may be postponed or the right of redemption suspended. Each prospectus lists the specific circumstances under which this may occur. (See Figure 9.12.)

This section also discusses reinvestment privileges following a surrender of shares. Shareholders who have redeemed shares and have not previously exercised this reinvestment privilege may reinvest any portion or all of the proceeds in shares of the fund. Reinvestment will be at the net asset value (without a sales charge), next determined after the order is received, and reinvestment must take place within 30 days after the date of the redemption. This privilege will not ordinarily affect the tax treatment of any gain or loss realized when the shares were first redeemed.

Distributions and Tax Information This fund will distribute annually to shareholders all of its net investment income (dividend and interest income). This fund will also distribute annually substantially all net short-term capital gains realized from the sale of portfolio securities and will determine annually whether or not to distribute any net long-term capital gains so received. (The money market funds should have no long-term capital gains.) Any gain or loss will be a long-term capital gain or loss if the securities have been held by the fund for more than six months and the shareholders have held their mutual fund shares for at least six months. If the fund holds the securities for less than six months, capital gain or loss is considered short-term.

In addition to short- and long-term gains, this section of the

Figure 9.12 How to Redeem Shares

HOW TO REDEEM SHARES

If stockholders wish to redeem some or all of the shares they hold in the Fund, these conditions must be met:

1. The request must be written.
2. All requests (whether or not represented by certificates) must be signed by the shareholder (or shareholders) exactly as they are registered including fiduciary titles, if any, and must specify either the number of shares or the dollar amount of shares that are to be redeemed.
3. Each of the signatures must be guaranteed by a member of a national stock exchange, a U.S. commercial bank or trust company (or one having correspondent relations with a U.S. bank or trust company).
4. If stock certificates have been issued for shares to be redeemed, such *stock certificates* and *additional documents* may be required for redemption by other organizations, executors, administrators, trustees, custodians, guardians, or if the redemption is requested by someone other than the shareholder of record.

A redemption request should include the shareholder's account number.

The redemption price will be the net asset value of the Fund shares next computed after all the documents required for the redemption request have been received by the Fund. Payment of the redemption price will be made by check within seven days after receipt of the request in proper form, except under unusual circumstances as determined by the Securities and Exchange Commission.

Redemption of shares that were recently purchased may be delayed in order to permit a determination whether the purchase check will be honored. The Fund may suspend the right of redemption when its Board of Directors declares a suspension of the determination of net asset value during any period described under the heading "Net Asset Value."

The value of the Fund shares upon redemption may be more or less than the investor's cost depending on the net asset value of the Fund's share at the time of redemption.

A former shareholder, within 30 days from the date of redeeming shares, may apply the proceeds to purchase new shares of the Fund without commission at net asset value.

prospectus addresses the shareholder's tax liability, whether paid in cash or reinvested. The section also describes how making distribution of substantially all income received qualifies the fund for specific federal income tax treatment.

The section describes the effect of a distribution on the net asset value per share and reveals that it usually would adversely affect a purchaser's tax liability to make a purchase immediately before a distribution is to be declared. It would be more advantageous to wait a day or two. The following example illustrates this.

Suppose your client has $1,500 to invest (after sales charges). The net asset value per share of the fund your client selects is $12 on the day before a dividend is to be declared. The investment is made, and your client receives 125 shares. The next day a $2-per-share dividend is declared. This reduces the share value to $10, assuming no other fluctuations. Your client now has a $250 distribution and 125 shares worth $1,250. If the distribution is reinvested, it provides 25 additional shares. Now the shareholder has 150 shares still worth $1,500. There is no loss of value. However, a $250 dividend must be reported for federal income-tax purposes.

Suppose, instead, that your client had waited a day to make the purchase. Your client's $1,500 at $10 a share would purchase 150 shares, which produces the same result, but in this case there is no dividend tax liability.

DESCRIPTION OF CAPITAL STOCK

This section includes a description of the fund's common stock shares and their characteristics, such as nonassessability, transferability, and redemption features (Figure 9.13).

Figure 9.13 Description of Shares

DESCRIPTION OF SHARES

The Fund's authorized capital consists of one hundred million common shares of $1 par value per share. All shares are of the same class, with equal rights and privileges. Each share entitles the holder to one vote for the election of Directors and on all other matters and to participate equally in dividends, distribution of capital and net assets of the Fund on liquidation. When issued, the common shares are full paid and nonassessable, and will have no preventive conversion, or exchange rights. The shares are transferable without restriction. Fractional shares entitle the holder to the same voting, redemption, dividend, distribution, and other rights as whole shares on a pro rata basis.

Custodian and Servicing Agency

Figure 9.14 Custodian

> **CUSTODIAN AND TRANSFER AGENT**
> The custodian of the assets of the Fund is New Boston National Bank, 16 Beacon Hill, Boston, MA 02108, pursuant to an Agreement dated as of January 2, 1979. Compensation for these services is based upon schedules of charges agreed upon from time to time.

The custodian of the fund, who also acts as transfer and disbursing agent, is identified in the prospectus (Figure 9.14).

Portfolio of Investments

This section of the mutual fund prospectus (Figure 9.15) describes the fund's portfolio of investments. It includes a breakdown of the specific types of investments that make up the mutual fund (common stock, short-term investments, etc.), the general field of the investment (cable television, computers, oil companies, etc.), and the specific securities that comprise the general fields of the investment (e.g., Tele-Communications, United Cable Television, which would be in the cable television field).

Note that, at the top of the first section, the *type* of investment is listed. To the immediate right is the total percentage of fund assets invested in each particular type. In this case, 5 percent of the fund is composed of corporate bond investments, 3.6 percent of preferred stock, and 91.4 percent of common stock.

The general field of investment and the percentage of the total funds allocated to that specific field are recorded next. For example, in the third group listed, common stock, 2.8 percent of the total common stock investment is in the field of banks and finance, 5.3 percent is merchandising, and 15.2 percent is in manufacturing.

Listed under the general field of investments are the specific securities owned. In the left-hand column, the number of shares owned by the fund is presented.

Figure 9.15 Portfolio of Investments

STT FUND, Inc.
Investment Portfolio
February 20, 1985

FACE AMOUNT	CORPORATE BONDS—5%	MARKET VALUE
765,000	Texas Air Corp. Cv. Sub. Debs., Reg., 8.375%, 9/15/00	$ 629,213
4,550,000	Xidex Corp., Cv. Sub. Debs., 8.5% 11/15/07	7,729,313
4,730,000	Comserv. Corp., Cv. Debs., Reg., 11%, 7/102	5,297,600
	Total Corporate Bonds (Cost 10,045,000)	13,656,126
SHARES	**PREFERRED STOCKS—3.6%**	
132,000	Flexi-Van Corp., $2.75 Cv. Pfd.	3,894,000
80,000	St. Regis Capital Corp., $50 Pfd.	4,000,000
136,000	Kinney Systems, Inc. 1.375 Cv. Pfd. Ser. B	2,108,000
	Total Preferred Stocks Cost 348,000	1,002,000
	COMMON STOCKS—91.4%	
SHARES	**BANKS AND FINANCE 2.8%**	**MARKET VALUE**
88,900	Chemical New York Corp.	4,967,288
11,449	Michigan National Corp.	191,771
100,000	Wells Fargo & Comp.	2,650,000
		7,809,059
SHARES	**MERCHANDISING 5.3%**	**MARKET VALUE**
160,000	Associated Dry Goods Corp.	9,600,000
156,250	Charming Shoppes, Inc.	2,207,031
73,305	May Department Stores	1,924,256
150,500	Supermarkets General Corp.	2,765,438
		16,496,725
SHARES	**MANUFACTURING 15.2%**	**MARKET VALUE**
200,000	Cessna Aircraft	4,350,000

Statement of Assets and Liabilities

A mutual fund prospectus contains various other financial statements; for example, a statement of assets and liabilities as of

Figure 9.16 Statement of Assets and Liabilities

STT Fund, Inc.
Statement of Assets and Liabilities
February 20, 1985

ASSETS

Investments in securities, at market value—280,005,010 (average cost 210,080,096)—see accompanying statement	
Cash	$ 22,970
Receivables:	506,349
Investments Sold	637,242
Fund Shares Sold	933,670
Dividend and Interest	3,465
Other	-0-
	282,108,706
LIABILITIES	
Payable for Investments Purchased	927,443
Accrued Advisory and Administration Fees	46,370
Other	32,667
	1,006,480
Net Assets—Applicable for 16,750,899 Shares Outstanding	$281,102,466
Net Asset Value and Redemption Price Per Share	$16.78
Maximum Offering Price Per Share (Net Asset Value plus Sales Charge of 8½% of Offering Price)	$18.21

a specific date (balance sheet) and a statement of operations (income statement) for the most recent period. In addition, there is usually a statement covering the most recent changes in net assets of the fund. These are all supported by notes to the various statements and a report by the independent auditors who have reviewed the statements. (See Figure 9.16.)

The financial statements in a mutual fund prospectus must cover a period ending no more than 16 months before the prospectus is presented to the prospect. For this reason, a prospectus is updated and reissued at least once a year. For example, a prospectus giving financial information as of December 31, 1981, could not be used beyond April 30, 1983.

SUMMARY

At the beginning of this chapter it was pointed out that a prospectus must precede or accompany all sales presentations. The information presented in the prospectus is detailed and provides a complete picture of the funds' features and policies. But remember, this level of detail is far beyond the scope of a sales presentation. During the sale, your attention and that of your clients' should be focused on a fund-specific brochure that highlights fund features related directly to your clients' investment objectives. The prospectus should be presented to your clients after you have reviewed the fund-specific brochure. When you hand the prospectus to your client, you may introduce it in this way:

> "This is a prospectus for the (NAME OF FUND), which will give you a detailed description of this funds' features and investment policies. I will leave it with you for your review and suggest that you keep it for future reference."

PART III

LIMITED PARTNERSHIPS

10

Tax Shelters and the American Economic System

The United States Congress has passed numerous pieces of legislation to encourage investments in key industries by providing tax incentives to motivated investors. This legislation affects such strategic industries as energy, housing, agriculture, and food, in which the traditional return on capital has not been high enough to attract sufficient money from investors. These congressionally mandated tax incentives thus entice venture and investment capital into these targeted industries. Though investments in these industries often carry with them a higher degree of risk, they may also offer attractive rewards to careful investors and an opportunity to cut their tax bite.

Investors who use tax shelters merely to protect ordinary income are missing the point of the shelter vehicle. In reality, tax shelters should combine tax advantages with investment benefits. Shelters lacking financial merit serve their owners poorly and can be characterized as "abusive tax shelters." Investors should be encouraged to use tax savings wisely—setting them aside in an interest-earning account, for example—and to anticipate an eventual economic return, at which time the shelter's gains would outweigh its cost.

The tax aspects of these investments are significant, but the economics of tax shelters are not simple. Tax shelters should be analyzed case by case, recognizing that some satisfactory relationship must exist between the tax features and the economic returns from the investment. Factors to be considered include:

- the type of tax shelter (real estate, oil and gas, etc.);
- the tax situation of the investor (e.g., the tax bracket and other technical tax considerations); and
- the objective of the shelter (e.g., tax deferral, conversion of ordinary income into long-term capital gain, tax elimination, or a combination of these).

We will discuss techniques such as special deductions, depreciation, borrowing, tax credits, and depletion and how they allow investors to shelter ordinary income from taxes through what is actually a "mismatching of income and deductions."

Income increases that offset inflation are forcing more investors into higher tax brackets (often referred to as *bracket creep*). The progressive income tax increasingly erodes after-tax purchasing power. Thus, tax shelters are being pursued by an increasing number of investors.

SUITABILITY AND DUE DILIGENCE REQUIREMENTS

Because tax shelters are often offered to investors who are unfamiliar with the business of a particular shelter, each shelter must be matched carefully to each investor's needs. Not all tax shelters are suitable for all clients. Consequently, two important criteria govern tax shelter decisions and determine whether an investor qualifies for a particular tax shelter and whether the specific investment appears to be economically viable. The first of these criteria is *suitability*, and the second is *due diligence*.

SUITABILITY REQUIREMENTS

Suitability is difficult to define in a single sentence. However, it can be summed up as follows: *Suitability* is a measure of the investor's ability to lose all or part of the tax shelter investment without suffering undue economic hardship. A tax shelter investment can be sold only to a suitable investor, that is, one who is able to assess the risks intelligently and assume a possible loss.

You, as a registered representative, must become familiar with suitability standards. Both program sponsors and selling representatives are required to make a suitability examination. *The North American Securities Administrators Association Real Estate Program Guideline*, formerly *Guide 60* and now known as *SEC Guide 5*, is a major document in this area. The following guidelines should be used to determine that the investor can reasonably benefit from the tax shelter:

1. The investor or the investor's representative should understand the fundamental aspects of the program. This may be evidenced by the investor's employment experience; the educational level achieved; access to advice from qualified sources, such as attorneys, accountants, and tax advisors; and prior experience with investments of a similar nature.
2. The investor should have an apparent understanding of fundamental risks and possible financial hazards of the investment, lack of liquidity of the investment, management of the investment by the sponsor, and tax consequences of the investment.
3. It must be shown that the investor can reasonably benefit from the program in view of his or her overall investment objectives and portfolio structure.
4. Investors must meet minimum annual gross income and net worth requirements (e.g., a net worth test). In other words, investors must be able to bear the economic risk of the investment.

DUE DILIGENCE REQUIREMENTS

Due diligence is a term used to describe the scrutiny of shelter offerings by sales personnel and other experts in an attempt to ascertain that the legal provisions, accounting projections, and practical economic aspects of the tax shelter appear to be sound and have a reasonable basis in fact. Due diligence also involves an analysis to discover any deceptive or abusive use of tax shelter monies by the general partner, sponsors, or other affiliated persons.

The SEC has a valuable *Due Diligence Checklist* (release #3, 4/83), which makes specific reference to particular types of shelters. The SEC raises a number of questions regarding each of the following:

- investor's suitability
- partnership and partnership agreement
- capital contributions and subscriptions
- economics of the program
- prospectus or private placement memorandum information
- profile of the sponsor organization
- management ability
- partnership management
- conflicts of interest
- documentation review
- selling agreement

BENEFITS OF TAX SHELTERS

Depending on the nature of a particular investment, the investor can derive many short- and long-term benefits from tax shelters. Some tax benefits can be gained through the following strategies.

- *permanent elimination of taxes* through the use of credits, (e.g., investment tax credits not subject to recapture)
- *deep-shelter write-offs* that generate losses sufficient to offset nonrelated taxable income created in a venture
- *sheltered (nontaxed) income* passed through to investors via the limited partnership vehicle
- *deferred taxation* over the early years of the program until a crossover point is reached
- *conversion of ordinary income* into long-term capital gain
- *leverage* (borrowing) to increase the investor's tax deductions beyond the actual cash outlay

The term *multiple write-off* refers to an immediate deductibility of more than the cash investment. Thus, a 2:1 or 3:1 write-off refers to initial tax deductions on the investor's income tax return of two times or three times the upfront cash investment. Such high multiple write-offs are often called *deep shelters*. A high write-off is most often accomplished by using borrowed dollars in the tax shelter to increase the amount of the investment. In this case, the taxpayer's initial investment is the "lever" or equity for obtaining a much larger investment. This is why borrowed money is referred to as *financial leverage*.

In addition to the tax advantages listed earlier, the taxpayer could reap economic benefits such as cash returns from investment, appreciated equity, and property value increases.

One of the most attractive advantages of tax shelter investing is the combination of *immediate* tax deductions (e.g., losses at the start of an investment program) and future tax savings.

CONVERTING ORDINARY INCOME INTO LONG-TERM CAPITAL GAIN

Income Conversion In computing taxable capital gains, the original cost is increased or decreased to an *adjusted cost basis* when the property is sold. The difference between the adjusted basis and the sales price is the amount of gain or loss realized. In order to be considered a long-term capital gain, the liquidated property must have been held for more than six months (24 months for cattle and horses).

The following is an example of a taxable capital gain computation:

Investment in program	$10,000
Sale price after four years	$ 5,000
Adjusted cost basis	-3,000
(after annual adjustments to basis)	
Capital gain or loss	$ 2,000

Part or all of the capital gain will revert to ordinary income upon disposition if there is a "recapture item." *Recapturing* occurs when a previous deduction, such as depreciation, must be returned (i.e., recaptured by the IRS). (More on recapture later.)

Capital Gains Capital gains are taxed at lower rates than is ordinary income and are thus advantageous to investors despite the possibility of a later recapture or an Alternative Minimum Tax calculation (more on this later). The maximum effective tax rate on long-term capital gains is currently 20 percent, as opposed to the maximum of 50 percent on ordinary income.

RETURN ON THE INVESTMENT

The investor employing tax shelters to protect income from taxation should measure the return *after* taxes. When determining the expected rate of return on an investment, the investor should consider all aspects of the investment, such as income reported but not actually delivered by a partnership to an investor (known as *phantom income*), appreciation, actual distributions, and several elements of risk, including future or "back-end" taxes, such as the Alternative Minimum Tax and others to be reviewed later.

INTERNAL REVENUE CODE PROVISIONS FOR DEDUCTIONS

To plan for the tax impact of tax shelter investments, investors must understand the Internal Revenue Service's tax treatment of certain expenditures. In determining taxable income, the Internal Revenue Service recognizes a number of deductions.

NONCAPITALIZED EXPENSES

The first of these is a noncapitalized expense deduction. Taxpayers are permitted to deduct certain expenses from income, rather than add them to the capital base, when computing income for tax purposes. (If added to the base, these expenses would be nondeductible.)

Examples of special expenses that can be deducted immediately, rather than capitalized, include:

- intangible drilling and development costs incurred in oil or gas drilling development activities
- interest and property taxes in a real estate venture
- expenses for feeding and raising cattle

In the case of cattle raising, supplies and materials deducted must have been consumed by the livestock within the tax year. Of course, normal business expenses such as salaries, rent, and insurance are deductible as expenses. In general, these expense items must be interpreted as being ordinary, necessary, and reasonable.

Depreciation Expenses

Depreciation is another deduction. Expenditures that are depreciated are said to be capitalized and depreciated over their useful life. Useful life is determined by the Accelerated Cost Recovery System (ACRS). This system, approved by Congress, allows a more rapid write-off than previous methods for assets placed in service in 1981 and thereafter. The ACRS rules allow for the selection of either an accelerated or a straight-line option. Under either method, the ACRS tables shorten the time over which assets can be depreciated, thereby allowing for larger tax deductions in earlier years.

ACRS Tables The ACRS tables group assets into five categories: three-year property, five-year property, ten-year property, 15-year property, and 18-year property. In straight-line depreciation, deductions are parceled into equal amounts and spread over the appropriate number of years. As an example, petroleum storage facilities are considered five-year property and can be written off over the ACRS period of five years by using either the accelerated or the straight-line option. With accelerated depreciation, the deductions are normally greatest in the early years and smallest in the later years. Under either system, the total amount of deductions will be equal. ACRS also eliminates from consideration such factors as salvage value, bonus depreciation, and component depreciation.

Though land cannot be depreciated, depreciation is allowed on such assets as buildings, improvements to the land (such as a parking lot or swimming pool), equipment, machinery, motor vehicles, and cattle. An item held for personal use, such as the family automobile, cannot be depreciated or deducted for tax purposes. In order to be eligible for depreciation, an item must be a tangible asset used in the investor's business, and it must have a useful life of more than one year.

Depreciation allows the investor to write off as an expense the cost of buildings, equipment, property, and other durable items over their useful life. A new provision (Section 179 ERTA) gives taxpayers an immediate write-off on the purchase of a capital asset up to $7,500 in 1984 and 1985 and $10,000 in 1986 and thereafter. Therefore, this "expensed" amount is not capitalized and depreciated as it normally would be. This amount, then, is not eligible for the investment tax credit.

Expense Allocations

As an overview, remember that most expenditures in business (excluding tax shelters) fall into four categories:

1. expense
2. capitalization and depreciation
3. capitalization and amortization
4. nondeductible capital expenditures

These four categories are listed in order of desirability to the taxpayer. That is, given a business expense as a tax shelter, immediate full write-off (deduction) of the expense (Category 1) provides the most advantageous tax treatment.

Expense If the Internal Revenue Code does not allow taxpayers to treat an item as an expense, it must be capitalized (added to the cost basis) and deducted over a specified period of time (Category 2 or 3) or treated as a nondeductible capital expenditure (Category 4).

Depreciation Capitalization and depreciation are used for *tangible* personal property used in a trade or business or for the production of income that has a useful life of more than one year. These tangible assets will be depreciated over the appropriate ACRS period. This depreciation deduction then allows the assets' cost to be written off (recovered) over a specific period of time.

Amortization Capitalization and amortization are used for *intangibles*. As with Category 2, the expenditures for these items are written off over a specified period of time. The time period is specified by Internal Revenue Code or IRS rulings, and the deductions must be computed using a straight-line method. Examples of intangibles that fit this category and the mandated amortization periods are:

- organization expenses of starting the business (five years)
- construction period interest and taxes in real estate projects (ten years)
- prepaid interest and loan standby or commitment fees (the standby period)

Nondeductible Business expenditures that cannot be assigned to the most desirable category (Category 1) and do not qualify for the next-best categories (Catcgories 2 or 3) belong to Category 4. These do not qualify as expenses.

Category 4 is used when there is no measurable, usable life of an expenditure because it is expected to last or have benefit for the life of the enterprise. Examples include land purchases and selling/syndication fees for the tax shelter offering. These may sound like expenses, but by IRS rule they are nondeductible. They do, however, add to the investor's capital base. When the enterprise is sold, the capital gain will be lower because the basis has been increased by these expenditures.

INTEREST

Interest on borrowing is a deduction that can be utilized in most tax shelters. Interest is usually considered an ordinary and necessary business expense of the tax shelter enterprise and is immediately deductible.

DEPLETION

The last important deduction is depletion. For tax shelters that qualify, depletion is a major source of tax relief. It is a means of allocating the write-offs of "wasting assets" (oil, gas, coal, timber, gravel, and various other minerals and natural resources). Land cannot be depleted.

Depletion may be calculated on either a *cost depletion basis* or a *percentage depletion basis.* Cost depletion may be used on any allowed wasting asset and is the only approach allowed for timber. Oil and gas depletion is most frequently calculated on a percentage basis because this method offers the investor greater tax benefits. Depletion allowances may be calculated both ways to determine which method affords taxpayers the best deduction.

THE INVESTMENT TAX CREDIT

The investment tax credit (ITC) allows investors to claim up to a 10 percent credit against taxes due for qualified investment properties in the year the properties are placed in service. A number of tax shelter investments qualify for the investment tax credit. Since the 10 percent credit is applied directly against taxes, it is much more attractive then a deduction against income.

This special credit is allowed only in the year the asset is actually placed in service and is for the cost of tangible personal property with a useful life of at least three years. For three-year recovery property under ACRS rules, the investment tax credit is 6 percent.

If the property has an ACRS useful life of five years or more, the investment tax credit is 10 percent. Do not be confused by the term *tangible personal property*. It does not refer to your personal property, which is nondeductible, but to property used in a business that is not real property (real estate). As you will see later, Section 38 of the Internal Revenue Code governs which property is eligible for the investment tax credit. If the property is one of the many listed in Section 38, it is eligible for the ITC.

REDUCE BASIS BY ONE-HALF OF ITC

If the maximum ITC is taken (either 6 percent or 10 percent), the taxpayer must reduce the depreciable base of the asset by one-half of the ITC taken. For example, a $10,000 computer (five-year property) would generate a 10 percent ITC or $1,000. One-half this amount ($500) must be subtracted from the $10,000 cost basis before depreciation deductions begin (i.e., only $9,500 can be depreciated).

The calculations are as follows:

Equipment	$10,000
1/2 ITC taken (1/2 × .10 × 10,000)	- 500
Depreciable base	$ 9,500

LIMITATION OF ITC

Use of the investment tax credit is limited. The maximum credit allowed per taxpayer for property that was purchased used is the cost of the property up to $125,000 through 1987 and $150,000 beginning in 1988. The maximum amount individuals may claim on their individual income-tax returns is 100 percent of the first $25,000 of tax due plus 85 percent of the amount that exceeds $25,000. Thus, if a taxpayer's tax liability is over $25,000, the amount cannot be wiped out completely with tax credits. The taxpayer can, however, wipe out 85 percent!

When the investment tax credits allow a taxpayer to exceed the total income tax due for that year, excess ITCs can be carried back three years. Previous returns can be amended to produce a refund. If a taxpayer paid no taxes in the previous three years, the excess ITC credit may be carried forward for 15 years.

When property is disposed of before the end of the useful-life period, part or all of the investment tax credit previously claimed will be recaptured. That is, a portion of the credit claimed in previous years must be paid back in the year of the premature disposition by adding it to the taxpayer's regular tax liability. The amount that must be repaid is 2 percent for each year the property was sold early.

RECAPTURE OF ITC

For example, if a 6 percent tax credit was claimed for three-year property, the taxpayer would be obligated to keep the property for three years. If the property was held for only two years, the recaptured amount would be 2 percent of the original tax credit (because it was sold one year earlier than expected). If the property was held for only one year, the recaptured amount would be 4 percent (because it was sold two years earlier than expected). The maximum penalty is a recapture of the entire credit if the property is sold before the end of the first year. For three-year property, there is no recapture penalty after three years. For five-year property, there is no recapture penalty after three years. There would be no recapture in these cases because you held the property for the length of time to which you agreed (i.e., three years or five years). As shown in Table 10.1, the recapture penalty decreases by 2 percent per year.

Table 10.1 Recapture Penalties for Property Sold Early

	Amount of ITC Previously Claimed That Must Be Recaptured	
Property-Holding Period	**For 3-year property**	**For 5-, 10-, and 15-year property**
Less than 1 year	6%	10%
1 year or more but less than 2 years	4	8
2 years or more but less than 3 years	2	6
3 years or more but less than 4 years	0	4
4 years or more but less than 5 years	0	2
5 years or more	0	0

For example, suppose a business purchases a delivery truck for $7,500. Light trucks are classified as three-year property. This business utilizes the maximum 6 percent ITC and after one year sells the truck. ITC recapture in the year of sale is as follows:

Purchase of 3-year property	$7,500
ITC utilized (6%)	$ 450

Property disposed of after 1 year requires recapture of 2% for every year sold too early	4% recapture percentage
4% of the 6% credit (2/3) recaptured in the year of sale	$ 300 recapture (4% of $7,500)

EXPLAINING TAX SHELTER CONCEPTS TO CLIENTS

The balance of this chapter provides answers you might give to questions clients commonly ask about tax shelters. These are only general sales explanations and are not meant to substitute for a thorough explanation of the offering memorandum. As you know from your licensing studies, tax shelter sales are rigidly regulated by the SEC. In answering any objection a client may pose, you must provide full disclosure to your prospect. The suggested answers on the pages that follow should help to *introduce* your prospect to tax shelter concepts.

Q. "In a paragraph or two, explain basically what a tax-advantaged limited partnership is."

A. "There is nothing inherently elusive or intimidating about limited partnerships. A tax-advantaged limited partnership is a direct investment in a business enterprise. It is different from other investments you make because it provides you with tax benefits *when you make the investment.*

"As a passive investor, you report the profits and the losses of the business directly on your own return. You use the deductions available from the tax shelter to offset taxable income from salary or any other source. This is perfectly legal; in fact, Congress has provided tax incentives for you to invest in businesses in order to encourage investment in certain industries. But you should always recognize that, first and foremost, tax shelters should be great *investments* that will make great profits."

Q. "Why are tax-advantaged investments partnerships instead of corporations?"

A. "The partnership form of doing business is ideally suited to tax-advantaged investing because in a partnership taxable losses and gains flow directly through the partnership to the partner, i.e., the investor.

"In contrast to a partnership, the corporate form of doing business does *not* allow the investor to pick up losses realized by the corporation.

"Tax shelters are usually *limited* partnerships. Limited partnerships have limited liability. A general partner has unlimited liability."

Q. "What is the difference between tax-advantaged limited partnerships and stocks or mutual funds?"

A. "Purely as investments, ignoring the tax implications, limited partnerships are generally riskier than stocks or mutual funds. However, when tax advantages of those investments are factored in, this relative risk is reduced.

"With stocks, you receive no tax incentive when you make the investment, and you receive a deduction in the future only if there is a loss.

"On the other hand, with limited partnerships you receive a deduction *initially* as if you lost your money, and then you pay a tax in the future if it turns out that you did not lose money. Generally, the losses are considered to be *ordinary losses*, while stock market losses are considered *capital losses*.

"For example, if you invest $100,000 in a limited partnership and sustain a *complete* loss, in the 50 percent tax bracket your loss is $50,000.

"On the other hand, if you invest the same $100,000 in a stock that goes down the drain and you hold the stock for more than six months, you have a long-term capital loss of $100,000. Capital losses may *not* be used to offset ordinary income on a dollar-for-dollar basis. Instead, they offset against ordinary income at a rate of only $3,000 per year. The $100,000 stock loss would provide $40,000 of deductions against your ordinary income, and it would take 14 years to use up that $40,000."

Q. "What is the concept of liquidity?"

A. "Liquidity is the ability to convert investment property quickly into cash. Limited partnerships are *not* liquid for both tax and nontax reasons. A need for liquidity and investment in limited partnerships is not consistent. You should not be in a tax-advantaged limited partnership in the first place unless you can afford to *lose* your investment (permanent illiquidity!). Partnership agreements provide for substantial limitation on your ability to resell or transfer units. In addition, a limited partnership investment is very difficult to sell because there is no formal secondary market for it.

"A high income tax bracket alone should not lead you to limited partnerships. You must be economically and emotionally ready for the risks in the long haul."

Q."What is the concept of leverage?"

A."*Leverage*, in the economic sense, means the borrowing of money for investment. When you invest with your own money *and* borrow additional money for investment, your potential financial reward is disproportionately greater than what you would have received merely investing with your own money. Borrowing additional money is the lever that allows your own dollars to do more work.

"Leverage, of course, can work in two ways: it may cause you to win bigger and faster in a *good* limited partnership, or it can work in reverse and make you lose faster.

"Investing with leveraged dollars gives you two direct tax benefits. First, because the amount of the investment has been increased, all of the deductions normally generated by the investment will, in turn, increase. Second, paying interest on the borrowed money in most cases entitles you to claim interest deductions."

Q."What is depreciation?"

A."Depreciation is a tax and accounting concept. It is a deduction for the amortization of the cost of improved real estate and certain other properties; i.e. the recovery of the property's cost. At one time, depreciation deductions were taken over the useful life of an asset. Today, assets are depreciated over three-, five-, ten- and 18-year recovery periods—depending on the type of program. For example, real estate is now depreciated over 18 years.

"No cash is involved directly in a depreciation deduction; i.e., it is a noncash expense. Since depreciation is an additional expense of a tax shelter, it can create a tax loss for you."

Q."What are recourse notes or loans?"

A."They are a way to substantially increase your tax deductions from a tax shelter. They are *also* additional amounts of money for which you are *personally* liable. This is because you personally sign a note that says that, if the investment fails, you pay up. Before you take on this greater risk, you must be very sure of the economics of the investment.

"Recourse loans are one reason that you should not invest in a limited partnership unless you are fully able to lose your initial investment *and* the recourse borrowing."

Q."What are the at-risk rules?"

A."*At-risk rules* mean that your income-tax deductions from a limited partnership cannot exceed the amount of money at risk in the venture.

"How much is at risk? What you actually put in plus any amount for which you are personally liable—amounts of recourse notes are included.

"The at-risk rules apply to all limited partnerships *except for real estate*."

Q."I hear people talk about 'hard dollars' and 'soft dollars.' What does this mean?"

A."This is jargon. Let me translate this into English: Hard dollars plus soft dollars equals your total investment.

"Hard dollars are your contribution—your investment *less* tax savings. Soft dollars are your tax savings.

"For example, if you are in the 50 percent tax bracket and you invest $10,000, which generates $9,000 of tax deductions, your tax savings, or soft dollars, are 50 percent times $9,000, which equals $4,500. Your hard dollars are your investment less tax savings, or $10,000 less $4,500, which equals $5,500 of hard dollars."

Q."What is the investment tax credit?"

A."The investment tax credit is a provision in the federal tax laws that helps subsidize many investments by permitting from 6 to 10 percent of the cost of certain outlays to be deducted from the first year's tax.

"A tax credit is better than a tax deduction. This is because a credit is a dollar-for-dollar *reduction* in your tax bill, whereas a tax *deduction* reduces your taxable income by only a dollar, thereby reducing your tax bill by only part of that dollar. The investment tax credit most often applies to tax-advantaged investing in equipment leasing, research and development, and real estate rehabilitation."

Q. "What are tax preference items?"

A. "For federal income-tax purposes, investors are subject to a tax over and above the normal income tax. It is equal to the excess of 15 percent of tax preferences over the greater of $10,000 or one-half of the regular federal income tax liability. This is important to limited partnership investors because tax preference items include such things as adjusted itemized deductions, depletion allowances, intangible drilling costs, and the excess of accelerated depreciation over straight-line depreciation on real property."

Q. "What is the alternative minimum tax?"

A. "The alternative minimum tax is an entirely separate tax that is applied if it exceeds the sum of the regular tax plus the minimum tax. It is an alternative way of having your tax assessed. It rarely applies to anyone. It applies only if you have capital gain that is disproportionately large as compared to your other income or if your itemized deductions are very large. In those cases, see your accountant."

Q. "What does *recapture* mean?"

A. "When the proceeds from the sale of a property exceed the basis of that property, all or part of the depreciation deduction is taxed at ordinary income tax rates. Part or all is recaptured.

"Most often, recapture enters the picture in real estate when the difference between deductions received for accelerated depreciation and deductions for straight-line depreciation are recaptured. The difference between these two kinds of depreciation is called *excess depreciation*. This excess depreciation is recaptured at ordinary income rates. On this portion, you have gained a deferral of the tax."

Q. "What is *phantom income?"*

A. "Phantom income results when the IRS says that you have received taxable income from your tax shelter but you have actually received no cash from it with which to pay that tax. As a result, you have income tax to pay *without* the cash to pay it.

"Phantom income occurs when deductible interest payments decrease and the nondeductible principal payment increases. This means that, as you pay off your loan (when money is borrowed in the tax shelter), you receive fewer tax deductions. Also, your principal payment amount is increasing (just like your home mortgage). In addition, the depreciation deduction decreases and eventually runs out. There will be a time when your tax shelter crosses over from producing losses to producing taxable income. This creates the phantom income, at the point when nondeductible principal payments become greater than depreciation deductions."

Q. "What happens if my partnership goes under?"

A. "Let's look at a real estate investment for illustrative purposes. The only potential amount of money that you lose is the total amount of your investment. The investment is structured as a limited partnership; therefore, you have limited liability. You lose only the amount you have invested in the deal. No one can come after you personally.

"Let's also look at the income-tax consequences. You will probably have income tax to pay, although you will not receive any cash with which to pay it. It may be a capital-gains tax, or it may be ordinary income, depending on the technicalities of how the property is conveyed to the lender (assuming leverage was part of the deal).

"Where does taxable income come from? Income is realized when your tax cost minus depreciation in the property is *less than* the mortgage on the property; the difference between the tax basis and the mortgage balance is the income you have. For example, assume that your real estate tax shelter cost $10,000, with a $2,000 down payment, the balance financed by an $8,000 mortgage.

"Depreciation of $4,500 has been taken so that your basis is now $5,500. At the time of the default the mortgage balance is $7,500. Your basis is below the mortgage balance. You have a negative basis of $2,000 ($7,500 minus $5,500 equals $2,000). When the property is foreclosed, you will have taxable income of $2,000 and will receive no cash with which to pay the tax."

SUMMARY

As a salesperson, you must understand, and be able to explain to your clients, the workings of the various tax shelter products you are selling. You are not likely to learn everything you need to know overnight, however, and neither is your client. Therefore, you should be prepared to answer a barrage of questions about tax shelter benefits, deductions allowed by the Internal Revenue Code, and complex but important matters like ACRS and investment tax credits. While you should be prepared to answer these questions clearly, remember always to stress that *no* tax shelter is a good investment if it does not provide a good return in addition to sheltering income from taxation.

11

Taxation of the Partnership Entity

A partnership is legally considered an organization created for the purpose of carrying on a business for profit. There are two forms of partnerships, general and limited, but we will be most concerned with limited partnerships. Partnership income and expense flow *through* the partnership to its members and are reported on the partners' individual income tax returns. Because of this flow-through, considerable tax benefits can result from participating in a partnership. The flow-through process is known as the *conduit principle.* This often results in tax savings when partnership losses are passed on to the individual partners.

FUNDAMENTAL OF INCOME TAXATION FOR A PARTNERSHIP

The fact that a business organization calls itself a partnership does not necessarily make it one in the eyes of the IRS. Taxation by the IRS is based on the characteristics of the business entity. If the business has the characteristics of a corporation, it is taxed as a corporation; if it has the characteristics of a partnership, it is taxed as a partnership. Thus, to maintain the flow-through tax treatment of a partnership, (as opposed to the double taxation potential of corporate dividends), one of the most important considerations for operation as a partnership is to ensure that it maintains its partnership status.

There are four characteristics common to corporations, and a partnership is allowed to have *no more than two* of these. They are:

- continuity of life;
- limited liability;
- centralized management; and
- transferability of interest.

Ordinarily, a partnership formed for tax shelter purposes already possesses two of these: limited liability and centralized management. Therefore, continuity of life and transferability of interest *must be avoided* in order to continue taxation as a partnership. Most frequently, this is accomplished by limiting the partnership agreement. That limitation stipulates that a limited partner's interest, if subject to a future sale, must be offered to the general partner or the other limited partners before it is offered to any other party. Often, the restriction stipulates further that, if none of the present partners purchase the interest, the limited partner can sell to another individual *only* with preapproval of the general partner and/or other limited partners.

Partners who allow their names to be used in the name of the partnership are "holding themselves out" as general partners and will be considered general partners by the IRS even if they are not legally so under the partnership agreement. Also, if a limited partner assumes a significant amount of the operational responsibility and day-to-day management of the partnership, that limited partner will be construed to be a general partner. Limited partners who believe they may be considered general partners, and wish not to be, can renounce all interest in the partnership (including all profits) in order to avoid the unlimited liability that attaches to general partners. If creditors might be harmed by this, a formal dissolution through the courts may be necessary.

THE INVESTOR'S BASIS IN THE PARTNERSHIP

The concept of *basis* is important to the investor. Generally, basis is the investor's cost, the amount the investor pays to invest in a tax shelter, plus future adjustments. Basis includes loans to the partnership for which the investor is personally liable. To be personally liable is said to be "at risk." Throughout this chapter, limited partnerships will be discussed in terms of the limited partner's basis and the changing adjusted cost basis of the limited partner when various financial activities occur. A limited partner's basis begins with the investment in the partnership. As a general rule, no gain or loss is recognized on the exchange of property or money for an interest in a partnership.

Importance of Basis

The computation of basis is of major importance because a partner's basis must be determined continually in order to calculate gains or losses in the investment. *A partner's loss deduction cannot exceed his or her basis at the end of the tax year in which the loss occurred.*

For example, if a partner puts up talent (rather than money or property) as the partnership interest, that partner cannot claim a loss during this initial period of the partnership's existence. For all partners, however, any unused losses can be recognized in future years when a partner's basis increases. This is called an *unlimited carryover of nondeductible partnership losses.* When the partnership has earnings, the basis of each partner increases. But if there is a loss, each partner can recognize the loss during that taxable year *to the extent of his or her basis above $0.* There is no such thing as a negative basis.

Adjustments to Basis—Continuous Fluctuation

After the initial investment, a number of financial transactions can either increase or decrease basis. On the partnership books, a capital account is assigned to each partner. An increase in the capital account, and thus in the partner's adjusted basis in the partnership, will occur when the partner:

1. puts more money into the partnership to help it grow;
2. receives a share of undistributed (K-1) partnership earnings; or
3. is allocated the appropriate share of liabilities assumed by the partnership.

When a partnership basis is increased, the partner may receive future loss distributions that can be offset against other ordinary income. This can continue until the basis has been reduced to zero.

A partner's adjusted basis in the partnership will decrease (but not below zero) when the partner:

1. receives a cash distribution;
2. receives a partnership loss distribution (K-1 form) at the end of the year; or
3. is allocated the appropriate share of liabilities relieved by the partnership.

Reducing a partner's basis has a twofold effect:

1. If it reduces to zero, the partner will no longer be able to utilize loss deductions from the partnership; and,
2. If it is low, and a partner sells his or her interest in the part-

nership in later years, a higher taxable gain (sales price minus adjusted basis) would result.

In either case, with a low basis, an investment has outlived its tax deferral advantage, and now may be the time to pay the tax collector. However, the prudent investor will have been able to defer taxes and convert the ordinary income into long-term capital gains. A key question is: How long can the investor maintain the tax deferral? This issue is of great importance to the investor and should be considered at the time of investment.

It is customary for a partnership to pass on losses to the limited partners in its early years. These losses shelter, or offset, the partners' other taxable income. However, a limited partner whose basis has been reduced to zero would not benefit from additional losses, although they can be carried forward. When a limited partner's basis is reduced to zero, the partner must find a way to increase the basis in order to take advantage of continuing loss distributions. One of three major techniques can be used to increase basis:

1. put more money into the partnership;
2. leave undistributed earnings in the partnership; or
3. have the partnership create additional liabilities for which the partners are responsible.

Recourse Loans and the At-Risk Rules The only types of liabilities that will increase one's basis are those loans known as *recourse loans*. This means that the limited partner is truly at risk on the loan, and, if the partnership cannot make payments, the creditors can attach personal assets of the limited partner. The only exception to this at risk rule is real estate investments. Nonrecourse loans to the partnership (for which the limited partner is not personally liable) that will increase a limited partner's basis are acceptable in real estate tax shelters.

Leverage *Financial leverage* means borrowing against the investment to create a greater asset value (i.e., adding borrowed money to the equity money invested). Thus, with a greater asset base, depreciation deductions, interest deductions, credits, and expenses can far exceed the upfront cash invested. While leverage is applied in most tax shelter investments, it has to be managed carefully, since it can magnify either the gain or the loss. Nonrecourse borrowing, where personal assets are not at risk, will not be treated as an addition to cost basis (except in real estate), thus severely limiting overall loss deductions.

Though leverage has the distinct advantage of reducing the amount of taxes paid by the investor, the approach is not without its pitfalls. One such pitfall that tax shelter investors should avoid is phantom income.

Phantom Income Early in a growing venture, most of the debt service is applied to payment of deductible interest, and little goes toward the reduction of principal. As the venture ages, income dollars begin to pay more and more of the principal on the loan, while little of this income passes to the investor. Repayments of principal are not tax-deductible, as are interest payments. When the venture is a partnership, a limited partner can be charged with taxable income that has been generated by the partnership but must be used to pay such nondeductible items as principal payments on indebtedness. In this situation, the limited partner will be charged with taxable income from the partnership investment, yet the investor never actually receives the income! This interesting phenomenon is undesirable from the investor's viewpoint and is referred to as *phantom income*. It is, nonetheless, a part of the price paid for upfront tax losses creating tax deferral and hoped for conversion of long-term capital gains.

Crossover Point A second problem is created as mortgage principal payments increase and the tax-deductible interest payments decrease. When this happens, the net taxable revenues will eventually exceed depreciation deductions designed to shelter the income flow. At the same time as the mortgage interest imbalance is developing, more and more debt service will be used for nondeductible repayment of debt principal. If accelerated depreciation is used, depreciation deductions will continue to shrink in later years. Eventually, taxable income will exceed deductions. This event is called the *crossover point*. The term implies that an investment has crossed over from sheltering income (using loss deductions) to manufacturing taxable income. As you can see, the crossover phenomenon is aggravated when the accelerated depreciation method is used.

At the crossover point, not only is the partnership's cash flow taxable, but part of it may be used to pay such nondeductible debt services as mortgage principal payments. This can create phantom income. Some shelters, such as equipment leasing, tend to generate phantom income earlier than others. This situation may be avoided by selling or refinancing the sheltered property before the crossover point is reached.

However, recapture of previous deductions may then become a problem. The individual investor may handle this situation by shifting this taxable into a later tax period that may be more favorable or by purchasing another tax shelter during the year the taxpayer is charged with phantom income or recapture.

To the thoughtful tax planner, deferral of taxes will result in tax savings, which can then be invested to earn money. A deferral can be considered effective tax planning, but the taxes deferred will have to be paid at a later date. Taxes may be postponed indefinitely by using a predetermined combination of different tax strategies scheduled over future years of expected income from previously deferred but currently taxable investments.

All of this requires careful financial planning that lays out the entire chronology *in advance* of the investment. The "sinking fund" concept of setting aside a portion of the tax savings to meet the postponed obligation is alway considered prudent.

TAXATION OF INDIVIDUAL PARTNERS

A partner will be taxed on his or her share of partnership income or loss realized in the taxable year of the partnership. Most partnerships report on a calendar year basis (January 1 through December 31). The partnership must have the same taxable year as its principal partners unless there is a good business reason for doing otherwise. The year-end report is referred to as each partner's *distributive share* and includes all gains, losses, deductions, and credits attributed to each partner's interest. This distributive share also includes any amount of money passed through the partnership to the partners. Usually, profits and losses are determined according to the partner's interest in the partnership. If the distributive share allocations under the partnership agreement are not proportionate to the capital contributions, the IRS will ask why and whether such distributive share allocations have "substantial economic effect."

The IRS does not allow partners' taxes to be avoided by intentional adjustment of items, such as assignment of all depreciation deductions to the partner in the highest tax bracket. This is a hot topic covered by both case law and IRS regulation, which imposes the test that the allocation must affect the dollar amount of the partner's share of income or loss *independent* of the tax consequences. This thwarts an attempt to allocate losses in a partnership to those partners for whom the losses are of greatest value.

A partner must report the items below on Form 1040 in addition to taxable income or loss from distributive share. Each partner's share will appear on the K-1 form if the partnership has any of these items:

- certain taxes paid or accrued that may be claimed as a credit;
- charitable contributions, which a partner claims individually;

- gains and losses, both long-term and short-term
- dividends and interest qualifying for exclusion, received by partnership from stock.
- IRS Section 1231 gains and losses (sale of real property used in a trade or business).
- other special items of income, gain, loss, credit, or deduction, including bad debt recoveries, intangible drilling and development costs, and exploration expenditures.

LIMITED PARTNERS' LIABILITY

The partnership agreement will stipulate that the liability of limited partners is limited to the amount each has contributed to the partnership, plus any agreed future amounts. In addition to the original contribution, a limited partner may agree to contribute added amounts, such as installment payments, staged payments, or mandatory assessments. If agreed to, the partner will be liable for these amounts to creditors.

CORPORATIONS AS GENERAL PARTNERS

Some tax shelter limited partnerships appear to resemble a corporation and thus attract IRS inquiry. One factor that may attract the attention of the IRS is a corporation as sole general partner. Most public real estate tax shelter partnerships have managing general partners that are corporations. This *is* legal, but the IRS will carefully scrutinize the relationship of limited partners and may litigate. Two leading cases in which the IRS litigated against a corporate general partner were *Philip G. Larson v. U.S.* and *Zuckman v. U.S.* However, the IRS lost both cases, supporting the contention that a sole corporate general partner is acceptable.

SALE OF A PARTNERSHIP INTEREST

A number of income-tax consequences are associated with a partner's sale of an interest, whether it is sold back to the partnership or to another approved person. The gain/loss from the sale will be broken into capital gain/loss and ordinary income/loss. A partnership interest is a capital asset; therefore, a sale or exchange results in a capital gain or loss. The gain/loss is figured according to this formula: sales price minus adjusted basis.

When a partnership interest is sold, the sales agreement often specifies that the sale price is made up of four components:

1. the partnership interest itself;
2. unrealized receivables;

3. inventory in the business; and
4. goodwill.

The last three of these items, if given a specific value in the sales agreement, could engender ordinary-income taxation and not capital gain. Let's investigate each of these items further.

The portion of money applied to the purchase of an *interest in the partnership property*—equipment, buildings, etc.—is treated as a payment for a capital asset and thus is treated as capital gain or loss.

Unrealized receivables are accounts receivable in the business that have not yet been received and will benefit the new owner when they are received. The portion of the sales price attributed to unrealized receivables is taxed as ordinary income.

Substantially appreciated inventory is goods on hand that are worth more than 120 percent of their adjusted basis. This generally means inventory that will be sold for 20 percent more than its cost! Any money allocated for substantially appreciated inventory is taxed as ordinary income.

That portion of the purchase price allocated to *goodwill* is treated as capital gain *only if the partnership agreement specifies* that goodwill is to be treated as capital property. If there is no mention of goodwill, it is taxed as ordinary income to the seller.

To summarize, a partnership sales price must be divided into amounts attributed to four categories. Tax treatment of each category is as follows:

1. partnership property: capital gain
2. appreciated inventory: ordinary income
3. unrealized receivables: ordinary income
4. goodwill: ordinary income, unless previously specified in the partnership agreement as a capital asset

SUMMARY

Before venturing into a limited partnership investment, your clients should understand not only the benefits, but also the pitfalls, of becoming limited partners. Such knowledge should begin with an understanding of what constitutes a limited partnership in the eyes of the IRS—and what will trigger an IRS challenge of that tax status. Investors also must have a good grasp of the concept of a continuously fluctuating basis, of the events or activities that will increase or reduce their basis, and of the tax ramifications of a sale of their partnership interest. The illiquidity of limited partnerships means that investors must foresee the tax implications of their investment over a relatively long term.

12

Rules and Regulations Governing Limited Partnerships

This chapter will briefly highlight the specific statutes and Securities and Exchange Commission rules for organizing and selling tax shelters in the United States. Legal requirements are vitally important to anyone connected, however remotely, with the offer or sale of tax shelter–type investments. Limited partnership interests of the tax shelter type are considered securities and, therefore, must comply with SEC rules. This means, generally, that they either have to be registered securities (registered under the Securities Act of 1933) or must meet one of the requirements for exemption from registration (e.g., Regulation D). If the securities are registered, each prospective investor must be provided with a prospectus, which is a synopsis of the registration statement filed with the SEC. After registration, these securities are considered to be public offerings.

Securities that are exempt from public registration are referred to as *private placements.* Instead of a prospectus, investors receive an offering circular that contains similar disclosure materials and information. Even a private offering under an SEC registration exemption such as Regulation D is considered a securities offering. It is merely private instead of public (no public solicitation, qualification of buyers, etc.).

Salespersons selling either a public or private offering are selling securities and may be required to meet the Securities Act of 1933 requirement for salespersons: they must be registered with the National Association of Securities Dealers, Inc. (NASD), pass the appropriate NASD exam, and so forth. We will begin our review of these securities laws in 1933, when it all began.

The Securities Act of 1933 was the first major securities act in the United States. It came about because of Depression-era abuses in the securities markets, through which unsuspecting or unsophisticated investors were fleeced and exploited. Since new issues were among those most abused, this act required that all new publicly offered securities be registered with the Securities and Exchange Commission through the filing of a registration statement. Unless a registration statement is in effect or an offering is exempt, it is unlawful for any person, either directly or indirectly, to sell a security through the use of interstate commerce or the mails. It is also unlawful to use the mails or interstate commerce for the transportation or conveyance of any security for the purpose of sale or delivery after a sale.

The SEC has rigid rules regarding prospectus distribution to potential buyers. A copy of a current prospectus must be delivered prior to a transaction involving any security affected. The act states that the prospectus must be delivered within 40 days of either the effective date of the registration statement or the first date which the security is offered to the public, whichever of the two dates is later.

REGULATION D

Regulation D is an SEC regulation under the Securities Act of 1933 that refers to limited offering exemption rules. This rule exempts certain offerings from the rigorous registration requirements of the 1933 act. Because the registration process required by the Securities Act of 1933 is time-consuming and can be extremely expensive, it is possible for the issuer and investor to benefit from the savings realized if an exemption to the registration requirements is available. Regulation D replaces the exemptions that had been provided under Rules 146, 240, and 242. Regulation D is actually a series of six rules from Rule 501 through Rule 506. Rule 501 sets forth definitions and terms applicable to the regulation. The most important definition is the term *accredited investor.* There are eight categories of accredited investors who are not counted for purposes of determining a purchaser limitation, each of which must be considered separately. Purchaser limitations are specified in the regulation and relate to the number of investors permitted in an exempted transaction. The eight categories of exempt investors are:

1. financial institutions such as banks, insurance companies and investment companies, small business investment companies, and employee benefit plans

2. any private business development company
3. any religious, charitable, scientific, or educational organization, including any college or university endowment fund, as well as other nonprofit organizations with assets of $5 million or more
4. any corporate or partnership "insider," such as any director, executive officer, or general partner
5. any purchaser of at least $150,000 of securities being offered, with a total purchase price not exceeding 20 percent of the purchaser's net worth at time of sale (including joint net worth with purchaser's spouse), for cash, marketable securities, a full recourse obligation that must be discharged within five years of sale, or cancellation of indebtedness
6. individuals with a net worth, or joint net worth with spouses, in excess of $1 million (including joint net worth with spouses)
7. individuals with income in excess of $200,000 in each of the last two years, with a reasonable expectation of having income in excess of $200,000 in the year of purchase
8. any entity 100 percent owned by an accredited investor or investors

For the purposes of Regulation D, a sale takes place when the purchaser enters into a commitment to pay for the securities. In a limited partnership situation, the sale takes place upon the issuer's acceptance of the subscription agreement.

Rule 502 describes the general conditions applicable to all Regulation D transactions. It provides a "safe harbor" from the integration of sales of securities by the issuer made six months prior to or six months after a Regulation D offering. Under Rule 502, all sales that are part of the same issue must meet the exemption requirements. Under this rule, two or more exempt offerings could be combined into one, possibly resulting in a violation. In determining which securities will be considered a single issue, those sales occurring more than six months prior to or six months after the subject offering are not considered.

The rule also describes when and what type of disclosure must be furnished in Regulation D offerings. Rule 502 limitations on resale require that the purchaser acquire the interest for his or her own account and require that there be a legend (i.e., a statement outlining the resale limitations) on each and every certificate. This legend is generally stamped on the face of the certificate of ownership.

Rule 503 provides a Uniform Notice of Sale Form (Form D) that the issuer must file with the SEC for exemption qualification in Regulation D offerings. This form is due 15 days after the first sale. The issuer must update it every six months after the first sale in the interim and 30 days after the last sale.

Rule 504, which concerns sales, indicates when specific disclosure is *not* required. Specific disclosure is not required in cases in which the aggregate offering price is limited to $500,000. It also provides for an unlimited number of accredited investors. Under Rule 504, commissions are permitted. Also under this rule, no general solicitation is permitted unless the issue is registered in a state that requires delivery of a disclosure document. This rule applies only to issuers that are not subject to the reporting requirements of the Securities Act of 1933.

Rule 505 is designed for offerings of between $500,000 and $5 million. Under this rule, the aggregate offering price limitation is $5 million in 12 months by any issuer that is not an investment company. The number of unaccredited investors is limited to 35 plus an unlimited number of accredited investors. Once again, commissions are permitted, and no general solicitation of sales is allowed.

Rule 506, which replaces Rule 146, pertains to offerings without regard to the amount of the offering. Again, the number of unaccredited investors is limited to 35, provided they meet the purchaser qualifications, plus an unlimited number of accredited investors. The difference between Rules 505 and 506 is that, under Rule 506, the purchaser must be sophisticated in relation to this particular type of investment if he or she is not accredited. If the investor is accredited (i.e., meets the financial requirements), he or she is presumed to be qualified. Once again, commissions are permitted, and no general solicitation is permitted. If only accredited investors are involved, Rule 506 eliminates the need to deliver disclosure documents. This rule contains a "purchase representative" concept whereby an investor lacking in knowledge or experience to evaluate this particular investment may secure independent representation.

Sound confusing? To summarize, there are three Regulation D rules that impose investor limitations—Rules 504, 505, and 506. Regulation D does not contain any prohibition against, or limitation of, sales commissions. Rule 504 provides an exemption from registration for any issuer for offers and sales of securities up to $500,000 a year to an unlimited number of accredited investors. As offerings go, $500,000 is not considered large, so that rule is seldom used. In addition, a public offering may be made under this ruling if the offering is made exclusively in states that require registration and if a disclosure statement is delivered to the investor.

Rule 505 provides an exemption from registration for any non-investment company issuer, including partnerships, for offerings in sales of restricted securities up to $5 million during any 12-month period to no more than 35 purchasers who are not accredited and to an unlimited number of accredited investors. This rule and Rule 506 are most often used in Regulation D to secure exempt status for a tax shelter private offering.

Rule 506, which has no dollar limitation and replaces Rule 146, provides an exemption from registration for any issuer for offers in sales of restricted securities to no more than 35 purchasers who are not accredited and to an unlimited number of accredited investors. To qualify under this rule, the issuer must reasonably believe, prior to making a sale, that the nonaccredited persons, either alone or with the purchasing representatives, understand the merits and risks of the investment.

For purposes of the Regulation D limit of 35 investors, a husband, wife, and any children living in the same household are considered one purchaser, even if they register the ownership in individual names.

REGULATION A

An exemption used primarily in stock offerings (not tax shelters) is known as Regulation A. This generally fits small businesses and issuers going public for the first time. This regulation exempts offerings of less than $1.5 million from SEC registration under the 1933 act.

Rule 147 provides an exemption from the registration requirements for intrastate offerings. An investor in these securities may resell to an out-of-state resident only after owning the securities for at least nine months. All securities of the issuer that are part of a single issue must be offered for sale in accordance with all of the terms and conditions of Rule 147. The issuer of the security must be a resident and do business within the state in which all of the offers and sales are made.

Also, in order to qualify under Rule 147, offers to sell must be made only to persons residing within the state or territory of which the issuer is a resident. An individual is deemed a resident of a state or territory if, at the time of the offer and sale, his or her principal place of residence is that state. Principal place of residence is determined by the address designation on one's federal income tax return.

During the period in which securities that are part of an issue are being offered and sold by the issuer, and for a period of nine months from the date of the last sale by the issuer of these securities, all resales of any part of the issue by any person must be made only to people who are residents within that state. This means that the investor cannot resell to any out-of-state person for at least nine months. The issuer must take precautions against interstate offers and sales. A legend stating the resale limitations must be placed on the certificate. Stop-transfer instructions must be made to the issuer's transfer agent. This is the person or organization responsible for transferring certificate ownership as needed from one person to another. Finally, written confirmation from each purchaser must be obtained by the issuer as to that purchaser's principal place of residence.

SUMMARY

It is important that you, as a salesperson, understand the provisions of the Securities Act of 1933 and other SEC regulations applicable to your offerings. Those regulations will affect both you and your prospective investors. Available exemptions from registration are particularly important to understand, since registration is a costly and lengthy process.

13

Real Estate Limited Partnerships

Real estate offers a familiar and tangible source of wealth for investors. It is popular because many investors are more comfortable with real estate than with other tax shelter programs. It is bricks and mortar; the investor can see, touch, and feel the investment. In addition, real estate has historically offered an effective hedge against inflation. In short, it has a strong history of providing investors with a method for achieving their goals of wealth accumulation.

Real estate has also become heavily regulated. Many state laws have been enacted to set safety requirements and building code standards and to protect investors. For example, real estate investments became popular in New York after World War II, but because promoters were often overzealous in their projections, the real estate investment market crumbled, leaving large numbers of unhappy investors. New York State followed with stringent securities laws governing real estate syndication.

CATEGORIES OF REAL ESTATE INVESTMENT

Real estate investments fall into three categories: residential, commercial, and government-subsidized. Examples of residential are multi-family apartment buildings, garden apartments, condominiums, etc. Commercial real estate generally refers to commercial office buildings and shopping centers. Government-subsidized real estate is real estate subject to special legislation under the Department of Housing and Urban Development (HUD), known as

Section 8 and Section 236. These investments include special residential development programs for the elderly, for low- or moderate-income residents, and for the handicapped. The following paragraphs describe considerations related to some of the categories of real estate investment.

Special Government Housing Programs

Several special government housing programs, authorized under Section 8 and Section 236 of the Housing and Urban Development (HUD) program, offer guarantees and subsidies that entice tax-oriented investors to new multi-family housing construction. These special HUD programs offer an inducement to finance low-income housing for the elderly, for low-income tenants, and for the handicapped. They offer the contractor a mortgage guarantee for 90–100 percent financing and special rent subsidy programs for tenants. In order to qualify for Section 8 or Section 236 projects, however, the housing project must be approved by local and regional HUD offices before construction, and the general partner must comply with all HUD requirements.

In recent years, funding for the origination of these projects has been cut back sharply by the federal government. While this means little new construction under these programs, subsidies and continuing funding for prior agreements still take place.

In a typical case, the developer gets HUD commitment and secures highly leveraged financing, often 90 percent of replacement value. The developer then sells 99 percent of the interest, usually at 115–118 percent of mortgage cost, to a limited partnership, retaining 1 percent interest. After giving the limited partnership various guarantees, such as on-schedule project completion, a specific occupancy date, and other considerations as part of the total package, the developer may retain up to a 50 percent "back-in interest." This means that the developer will take 50 percent of the net revenues after investors have been repaid their original investment. Once approval has been obtained and financing has been arranged, a package is put together, or syndicated, and is then sold to investors in the form of a limited partnership.

Housing assistance payments, known as *HAPs*, are direct rent payments by HUD on behalf of families who occupy a qualified property. Rental rates are set at fair market levels and often are subsidized up to 100 percent for certain preferential tenants; for example, the elderly or handicapped. In most cases, the tenant does pay a minimum of rent, an amount based on approximately 25 percent of gross income. The HUD program pays the balance. For occasional vacancies, HUD pays 80 percent of the rental for a period of 60 days. Rents are set by an agreement between the developers and HUD and normally on a contract basis subject to an adjustment for inflation, property taxes, utility rates, and certain other costs.

As with any investment, there are risks to be analyzed. The appreciation of low-income housing projects has not been up to the levels commonly associated with other real estate investments; in fact, many have actually depreciated. A special provision in Section 236 provides an inducement that helps offset the lower rate of appreciation—a rollover provision that allows the investor to move investments from one project to another, thereby deferring taxes on the capital gain upon sale.

When subsidized property is sold, the accelerated depreciation deductions allowed, which can be 200 percent declining balance over five years, must be recaptured. This can be a significant problem for an investor. The recaptured amount is the difference between the excess of accelerated over straight-line depreciation. As always, gain is computed as the sales price minus the adjusted cost basis.

Rehabilitated Property

Rehabilitation of older structures and certified historical structures offers a special kind of investment tax credit. The credit is 15 percent for buildings 30–39 years old, 20 percent for buildings 40 or more years old, and 25 percent if the property is certified historic. To qualify, the building must be substantially rehabilitated, but generally, 75 percent of the outside walls remain intact. Substantial rehabilitation means that expenditures over a two-year period ending on the last day of the taxable year must exceed the adjusted basis of the property or $5,000 per unit, whichever is greater. The maximum allowable depreciation for rehabilitated residential properties is $40,000 per dwelling. Depreciation is allowed over 60 months.

In order to be classified as a certified historic property, a property must be approved by a local or state historic society, which has in turn been approved by the National Historic Society. Certified historic structures must be depreciated as 18-year property, but they qualify for a 25 percent investment tax credit.

Raw Land

Land development normally takes place in six stages. Raw land is first developed as recreational land; recreational land is then developed into agricultural land; agricultural land is converted to predeveloped land; predeveloped land is turned into developed land; and, finally, developed land is redeveloped. In redeveloping land, buildings are destroyed and new ones are built in their place.

Developing raw land can be a risky endeavor, and it is more difficult to evaluate raw land investment than conventional real estate investments. There are several reasons for the high risk in raw land investment. First, it is easy to misjudge the eventual development potential of raw land. Even if the development potential is assessed accurately, much of the available raw land is already priced beyond the development market. Interim agricultural or ranching plans may not make good economic sense as a fiscal stopgap while the development potential is being realized.

Finally, agricultural, timber, and ranching syndications formed to acquire extremely speculative land must have a well-thought-out business plan, well-conceived economic potential, and proven experienced management. All in all, investment in raw land requires much more effort and entails far greater risk than conventional real estate investment.

Real estate investors must understand how raw land investments differ from conventional real estate investments. Raw land does not offer a deep shelter, nor does it result in a cash flow. Further, raw land acquired for investment normally must be held for a considerable time before it can be developed or resold. It can, therefore, be dangerously speculative unless the investors have great staying power. Holding raw land until the development potential is realized or until it is resold requires additional capital for taxes, for interest, and for debt-service. In addition, there is no cash flow from the investment.

Raw land, though it may be acquired through syndications or limited partnerships, is not normally bought this way. Land values in many areas are extremely high, adding to the difficulty of financing new construction on the land. This increases the risk and reduces the chance of a high return on the raw land investment.

COMMERCIAL/INDUSTRIAL REAL ESTATE

Income is produced from commercial properties through leases for space in such facilities as shopping centers, office buildings, apartments, and hotels. Major long-term tenants are solicited who will occupy the property on a net lease or triple net lease basis. A prime quality lessee arranges to rent under a long-term lease and to pay all utilities. This arrangement offers the investors the highest degree of rental security, although it results in the lowest rate of investment return.

In the triple net lease, the tenant agrees to pay for all maintenance, insurance, and property taxes. Total payments to the lessor under a triple net lease are less than under any other type of lease agreement. Thus, the lessor's only financial responsibility is the payment of the indebtedness (mortgage). Net lease and triple net lease have now come to mean the same in the real estate market (i.e. *net* means *triple net*).

The rate of return an investor should seek for income-producing commercial properties is determined by the kind of lease and the nature of the property. Net leases offer the greatest degree of security. The net lease, though, is a common form of lease, particularly for shopping centers. The major portion of space leased in a shopping center is rented to large chain stores on long-term leases, usually with an escalation clause for rental payments based on gross revenues of that store in the shopping center. The AAA-rated tenant (Sears, Montgomery Ward, K Mart, etc.) attracts the traffic, so other smaller space can be rented at higher per-square-foot rates.

Office buildings usually have a broader mixture of tenants who lease on a shorter-term than do shopping center tenants. They should afford a greater rate of return, which goes along with their higher risk. Apartments are rented for still shorter periods of time to a large range of individual tenants. These require an even higher rate of return to compensate for lower rental security.

SUITABILITY OF INVESTMENT

As with any other mutual fund or limited partnership investment, investors must be sure of the suitability of the particular investment being considered. When evaluating real estate as an investment, whether the program is registered or unregistered, investors (with the registered representative's assistance) should look for economic soundness and examine program management, program structure, and investment potential. Projects that make good economic sense and have investment potential within the broad economy are considered the most viable. Investors should examine management's supervisory services in construction, refinancing and rehabilitation, and day-to-day operations, as well as learn the method and amount of investor compensation, the front-end fees and ongoing charges, and the promoter's share of compensation and how the proceeds from a sale are shared. They should look for a program structure that is fair and reasonable with a clear statement of rights and privileges regarding taxes and economic benefits.

Careful investor evaluation alone will not ensure a sound investment. It is recommended that investors consider confirming investment potential using financial counselors, advisors, and tax accountants who will examine the investment for tax purposes in light of the investors' present investments and tax position.

If potential investors are unsophisticated in real estate investments or tax law, a purchaser representative may be used to judge the program for them.

Period Risks

There are three identifiable periods of risk in new real estate investments:

1. construction period risk
2. rent-up risk
3. operation risk

During the construction phase, for example, the contractor may declare bankruptcy and never complete the project. Delays resulting from labor problems, strikes, and material shortages may result in delayed completion dates, cost overruns, and even loss of a mortgage commitment.

The second phase and risk period is rent-up risk. Anticipated rentals may never develop because the property is not suitable for the planned market, has a poor location, is caught in a changing market, or for some other reason. Full occupancy may be difficult or impossible to achieve. If this happens, operating costs will get out of hand and money will run out before the property can reach the operational period.

The last, or mature, stage is the ongoing operation of the rented facility. If the project does not have astute and hardworking management, it may not operate profitably. Unanticipated costs may result in a property's being operated at a loss, even when operated to the best of management's ability. This is an ongoing risk and is referred to as *operation period risk*.

Program Structure

Real Estate Syndications Real estate syndicates offer investors a wide range of tax-sheltered investment programs. These include new multi-family residential projects; existing multi-family residential parcels; new or existing commercial buildings; recreational real estate, such as condominiums and ski resorts; and raw land, including orchards and farms. To develop these properties, syndicates have front-end charges. Since these increase the initial deduction that can be claimed by investors, they offer attractive, though sometimes risky, investment opportunities.

Real Estate Investment Trusts An additional form of real estate investment is the real estate investment trust (REIT). A real estate investment trust is a legal trust created within a single state (as opposed to a corporation, partnership, or other form of business organization) whose purpose is to invest monies on behalf of the "beneficial owners" of the trust. A trust operates under the conduit principle and generally distributes all net income. There are two types of REITs. The first is the more conservative and invests for equity in the real estate holdings. This type of trust involves little borrowing. The second type of REIT is debt-related and lends funds for the development and operation of real estate holdings. Equity interest is obtained as part of the financing. This type of trust is a creditor, rather than an owner, and, hence, there is extensive borrowing. The risk with this type of investment is that a real estate project that is in trouble may not be able to repay its indebtedness.

REITs were extremely popular in the 1970s, but because of skyrocketing construction costs, high front-end load, overpayment for properties, overleveraging, and inadequate fiscal reserves, many of these trusts ran into serious financial trouble. Most of these were *not* the equity type, but the lending or debt type. REITs are now making a comeback and appear to be managed much more conservatively.

Corporation as General Partner Frequently the general partner in a real estate investment program is a corporation. The corporation functions as a general partner and a management company, providing the experience and staff necessary to manage the real estate project.

While in a partnership the general partner must have unlimited liability, a corporation, by definition, has limited liability. Though the security rules that govern corporations require the general partner to have a net worth of at least $1 million, only this amount of corporate assets is available to satisfy a litigated obligation. Within these corporate limits, a limited partner can sue for recovery of investments or income. In addition, in a corporation, a limited partner can own no more than 20 percent of the corporate stock.

Another common practice in real estate investment programs is "shifting interest." In most real estate investment programs, for example, the formula for allocating profits and losses gives 90 percent to limited partners and 10 percent to the general partner. As the project grows, this sharing formula is often altered to the benefit of the general partner for ongoing management responsibilities. In a typical case, the formula is changed to a sharing rate of 50 percent for the limited partner and 50 percent for the general partner five to seven years into the project.

TAX CONSIDERATIONS

TREATMENT OF EXPENDITURES

For the purpose of computing taxes, investments and expenditures for real estate shelters are divided into three categories: expenditures incurred in acquisitions, ordinary and necessary operating expenses, and special allowed expenses.

Acquisition Expenses Certain costs, such as the acquisition of land, are completely nondeductible. Some costs, called *soft costs*, are deductible as they are incurred. These soft costs are normal operating expenses such as wages, management fees, and some interest deductions. Other costs, such as material and labor, must be capitalized and amortized along with other depreciable assets over the ACRS depreciation period. This capitalization increases the adjusted basis for an investment.

Ordinary and Necessary Expenses The costs of running a real estate business are referred to as *ordinary and necessary* business expenses. These include salaries, interest, repairs of a minor nature, taxes, utilities, management fees, insurance, and supplies. These are considered soft costs and are deductible as they are incurred. *Hard costs* are expenses for items that require upfront cash now, but for which little or no write-off of the assets purchased is immediately available.

Special Allowed Expenses Certain expenditures are subject to special rules. For example, interest and taxes incurred during the construction period must be capitalized and amortized over a ten-year period. Prepaid interest and points must be capitalized and amortized over the length of the loan. Special allocations of partnership income or loss are restricted. Limited partners are not eligible for retroactive allocation of losses and income. Expenditures that increase the value of a building are considered betterments and must be capitalized and deducted over the ACRS life. All materials and labor used to improve the building must be allocated in this manner. Repairs of a minor nature are immediately deductible, while those of a major nature are considered improvements and must be capitalized. Changing two locks in a building, for example, would be deductible as a repair, but changing all the locks in a building is considered a betterment that must be added to the capital value of the building and written off over its remaining useful life or ACRS period.

ACCELERATED COST RECOVERY SYSTEM

Using the Accelerated Cost Recovery System (ACRS), real property can be depreciated over an 18-year period using a schedule that approximates 175 percent of straight-line depreciation. (This does not apply to low-income housing.) If the straight-line schedule is selected, property can be depreciated over 35 years or 45 years or over 18 years with a level annual depreciation amount applicable each year.

When an accelerated ACRS schedule is applied to a mortgaged real estate investment, the amount of both the depreciation and interest deductions on the mortgage steadily declines. At some time in the future, a crossover point is reached when the excess write-offs created cease to shelter the income produced by the property, and positive cash flow results.

Investment Tax Credit (ITC) In Real Estate Investments

Internal Revenue Code Section 38 defines properties that are eligible for the investment tax credit. The investment tax credit is normally 6 percent for three-year property and 10 percent for five-year or longer property and is available only for "qualified tangible personal property." You might remember this as Section 1245 property. While 10 percent is normal, an additional 10 percent federal energy credit can be applied to qualified solar, wind, and geothermal investments made by a business. While some state laws allow additional deductions for energy-related investments, federal law does *not* include residential property for these special tax credits. The extra energy tax credit can be used only in a business for the production of a tangible product.

Real estate investments offer several sources for investment tax credits. Such tangible personal property items as equipment, machinery, furniture, and appliances are eligible for the credit. Note that land and buildings are not eligible for tax credits. Additional tax credits can be applied in real estate if a building can be certified as a historical landmark or because of age.

There are, however, some limitations on the use of investment tax credits. Property placed in service in December qualifies for the full investment tax credit. For used property, the investment tax credit is limited to a cost up to $125,000.

Individual taxpayers may claim a 10 percent credit for investments in qualified business property. The corporate taxpayer may claim a 10 percent tax credit for a qualified investment in corporate property. Corporations may elect an 11 percent credit for qualified investments if an amount equal to 1 percent of this investment is contributed to an employee stock ownership plan (ESOP). Since 1977, an additional 1/2 percent employer contribution can be claimed if it is matched by employee contributions to the employee stock ownership plan. This makes a total potential investment tax credit of 11½ percent for corporations.

The investment tax credit is limited to the amount of tax due and may not exceed $25,000 plus 85 percent of the amount in excess of $25,000. Investment tax credits may be carried back three years or carried forward 15 years. These must, however, be applied in the earliest possible years. If you cannot use your ITC this year, you must go back three years and claim it then, if you paid any taxes. If not, then you go back two years and apply it if possible, and then one year, before you are allowed to carry it into future years.

SUMMARY

Because real estate usually offers a hedge against inflation and is familiar to your clients as a tangible entity, many of your investment prospects may wish to put their investment dollars into this medium. Even though real estate investments may seem "comfortable" to your clients, they must understand that the real estate market is broad and complex. The different forms of investment, such as syndication and REITs, and the various types of real estate in which prospects can invest offer widely disparate benefits and have different tax implications. Be sure that prospective real estate investors understand the risks they will face during different stages of the investment's life.

14

Oil and Gas Limited Partnerships

A number of tax shelter benefits are associated with oil and gas programs. These programs are public in nature, and, in contrast to real estate investments, the majority are registered with both the SEC and NASD. The two types of direct participation programs (DPP) offerings are drilling partnerships and income partnerships. The total amount of investments raised annually for both types now exceeds $7 billion. This chapter will focus on partnership operations and tax treatment of these investments.

DRILLING PROGRAMS

PROGRAM STRUCTURE

General Partner–Limited Partner Relationship Even in the best-structured drilling programs, conflict of interest between the general partner and the limited partners may arise. To the extent that the general partner is selling leases to the program at a mark-up or is performing drilling or other services for the program at a profit, he or she stands to make money whether the investors do or do not. Even in the best programs, the sponsor will receive a promotional interest, that is, an interest in revenues either cost-free or as a share of program costs smaller than the share of revenues with which the sponsor is credited. This promotional interest means that wells may be drilled that are profitable to the sponsor but not to the investors. Finally, a possible conflict arises when the general partner wants to cap the well because it has only limited commercial value, but the limited partners may wish to prepare it for production.

In many ways, the greatest danger for the limited partner concerns how intelligently the sponsor will expend monies in the oil or gas search. This is the chief pitfall, because it may take years to determine whether or not the program will be financially successful. Consequently, the track record of the promoter may be the single most important factor to consider in deciding whether or not to invest.

Oil and Gas Program Sharing Arrangements Sharing arrangements refer to the difference between the percentage of revenues from the program to be allocated to the sponsor and the percentage of costs the sponsor is to bear. This difference is known as the *promotional spread* and is expressed in points. For example, a sponsor may have a 15-point spread. The sharing arrangement can assure a profit to the sponsor even if the investor receives none.

Types of Sharing Arrangements The four most common sharing arrangements in oil drilling programs are:

1. *Functional allocation*—an arrangement whereby the nondeductible costs (i.e., the capital costs, or tangible costs) of drilling are borne by the general partner and all intangible costs are borne by the limited partners, making their investment *fully* deductible.
2. *Overriding royalty interest*—occurs when the sponsor or general partner bears no part of the drilling costs but shares in revenues according to a certain percentage from the beginning (e.g., 10 percent of revenues).
3. *Reversionary interest*—sometimes known as *subordinated interest,* occurs when the sponsor or general partner bears no program costs but does not share in the revenues *until* all investors have recovered their entire costs or more. For example, investors receive back 125 percent of their investment before the sponsor begins to receive revenue sharing (specified percentage).
4. *Disproportionate sharing*—an arrangement whereby the general partner or sponsor bears a portion of the costs of drilling the well but has a higher percentage of revenues shared. The sponsor's economic interest in the well (revenues) is disproportionate to the amount of costs shared. For example, the sponsor will bear 10 percent of the costs of drilling but receive 35 percent of the production revenues.

Pros and Cons Each type of sharing arrangement carries with it inherent advantages and disadvantages. Let's look at each type separately.

In the *functional allocation* arrangement, a large share of the revenues, normally 40–50 percent, is received by the sponsor. This may tend to overcompensate the sponsor for his or her share of the costs, since most functional allocation programs do not require the sponsor to bear any of the dry hole risk. Also, the casing point conflict may arise. This occurs when a decision must be made as to whether or not to complete a well that might prove profitable to the investor but not to the sponsor, who must now bear a majority of the completion costs. This situation could reduce or eliminate profitability for the investor.

There are, however, some advantages for investors who participate in a functional allocation arrangement. This arrangement offers 100 percent deductibility to the investor. While the sponsor bears no portion of the dry hole costs, he or she does share in the cost of all productive wells. Therefore, his or her money is at stake from a time value standpoint. The investor must also share in the risks of a well that is productive but not really profitable. Finally, the problem of the spread between the sponsor's share of the cost and the revenues can be reduced by requiring the sponsor to agree to bear a specified minimum portion of the program costs. This requirement is included in the current version of the North American Securities Administration Association's Oil and Gas Guidelines.

The *overriding royalties* sharing arrangement carries two major disadvantages. First, it encourages drilling of wells without regard to their profitability to the investor (no sponsor money involved). Second, it has no consideration for the time value of the investor's money. Abuses of this arrangement arising from the drilling of numerous productive but unprofitable wells led to the discrediting of this approach by the end of the 1970s. It is "looked upon with disfavor" under the Oil and Gas Guidelines of the North American Securities Administration Association.

Something investors should consider with regard to the *reversionary interest* arrangement is that it does not take into account the time value of money. A sponsor has nothing to lose because he or she has nothing to risk. All expenses, including administrative overhead, will be reimbursed. If the well eventually pays out, the sponsor will back in for a share of revenues after the pay out. The pay out does not, in fact, "make the investor whole," since he or she has lost the use of the money in the meantime. An even more significant disadvantage of this arrangement is that the reversion is normally figured on a well-by-well or prospect-by-prospect basis and not on a whole-program basis. For example, suppose a program has drilled ten wells, seven of which are dry and three of which have returned three times their original investment. The sponsor will have received a significant profit even though the investor has not made money (i.e., been "made whole").

In some cases, however, some of these shortcomings can be rectified. A sponsor may be required to bear a greater-than-proportionate share of the development well costs, thus putting his or her money at risk. Also, it may be that the sponsor backs in only after the investors have recovered 120 percent of their costs. In addition, the program may compute the sponsor's reversion on a whole-program-payout basis.

A key investor consideration with *disproportionate sharing* is that the investor shares in the nondeductible, as well as deductible, costs. In this case, the investor will not likely come out whole if the spread between the sponsor's share of the costs and the sponsor's share of the revenues exceeds 10–15 percent, unless it is an unusually successful program. The major advantage of disproportionate sharing is that it puts the sponsor, as well as the investor, at risk and subjects both to the consideration of the time value of money. Also, unlike most functional allocation programs, the disproportionate sharing arrangement subjects the sponsor to a share in the dry hole costs.

Funding the Oil or Gas Program How do drilling program sponsors expend and raise funds from investors? Part of the monies raised go for front-end costs—sales commissions and costs of making the offering. Some of the remaining net proceeds of the offering are used to reimburse the sponsor for costs of lease acquisition. In functional allocation programs, which will be discussed in this chapter, the sponsor usually bears these costs, at least as long as the well is productive. Net proceeds are further used to drill one or more exploratory, or test, wells on other prospective sites. This is done in order to operate those wells that appear to have commercial potential. A portion of the net proceeds may also be used to develop further any exploratory prospects that prove to be productive. Such developments may require bank borrowing or additional assessments. Finally, a portion of the funds raised and a portion of the production revenues will frequently go to reimburse the program sponsor for his or her general, administrative, and overhead (GAO) expenses. The GAO refers to any expenses necessary for the conduct of the oil and gas operation that do not relate directly to a particular drilling prospect.

There is potential for abuse under the GAO category of expenses. GAO is a necessary part of any successful oil or gas operation, but it can be abused when it is used to hide salaries or extravagant expense reimbursements for principals and general partners. The GAO can also be used as a mechanism to keep the sponsor in business, whether operations are successful or not. Different companies use different methods for allocating costs. It is difficult, therefore, to evaluate whether or not GAO reimbursement is being abused by comparing cost levels from sponsors. A high GAO may simply reflect the fact that a sponsor has an effective, well-staffed operation. It may mean more productive drilling and, therefore, more success for investors.

Assessments Many programs contain an assessment feature for limited partners. Upon completion of exploratory wells within a program, additional drilling may be required to develop fully those prospects in the partnership's oil field area that appear to be commercially productive. In this case, additional capital may be needed to complete these wells. This is a *good sign* for the investor. An assessment call, usually 25–100 percent of each partner's initial investment, is made to complete the wells in order to prevent the limited partner from being forced to sell or farm out promising well locations. The call may be voluntary or involuntary. Usually, it is advantageous for the limited partner to submit to the call. If the program is of the nonassessable type, the limited partner may find that the profit and certain tax-sheltering opportunities are lost because of the lack of finances needed to continue the drilling.

Right of Presentment Limited partners can sometimes realize a gain by selling their interests back to the general partner. Many public oil and gas programs offer what is called a *right of presentment*. In granting a right of presentment, the general partner agrees to *buy back* a certain number of partnership interests each year from limited partners who want to sell. Exercising a right of presentment does not guarantee that a limited partner will realize a gain on the sale of the interest.

FORMS OF DRILLING INVESTMENT

Specified Drilling vs. Blind Pool Programs The two major types of drilling programs are known as *specified drilling* and *blind pool programs*. In a specified drilling program, the general partner has the lease rights in hand prior to raising the money from the limited partners, so they know exactly where their money will go. In blind pool programs, the general partner identifies only the type of drilling and the general area in which drilling will take place (e.g., the Eastern Overthrust Belt or the Oklahoma Basin). The majority of oil drilling programs are carried out on a blind pool basis.

Exploratory vs. Development Drilling Three basic types of oil drilling programs are available to the general public—exploratory (wildcat) drilling programs, developmental drilling programs, and a combination of the two. *Exploratory,* or *wildcat,* drilling refers to drilling in unproven areas for the possibility of a significant find. *Developmental* drilling refers to drilling in proven areas where more and more wells will be tapping the same reservoir. Developmental drilling carries with it less risk of dry hole drilling. On the other hand, the barrels-per-day production may be somewhat limited because of the other drains on the reservoir. As a rule of thumb, an average of one in ten wells drilled find oil or gas in wildcat or exploratory drilling, and six to eight wells drilled are successful in developmental drilling. An increasingly popular type of oil drilling program is the balanced program, which may be, for example, 60 percent developmental and 40 percent exploratory.

There is a difference between drilling development wells on an exploratory prospect and drilling development wells on a development prospect. In the case of development wells on an exploratory prospect, when the exploratory well is successful, it is normally surrounded by a number of equally lucrative drilling locations. Exploitation of this prospect continues until the less profitable portions of the reservoir are all that remain to be drilled.

Farm-out and Farm-in Interests Sometimes oil drillers have interests known as *farm-out* and *farm-in* with oil wells. The farm-out involves another oil drilling operator actually drilling the well on behalf of a partnership and receiving an interest in any oil or gas found. Thus, the expense of drilling the well itself is farmed out in return for the carried interest of the actual driller. A farm-in is just the opposite. In this case investors bear the expense of drilling on someone else's lease in return for the potential carried interest that they receive. *Carried interest* refers to an interest in the production or economic value of a well (usually expressed as a percentage). This term means that investors do not pay directly for their interest but have received it for services performed. A step-out well is one in which the partnership drills its own well but is drilling outside a proven area.

Investment Suitability

Several facts about oil and gas drilling programs must be taken into account by prospective investors before investing.

Cash Flow Problems Oil and gas programs can often cause serious cash flow problems. Because the drilling phrase of an oil or gas well may last from a few months to several years, wells will generate no cash flow until the production is actually sold. Also, additional development drilling needs may eat up cash flow of the wells already on stream. Cash flow may also have to be used to finance program borrowings for additional drilling. For these reasons, cash flow may not become available for several years after the initial investment.

Cost Consequences of Risk There are other important factors to consider when investing in a gas or oil program. For example, there is a very good reason why these programs are set up as limited partnerships. A well blowout or a similar disaster could have enormous cost consequences resulting from third-party damages to persons, property, or the environment. It is not possible to insure against all such risks. For this reason, limited partnerships are used to reduce investors' liability to the amount of capital invested.

Investor Qualifications Another factor to consider is the *investor's* suitability. Five questions must be answered by the client prior to investing:

1. Are you in a high enough federal income-tax bracket?
2. Can you afford the risk of losing *all* your investment?
3. Can you afford to make a similar investment for an extended period for time-line diversification?
4. Can you afford to meet an additional assessment if required?
5. Can you wait a substantial period of time for any cash flow?

TAX CONSIDERATIONS

Oil and gas drilling programs carry with them two special tax benefits to attract investors. The first major tax incentive is the intangible drilling cost (IDC) deduction, which allows 80–90 percent of the entire cost of drilling for oil and gas to be written off during the drilling process, whether or not oil or gas is found. The other benefit is the depletion allowance.

Intangible Drilling Cost Deduction Intangible drilling costs (IDCs) represent the majority (often up to 80 percent) of costs involved in drilling a well. Intangible drilling and development costs are expenditures such as wages, fuel, repairs, hauling, supplies, etc. incidental to and necessary for the drilling. IDCs are deductible only by the entity or individual who *owns* or holds the *working interest* in the oil or gas property.

IDCs are the costs associated with drilling the well for which there is no salvage value after the drilling process. Any equipment or machinery that can be moved from one well site to another is considered tangible drilling equipment. The intangible expenses associated with the cost of drilling the well become IDCs. The following are examples of these.

- location/surface preparation
- labor utilized in drilling
- drilling mud and chemicals
- drill stem tests and core analysis
- footage and day-work drilling costs
- engineering and well site geographical expense
- daily rental costs
- abandonment loss costs

Under the Tax Equity and Fiscal Responsibility Act of 1982, a special rule applies to integrated oil companies. These companies are allowed to take only 85 percent of the IDCs. The remaining 15 percent must be amortized over three years. This limitation generally does not affect DPP programs.

The drilling phase of an oil or gas program produces no income. Lease acquisition or the right to drill on the property is first obtained. The landowner who grants the lease will usually receive upfront cash and a percentage (e.g., 3 percent) of all oil and gas found and sold. The costs of acquiring rights, called *lease acquisition costs,* are written off according to a special set of rules. Lease acquisition costs must be capitalized; i.e., they are not currently deductible expenses. If the leased area turns out to be productive, the lease acquisition costs are recovered only through the depletion allowances. If the drilled well is not productive, the lease acquisition costs are deductible when the partnership abandons the drilling site.

Depletion Allowance The second, and possibly greater, tax benefit is the depletion allowance for oil and gas production. There are two types of depletion allowances: *cost depletion* and *percentage depletion.* Depletion is a deduction for the recovery of capital invested in wasting assets as those assets are removed and sold.

The Internal Revenue Code allows an owner/investor to select either cost depletion (IRC Section 612) or percentage depletion (IRC Section 613) as oil and gas is removed from the well and sold. A partnership is allowed to calculate each method and use the most favorable, even switching from year to year. Depletion allowances are available each year only for the quantity *sold.* Thus, there are no allowances for amounts used in production, amounts produced but not sold, or amounts lost or destroyed before sale.

Cost Depletion Cost depletion permits an annual deduction representing that portion of oil or gas actually removed and sold as a proportion of the total estimated recoverable reserves of the wells. This percentage (of removed reserves) is applied to the cost of the program. Investors must stop taking depletion allowances when their entire investment in the well has been written off.

The formula that is applied each year is:

$$\text{Cost depletion} = \frac{\text{Adjusted Basis}}{\begin{array}{c}\text{Amount of bbls.}\\ \text{remaining including}\\ \text{those sold this year}\end{array}} \times \text{Amount of bbls. sold}$$

Percentage Depletion Percentage depletion has a potentially greater benefit to the taxpayer, since it is unlimited. As long as oil or gas continues to be produced and sold, the percentage depletion allowance may be continued, even beyond the investor's cost in the program. Percentage depletion is a fixed percentage (15 percent after 1986) of the amount of gross income produced by the well. The actual benefit to the investor is even greater than 15 percent (upward of 20 percent–25 percent) because percentage depletion allowance is allowed against gross rather than net income. Percentage depletion does allow the write-off to continue, regardless of the adjusted cost basis. Thus, potentially, investors can gain deductions that far exceed their investments in the drilling program.

Percentage depletion, as discussed, is applied against gross income. Gross income is defined as the amount for which the taxpayer sells the oil or gas in the immediate vicinity of the well. Gross income does not include any rents or royalties received from the land. Also, the percentage depletion allowance, once computed, is limited to no more than 50 percent of the taxpayer's taxable income from the property.

Background of Depletion Allowances A portion of income from productive wells is considered a return of capital. The IRS recognizes that, as production continues, an oil or gas reserve is a wasting asset. Therefore, the capital invested in the well is also a wasting asset. This is equivalent to depreciation in a real estate investment.

As oil and gas are produced and sold, cash flow will be generated by the partnership and passed through as distributions to the individual limited partners. Approximately 20–25 percent of the cash flow will be sheltered from federal income taxation by the depletion allowance. The exact amount of cash flow and the exact period of time over which it will be distributed will depend on three factors:

- the success of the drilling program;
- how quickly wells can be connected to pipelines; and
- the producing characteristics of the oil and gas formations.

When discovered, oil and gas reserves are sold in place, as opposed to being produced and sold by drilling programs; *no* depletion allowance is available on the proceeds from the sale. Proceeds will normally be taxed as a long-term capital gain if held for more than six months. There is a possible IDC recapture of previous deductions at this time (i.e., when the well interest is sold).

DRILLING CONTRACTS

It is the general partner who will select the drilling company and execute partnership contracts. Drilling is usually accomplished through a turnkey drilling contract or a per diem drilling contract.

A turnkey contract, as the term implies, contemplates a single fee for the drilling operator to drill to a certain depth. This is not the most popular arrangement because drillers may experience difficulties for which they are not paid. The IRS will allow deductions for drilling costs prepaid through a turnkey contract if:

1. there is a binding contract with the drilling contractor;
2. the partnership has paid the contractor; and
3. the contractor is not an affiliate of the partnership's sponsor.

The most popular form of contract is per diem, and the driller stays on site only as long as it takes to drill the well to the required depth. Each party knows how much it is costing per day for the drilling.

OIL INCOME PROGRAMS

Oil income programs differ from oil drilling programs in four important respects. First, income programs are characterized by significant cash flow. This may be contrasted with the deep-shelter feature of drilling programs. Second, acquisition costs of such properties are required to be capitalized for federal income tax purposes. This differs from drilling programs since there are relatively few front-end tax write-offs. Third, income programs involve acquisition of producing properties to provide a steady stream of partially tax-sheltered income (through cost depletion) to the limited partners. Because income programs buy proven reserves, they must use cost depletion rather than percentage depletion. Fourth, no drilling is involved in oil income programs. Instead, established reserves are being purchased. This is considered to be lower-risk than drilling.

Risks of Oil Income Programs

Oil income programs, of course, are not completely free of financial risk. The downside risks of leverage may be very great. Current oil or gas prices may be reduced. There may be unanticipated difficulties in recovering the reserves. Estimates of recoverable oil and gas reserves may be inaccurate. Finally, a sufficient number of attractive properties may not be available to a blind pool program.

Evaluation of Producing Properties

The evaluation of a price to be paid for an existing producing well is accomplished in three steps. First, an estimate is made of the amount of recoverable oil or gas reserves remaining in the ground. Next, the present value of the estimated future net revenues from such reserves is discounted. Finally, this present value of the future income stream is further discounted to take into account other risk factors.

CONFLICTS OF INTEREST: DRILLING AND INCOME PROGRAMS

The conflicts of interest inherent to oil and gas programs are also related to other tax-sheltered investments. The fact that the syndicator can profit even though the investor does not is a conflict in itself. A more serious conflict involves self-dealing with programs by sponsors or their affiliates. This situation creates an opportunity for a potential profit, irrespective of the profitability of the program. Also, the conduct of operations in many oil and gas programs is such that there is an unnecessary potential for loss on the part of the investor.

The key conflicts of interest in an oil and gas drilling operation are as follows:

- sale of leases or producing properties to or from the program by sponsors, especially when sales are not supported by independent appraisal or when there is a markup
- transfer of less than all drilling locations on a prospect, possibly resulting in investor's funds being used to "prove up" surrounding drilling locations for the sponsor
- performance of services for the program for compensation other than at cost

- farming out of undrilled locations when the effect of such a farm-out will be to reduce the sponsor's obligations
- commingling of program funds with the general funds of the sponsor
- loans of monies by sponsor to the program at unreasonable interest rates
- redemption of investor program interest except when based on appraisals by qualified independent petroleum experts

These conflicts of interest rarely occur in income programs.

WINDFALL PROFITS TAX

When the price of oil was decontrolled in 1980, Congress imposed an excise tax on increases in the price of domestic crude oil that resulted from the decontrol. This is known as the *windfall profits tax.* Congress established a base price for each of three kinds of oil:

1. "old" oil
2. oil from stripper wells (wells that produce less than ten barrels a day)
3. newly discovered oil

The amount that the sales price exceeds the base price is subject to a windfall profits tax. The tax is imposed on the producer, so it decreases a partnership's gross revenues. The oil produced by stripper wells is no longer subject to the windfall profits tax. The windfall profits tax is exacted on newly found oil known as "Tier 3" oil.

The windfall profits tax is levied on the oil as it is actually removed from the ground. The tax rate is currently being scaled down from 22.5 percent for 1984 to 20 percent for 1985 and 15 percent for 1986 and thereafter. When oil has been found, the partnership has the option of leaving it in place and, therefore, delaying the windfall profits tax.

EVALUATING A SPECIFIC PROGRAM

Once investors have decided that oil and gas drilling programs in general are appropriate for them, they must apply the same scrutiny to the specific program being considered.

TRACK RECORD OF THE SPONSOR

Although it is often difficult, the investor must perform an analysis and review of the sponsor's track record of past performance. Good past performance is no assurance that a particular future program will succeed, but it is unwise to invest without a review of the sponsor's previous results. The interested investor must also look for indications of fairness in sharing arrangements and resolution of conflicts of interest.

Box Score for Drillers

One form of assistance in this area is the SEC-required "box score," which enables all publicly registered programs to show an investor the past performance of the general partner. It shows how many wells have been drilled each year and the wells that eventually came on line for production. A major shortcoming of these box score tables is that they do not measure the reserves of oil and gas found. This would be the best determinant of the success of the program. The box score tables are simply measures of the number of hits and misses.

Net Cash and Payout Tables

A set of tables that may prove more useful to the potential investor includes the net cash and payout tables, which indicate the dollars expended and revenues received by investors in past programs. Such tables contain information on both a cumulative and a last-three-months basis. With these tables, the investor can gain some idea of the profitability of the previous programs. A conspicuous shortcoming, however, is that the tables do not reflect reserves discovered in previous programs. The SEC does not require the disclosure of reserve data in the prospectus. Few sponsors have offered this information, since it is difficult to estimate without "sufficient producing history."

SUMMARY

Oil and gas drilling and income programs are unique among limited partnership investment vehicles. Suitable investors are those in a high income-tax bracket who can risk the total loss that is often suffered with this type of investment. Perhaps more than in any other type of limited partnership, investors should thoroughly understand the relationship between general and limited partners and should be aware of the potential for conflict of interest. For this reason, and because of the high-risk nature of drilling programs, investors *must* thoroughly investigate the track record of the sponsor of any specific program being considered.

15

Equipment-Leasing Limited Partnerships

Equipment-leasing limited partnerships have become one of the most popular and conservative methods of tax deferral. Many of these programs are large national public programs raising millions of dollars for investment in expensive equipment leased to major U.S. corporations. An untold number of smaller, private (exempt from SEC registration) limited partnerships are organized for the purpose of owning and leasing anything from naval ships to barges and boxcars. This chapter will discuss the tax impact and procedures to be followed with these various types of leases.

LESSOR/LESSEE

In equipment-leasing limited partnerships, it is important to master the terminology. A *lessor* is the owner of the equipment (limited partnership), and the *lessee* is the user (business) who is obligated to make the lease payments to the lessor for the use of the equipment. Virtually any type of equipment can be leased. Some examples of leased equipment are aircraft, computers, railroad rolling stock, oil drilling rigs, entire industrial plants, and even huge oil tankers and liquefied natural gas tankers. The advantage of leased equipment to the lessee is that capital and financing for the initial purchase price are not needed.

Frequently, the financing is "off balance sheet" financing (indebtedness appears only as a footnote) and will eliminate the risk to the business of being stuck with obsolete equipment. The business has retained working capital for other purposes. Equipment leasing provides a good potential tax shelter investment, if structured correctly, because all the tax benefits of ownership go to the lessor (owner), which is a limited partnership passing these tax benefits to the partners.

HOW LEASING AS AN INVESTMENT WORKS

In the typical equipment-leasing investment, a syndicator/sponsor arranges, in advance, for a lease commitment with a creditworthy corporate client. The syndicate/sponsor purchases the equipment for a cash down payment, completing the financing through *recourse* or *nonrecourse* borrowing (usually on a 4:1 ratio, i.e., 80 percent borrowing and 20 percent cash). The equipment is then leased to the user or lessee for fixed lease payments. The lease payments, as made, are used to retire debt and, occasionally, to provide some cash flow. Upon termination of the initial lease period, the residual value of the equipment permits releasing or resale (ideally for a profit). Most often, the initial lease period is for less than the useful life of the property and the period necessary for mortgage retirement (operating lease).

TYPES OF LEASES

Equipment leasing programs use two types of leases: full-payout leases and operating leases. The operating lease is a short-term lease in which total rental payments are less than the original cost of the equipment. The operating lease can be use *only* if the lease period is *less* than 50 percent of the depreciable life of the property. The full-payout lease is usually a longer-term lease. The aggregate lease payments are sufficient to cover the entire purchase price of the property and the financing costs for that period of time.

If the cumulative payments made under a lease are equal to or greater than the purchase price of the equipment, the lease is a full-payout lease. Full-payout leases are safer than operating leases, but in a full-payout lease the lessee (the user of the equipment), not the lessor (the partnership), is eligible for the investment tax credit (ITC). A partnership qualifies for ITC only on equipment it leases under an operating lease. From the partnership's viewpoint, this is a major disadvantage of a full-payout lease.

An operating lease has two main characteristics:

1. It is *short-term*. The term of an operating lease cannot exceed one-half of the depreciable life of the equipment. When the lease expires, the partnership must release the equipment to

the same lessee, lease it to someone else, or sell it for its residual value (i.e., the best price the equipment will command on the open market).

2. It must have *active management.* The partnership, not the lessee, must be responsible for managing and maintaining the equipment, if the partnership is to claim the ITC. *Active management* means that the equipment-leasing partnership must spend at least 15 percent of its gross revenues in the first year to maintain and insure the equipment.

BENEFITS OF EQUIPMENT-LEASING TAX SHELTERS

MINIMUM RISK

Many investors like equipment-leasing tax shelters because they are conservative, deal in tangible goods, and are more liquid than real estate. They also demand little day-to-day management once in place and running smoothly. The lease payments provide predictable cash flow, with relatively minor speculative considerations. Other advantages include the potential resale value of the equipment and the fact that the equipment can easily be used to collateralize borrowing.

TAX BENEFITS

The major tax benefits of equipment leasing include depreciation deductions under the accelerated cost recovery system, deductible interest payments, investment tax credits, and normal operating expenses. Other advantages are available to corporate investors but not to individual investors. For example, the financing of the equipment can be nonrecourse, because the at-risk rules do not apply to corporate investors. Also, the net lease on the personal property of corporate investors is *not* a tax preference item. Finally, the investment interest limitations ($10,000 plus net investment income) are not applicable to corporate investors.

Under the accelerated cost recovery system, both new and used property are treated alike. An additional benefit of equipment leasing is the fact that the salvage value of depreciated equipment is not considered under ACRS. This means that the entire (unadjusted) basis may be depreciated.

TAX CONSIDERATIONS

THE CROSSOVER POINT

One of the major tax planning concepts of equipment leasing is the crossover point. This means that, just a few years into the tax shelter, the limited partner will be charged with taxable income. If an individual is going to remain in a high tax bracket for a long time, this creates additional problems. The crossover begins to evolve with the steady decline in depreciation deductions available under the accelerated depreciation schedules. It also increases over time in the amount of nondeductible principal amortization payments made to service the debt and the correspondingly decreased amounts of deductible interest payments. At the crossover point, a combination of these two factors produces taxable income.

The ACRS depreciation schedule permits larger deductions in the early years of a program and a decline in later years. For example, ten-year property would be subject to an 8 percent first-year deduction, 14 percent in the second year, and 12 percent in the third year. In years four through six this is reduced to 10 percent, and in years seven through ten, only 9 percent is permitted.

Similarly, as principal and interest are paid on loans, the early years will produce substantial interest deductions that will decrease steadily over time as a larger percentage of the loan payments is contributed to the principal. The net result of these two factors is to decrease the positive effects of deductible depreciation and interest expenses, thus limiting the investor's ability to offset income produced by the program. The point at which income exceeds deductions is the crossover point.

While the ramifications of the crossover point should be considered, they should not necessarily deter prospects from investing in equipment-leasing ventures. With proper planning in regard to the crossover point, another tax shelter can be arranged to offset the taxable income produced after the crossover point. In the tax shelter world, it is often said that one sale begets another sale three to four years later.

Investment Interest Limitations

The investment limitation restricts a taxpayer's deductions for a given year. Investment interest creates a significant part of the write-off. Potential investors should make sure they can fully use these deductions prior to buying an offering. If the investment interest deduction cannot be used in the current year, it may be carried forward and used in future years.

Tax Preference Items in Equipment Leasing

Equipment leasing carries with it some tax preference item consideration (alternative minimum tax). Remember that the three major tax preferences in tax shelters are accelerated depreciation, depletion, and intangible drilling costs.

Equipment leasing tax shelters have accelerated depreciation; as such, this is a tax preference item for client consideration prior to investing. Of course, there are no depletion or intangible drilling cost deductions. The preference item to be calculated is the excess of accelerated depreciation over straight line.

RECAPTURE

All depreciation taken out on equipment is subject to recapture as ordinary income to the extent of any gain over the adjusted basis of the property when sold, given away, or foreclosed. This recapture means that equipment leasing is, at least partially, only a deferral tax shelter.

PHANTOM INCOME

Recall that phantom income occurs when a limited partner is charged with income not received. There are two major circumstances that lead to phantom income. The first occurs when partnership monies are being used to repay principal on an indebtedness, and this is nondeductible to the partnership. This means that the limited partners are charged with taxable income because the partnership is profitable even though no money is actually distributed.

The second area that generates phantom income is the sale of an asset. If the adjusted basis of the asset has been reduced significantly through tax deductions and losses, then it may actually be reduced below the existing indebtedness. This is a common practice in equipment-leasing tax shelters. The difference between the adjusted basis and the indebtedness of the property is the amount of the phantom income that will be charged to the owners upon a sale or an other disposition. This is the case even if a new purchaser is picking up the indebtedness continuing those payments. This could have a significant tax impact for the investor in a single tax year. Figure 15.1 shows an example.

Figure 15.1
Equipment Leasing—Sale of Equipment after Lease Period

(1)	$500,000	Sale proceeds
(2)	-200,000	Adjusted basis
(3)	$300,000	Taxable gain
(4)	$500,000	Sale proceeds
(5)	-450,000	Indebtedness (principal remaining)
(6)	$ 50,000	Cash realized from sale

Note: Line 3 minus line 6 equals $250,000, so phantom income of $250,000 was produced: $300,000 of *taxable* gain, but only $50,000 of cash, was actually realized following repayment of debt.

Note in this example that the adjusted basis, through depreciation, is $200,000 and that the loan principal repayment is $450,000. This situation leaves the investors with $250,000 of phantom income (taxable but no cash).

CONDITIONAL SALES

Rental payments for equipment are normally structured in such a way that relatively little, if any, profit is made on the lease. Any economic benefits produced will come from the residual value of the equipment. If the user, or lessee, continues to renew the lease indefinitely, or purchases the equipment at the end of the lease return, the IRS may determine that the transaction is a *conditional sale.* In this case, the lessor (DPP) would be denied depreciation deductions and ITCs. Equipment-leasing arrangements, therefore, must be structured so they are, in fact, valid leases and not conditional sales.

For a valid lease, the IRS requires the lessor to have an investment of at least 20 percent (the balance can be borrowed), and any borrowing should not come from the lessee, but rather from outside lending organizations. Any purchase arrangement in the lease must be based on fair market value, and neither the lessee nor any related party can guarantee any of the lessor's indebtedness. An additional requirement is that there must be a residual value to the property at the end of the lease term.

PROGRAM STRUCTURE

THE LEASEBACK

An important consideration in equipment-leasing operations is the sale leaseback or gift leaseback. This can occur when the property owner wishes to retain the benefits of ownership, which have now been exhausted from a tax standpoint. Consider the doctor's office with expensive equipment that has already been depreciated and for which the tax deductions are now low. This doctor could sell the equipment to an equipment-leasing entity and then lease it back. The equipment would never have to move! This would provide the doctor with immediate cash plus deductible lease payments in the future, if the lease payments are reasonable. This would also allow the new lessor or owner the depreciation and investment tax credit benefits of the purchased property.

Gift leaseback is a similar transaction in which the property is not actually sold, but gifted. Frequently, a trust is set up, and the property is gifted to a trust. To continue the previous example, the beneficiaries of the trust might be the children of the doctor. Lease payments would be made to the trust, and these would be deductible by the lessee. The advantages to the seller in a sale leaseback or to the grantor in a gift leaseback are the immediate cash and the deductibility of the lease payments. The disadvantages are the lack of ownership interest, a long lease, and compulsory lease payments.

SALE LEASEBACK, USER LEASEBACK, AND OPERATOR LEASEBACK

In a sale leaseback arrangement, an owner sells property to a limited partnership and then immediately leases it back. If the seller/lessee intends to continue to occupy the property, the arrangement can also be called a *user leaseback*. If, on the other hand, the seller/lessee plans to subdivide and sublease the property—a shopping center, a warehouse, or an apartment building, for example—it is then called an *operator leaseback*.

FINANCIAL LEASES

Financial leases are those leases in which the lessee has an option to buy the property at the end of the lease for 10 percent or more of its original cost. Under the new restrictions of the Tax Equity and Fiscal Responsibility Act of 1982, the lessor must be a regular corporation. Only new property can be the subject of the lease. The lessee is limited to no more than 40 percent of the property placed in service that year as leased property. The lessor cannot have more than 50 percent of its tax liability offset by lease deduction and credits, and the ITC must be amoritzed over five years. One less restrictive outcome of TEFRA, that ACRS recovery periods and methods can be used.

ADVANTAGES FOR CORPORATE LESSORS

As reviewed earlier, a number of factors make equipment leasing more attractive to the corporate lessor than to individuals (See Table 15.1). For example, at-risk limitations do not apply to corporations unless more than 50 percent of the stock is owned by five or fewer individuals. Even for these closely held corporations, the at-risk rule does not apply if 50 percent or more of the gross receipts come from the leasing of equipment. Also, there is less likelihood that a corporate lessor's lease arrangement will be considered a sale rather than a rental.

Corporations also qualify for additional first-year expenses on leased equipment. Finally, corporations are not subject to limited deductibility of interest. This all means that equipment leasing is even more favorable to a corporate lessor than to an individual, limited partnership, or S-type corporation.

Table 15.1 Corporate vs. Limited Partnership Equipment Leasing

	Corporate	Limited Partnership or Individual
Loans	Nonrecourse loan will add to basis	Only recourse loans will add to basis
Interest	No interest deduction	Limit of $10,000 plus net
Deductions	Limitation	Investment income

SUMMARY

Equipment leasing is an appropriate vehicle for limited partnerships seeking a conservative investment with significant tax shelter benefits. In general, such investments offer minimal risk, predictable cash flow, and opportunities to resell the equipment or use it as collateral for loans. Investors should note, however, that equipment-leasing limited partnerships are more suitable for corporations than for individuals.

16

Cattle, Ranching, and Agricultural Investments

Cattle have become a highly visible and widely discussed tax shelter investment. The two main types of programs structured for cattle investment are, however, quite different. Indeed, the only element they have in common is cattle. Other than that, cattle-feeding programs are quite different from cattle-breeding programs. Agricultural and ranching tax shelters usually combine the cash flow of crop sales with the expected appreciation of the underlying land as the major attraction for investors.

THE CATTLE INDUSTRY

The basis of all cattle investment (feeding or breeding) is that, eventually, beef will be produced for consumption. This industry has been characterized by declining beef preferences in the U.S. on a per capita basis and low profitability over the last ten years. Investors are provided with tax shelters in the cattle industry via farming syndicates, corporations, and agency arrangements in which ranchers manage the program on behalf of investors. These shelters may be designed to achieve the following objectives:

1. defer taxes in the short-term, as in cattle-feeding programs;
2. defer taxes in the long-term and achieve long-term capital gains, as in cattle-breeding programs;
3. achieve tax deductions not normally available on land investments by combining cattle investments and long-term land speculation.

There are three kinds of investments in the cattle industry:

- feeding programs
- breeding programs
- ranching programs

In feeding programs, grain or grass is converted to edible beef through systematic feeding designed to increase beef weight. In feeding programs, taxes are deferred in the short term, and beef sales, if all goes well, generate profits. The goal of cattle-breeding programs is to increase herd size and quality. These shelters are used to defer taxes in the long term as well as to achieve long-term capital gains when the livestock born to the herd is sold. Ranching programs combine the benefits of cattle investment with long-term land speculation. These are designed to produce an eventual profit and achieve tax deductions during the holding period that are not otherwise available in raw land investment.

Feeding Programs

In most cattle-feeding programs, feeder cattle are purchased in the spring, fattened throughout the spring and summer, and sold for slaughter in the fall. The general partner, usually the rancher, buys cattle and feed and then manages the feeding operation for four to eight months before the cattle are sold for slaughter. The feeder cattle usually weigh 300–500 pounds at purchase and will increase in weight to 1,000–1,400 pounds when they are sold. The added weight is the object of feeding, for it increases the value of the animal at slaughter. Consequently, cattle-feeding operations do not hold the cattle through winter because they must be housed and fed, and winter weight gain is not sufficient to offset the expenses.

Kinds of Feeding Programs There are two types of cattle-feeding programs: *agency arrangements* and *farming syndicates.* In any agency arrangement, the investor works directly with a feedlot manager who acts as an agent for the investor. This arrangement entails a great deal of effort because the investor must work extensively and directly with the feedlot manager. Advantages of an agency arrangement, however, often compensate the investor for the additional work. In an agency arrangement, there is less risk of an IRS audit, administrative costs are typically lower, and conventional financing is easier to secure, mainly because it is recourse financing. In this type of arrangement, investors are actually considered to be farmers for tax purposes because they do not operate through a third party. We will see later in this chapter that being deemed a farmer can carry with it an extra tax advantage.

In the syndicate arrangement, a syndicate serves as an intermediary that works with the feedlot managers on behalf of the investors. Because this arrangement requires the investors to spend no time working directly with the feedlot manager, the costs are higher than they would be in an agency arrangement. A farming syndicate includes any farming enterprise other than a corporation in which 35 percent or more of the losses are passed through a partnership to the limited partners.

In a syndicate, the cattle raiser serves as the general partner and the investors serve as limited partners. Initial deductions are allowed for expenditures made before production. However, it should be noted that expenditures for feed can be deducted only if the fund is consumed before the end of the tax year. Farming syndicate offerings must be registered (or filed for exempt status) with the federal and state securities agencies. The at-risk rules *do* apply to syndicated farming investments. While it is a rare occurrence in cattle-feeding programs, animals owned for more than one year become a capital asset and thus are available for depreciation, ITC credits, and long-term capital gains upon sale.

Goal of Feeding Programs The goal of cattle-feeding programs is to defer income tax from one year to the next. The investor provides as little as 5–10 percent of the initial cost. Additional monies needed as cattle are purchased are obtained through recourse or nonrecourse borrowing. In most feeding programs, about two-thirds of each investment dollar goes for the cost of buying cattle, a nondeductible expense. The remaining one-third is spent on feed, feedlot services, and insurance. Feed is deductible if it is used or consumed before the end of the tax year in syndicate arrangements. Tax deferrals as high as 70–130 percent of the limited partner's equity may be generated in well-planned cattle-feeding programs. However, these programs are subject to the at-risk rules (i.e., recourse financing must be used if it is desired to include the debt as part of the investor's basis).

In short-term cattle-feeding programs, proceeds from the sale of cattle are taxed as ordinary income and thus create no special tax preference items (i.e., no alternative minimum tax items). It is possible to structure the proceeds from the sale of one investment to be rolled over into a new cattle-feeding program, thereby providing continuous deferral of taxes.

Tax Benefits of Cattle-Feeding Programs The major tax benefit of cattle-feeding programs lies in shifting ordinary-income tax deductions from one year to the next. Deductions allowed for operating costs and feed consumed are expected to be less than the income in the next tax year from beef sales. Cattle-feeding programs hope to generate ordinary income through beef sales.

Tax Drawbacks Those who invest in cattle-feeding programs should be aware of several potential drawbacks:

- Tax legislation relating to agricultural investments requires that prepaid interest be amortized over the period of the loan.
- Investors in farming enterprises may not deduct more than they have at risk.
- Retroactive allocations and special allocations are not allowed.
- Any organization expenses must be amortized over five years.

Deciding whether to use the cash or accrual basis for accounting is of critical importance. Corporations must capitalize rather than deduct any expenses incurred before production, even if the corporation is an investor in a limited partnership. However, farms engaged in a business for profit and using a cash basis account method may deduct all expenditures for the care of cattle. Thus, as we discussed earlier, if an investor is deemed a farmer (agency arrangement), *all* expenditures for feed are deductible, even before consumed, as regular farmers are allowed. Thus, if the investment is structured this way, prepaid feed in December is deductible. Cattle and farming syndicates, on the other hand, must use accrual accounting. In accrual accounting, expenses—even prepaid expenses—are not deductible until they are incurred. Feed is deductible in the year it is consumed, not in the year it is paid for.

Opportunities and Pitfalls in Cattle-Feeding Programs If the cattle weight gain is sufficient and market conditions are favorable upon sale, cattle-feeding programs can result in substantial profits for the investor. But even the best programs entail several risks. The spot price of beef can vary widely, depending on market supply. Market price, in turn, is affected by such factors as weather, feed supply, and consumer demand. Gain prices, too, can vary widely. An investor can get "whipsawed" if beef prices go down and grain prices go up!

Market conditions set beef prices, and cattle cannot be withheld from the market to wait for better prices. If cattle are held too long, the quality of the beef deteriorates, further reducing profit potential. These conditions can wipe out investors' equity; thus, investors are generally "price takers" when they arrive at the pens with their cattle.

Stop-Loss Provisions There are several techniques for minimizing losses and maximizing profits when market prices fluctuate. The tactics for preventing loss are usually referred to as *stop-loss provisions.* For example, the investor may make an agreement with the feedlot operator to guarantee that the loss per head will not exceed a specified figure. In return, the investor agrees that the feedlot operator will get a percentage of profits when the cattle are sold. That percentage may be as high as 50 percent.

This technique for reducing risk is subject to some drawbacks. The operator usually sets the guarantee figure so that a profit would result in any normal market. Thus, the guarantee is of little value in bad economic times, as was the case in the mid-1970s, when the operators suffered financial collapse. Finally, since the investment may not be considered held for profit, there is some risk that the investor may lose the deductions available under the Internal Revenue Code.

Risks can also be reduced by using feeding program structuring techniques. In long-term revolving programs, for instance, investors agree to reinvest yearly proceeds for up to five years to balance out the highs and lows of the marketplace. Using steer-averaging, the investor invests a fixed amount of money over a substantial period of time and benefits from a form of price averaging. In a prolonged program, taxes can be postponed indefinitely. While this method is useful as a structuring technique, the advantages can be negated by large disparities between beef and grain prices. Sometimes, it is too big a risk to take from year to year.

Hedging Systematic hedging is yet another technique to reduce risk. Hedging involves selling cattle futures in the commodities market (via a futures contract) to lock in a set beef price and to limit losses. While hedging guarantees that the investor will know exactly for what price the beef will sell, trading in commodities is also risky and involves commissions on trades. The additional costs of purchasing futures and forgoing potential profits, should the market price be higher at the time of sale, must be weighed. Note that grain price fluctuations can sometimes be successfully combatted by locking in the price of future grain deliveries via the futures market.

There are also techniques for limiting or distributing losses. In some agreements, a certain dollar amount of loss per head is applied to the limited partner. Another amount of loss is applied to the general partner, who is usually the feeding program sponsor.

All subsequent losses are applied to the limited partner. In such agreements, it is likely that hedging will be used to protect both the general partner and the limited partner against a serious loss. It is worth noting that legal interpretations to date make it unclear as to whether this technique can be used to avoid the prohibition against guarantees in the at-risk rules or whether they will satisfy the substantial economic effect required for partnership allocation.

Feedlots can be placed in different geographical areas so that cattle can be brought to market at different stages; the effects of geographical market price fluctuations can be minimized; and the risks of loss through natural or manmade catastrophe can be reduced by judicious herd distribution.

CATTLE-BREEDING PROGRAMS

The investors in cattle-breeding programs are seeking upfront deductions, long-term deferral of taxes and, eventually, long-term capital gains. There are two types of cattle-breeding programs: purebred breeding herds and commercial breeding herds.

The objective in purebred programs is to produce calves for sale to other breeders or calves to be used in improving the quality of the herd. The objective in commercial breeding programs is to produce and prepare calves for sale to feedlots or meatpackers. Purebred cattle programs are the most popular for tax shelter purposes.

Structure of Breeding Programs Cattle-breeding programs are generally designed to run from five to seven years. In these investment programs, the general partner or sponsor purchases breeder cattle and attempts to increase the value of the herd through: (1) normal births to the herd and (2) the increased value of the purebred cattle. Achieving a higher quality of purebred cattle is worth more per animal than in the original herd. The herd is purchased by borrowing up to 90 percent of the animal purchase costs from a commercial bank. A common technique is for the program sponsors actually to sell cattle to the syndicate, at a markup over their cost, to establish the herd.

The breeder's goal is to have cows drop one calf every spring. The calves will be inspected, cared for, and culled. The new calves that will benefit the herd will be kept. Bulls and any cows that will not improve the strain of the herd are usually sold to feedlots for fattening or directly to slaughterhouses. Feeding and breeding are supervised by a cattlebreeder who assures maintenance of the quality of offspring necessary to build a valuable herd.

Management expenses and veterinary bills for cattle-breeding projects are high because it is essential to maintain the health of the herd. Since expenses are high, occasionally sales are necessary to finance management operations throughout the normal five- to seven-year period of the program.

Tax Benefits of Cattle-Breeding Programs There are three sources of deductions for investors in cattle breeding operations:

1. capitalized and depreciated purchase costs of the cattle
2. investment tax credits
3. operations and maintenance costs

Cattle are depreciated using the ACRS method as five-year property. In addition to the depreciation, an investment tax credit may be claimed for "first user" cattle (i.e., the first time the animal was sold). Since there is no cost basis in cattle born to the herd, new calves are *not depreciable* and are *not eligible* for investment tax credits (only purchased animals are eligible). Using ACRS depreciation and taking advantage of the investment tax credit, it is not uncommon for an investor to receive 2:1 and 3:1 or higher ratios or write-offs of their investments. In addition, capital gains are expected in the fifth, sixth, or seventh year when a limited partnership's cattle are sold. The objective is to have a larger herd to sell (each cow dropping a calf every year) and a herd that possesses a highly desired strain of cattle.

In planning breeding program investments, the investor should take into account these tax considerations:

1. Upon sale, depreciation deductions are *fully recaptured* as ordinary income up to the extent of the taxable gain.
2. For the transaction to qualify for long-term capital gain on the sale, the cattle must be held for more than 24 months.
3. Calf drops are not eligible for investment tax credit or depreciation deductions, since they have no cost basis.

Opportunities and Pitfalls in Cattle-Breeding Programs Profits in cattle-breeding operations are derived from sales of culled cattle to feedlot operators or slaughterhouses, from sales of breeding stock to other breeders, and from the sale of complete herds. Sales of culled cattle alone are usually not sufficient to generate substantial income. Cattle are not sold to other breeders in large numbers, and complete herds must sometimes be sold at a loss, often among DPP breeders themselves! Further, the lack of cash flow during an extensive holding period of five to ten years makes it difficult to maintain the investment long enough to realize the profit. Parts or all of a herd are sometimes sold just to meet expenses. Effective organization and management are essential to achieve a profit.

To get started, premium prices are often paid for purebred animals. Several factors combine to limit the liquidity of purebred herds. Maintenance and syndicate fees for managing purebred animals are usually at least twice those charged for commercial animals because they require more work and care. Changes in consumer beef preferences can cause the value of high-priced, purebred animals to tumble. The demand for purebred animals is variable, and purebred animals command no higher price than commercial animals at the slaughterhouses!

Management and purchasing techniques can be used to minimize risk. For example, herd diversification can be achieved by purchasing cattle at different stages of development; mortality can be reduced by taking all possible health, maintenance, and management precautions; and the latest in scientific technology can be used to breed and feed the animals.

Those who invest in cattle breeding as a tax shelter should be appraised of these risks. Poor or careless health maintenance programs, low calving rates, and high mortality rates can severely limit or even decimate cattle herds. Adverse weather conditions or poor geographical dispersion can either destroy a herd or severely limit profits in the marketplace. The extremely cyclical nature of the cattle industry, changes in tax laws during the holding period, excessive markups on cattle sold, and stop-loss or hedging guarantees can eliminate profit potential.

The Economics Of The Cattle Industry

More so than in other industries, the cattle industry is characterized by cyclical overproduction with many peaks and valleys in market prices. Beef consumption per capita in the U.S. has declined over the past ten years. The price sensitivity of cattle investments clearly accentuates the necessity of assuring that these investments are managed with the greatest of care. Potential investors should consult guidelines for registering publicly offered programs, such as those adopted by the Midwest Securities Commissioners Association. These provide an excellent start for investors in evaluating a cattle industry tax shelter.

OTHER AGRICULTURAL INVESTMENTS

Kinds Of Agricultural Investments

In addition to cattle programs, other agricultural investments are available for use as tax shelters. Syndicate investments in orchards, vineyards, and vegetable crops, for example, are considered valuable sources of investment for tax shelter benefits. These nonlivestock farming operations can be divided into two categories: perennials and annuals.

The *perennials* are those that involve trees, vines, or the like, which produce their fruits or nuts every year. Apple orchards, peach orchards, vineyards, pecan groves, and citrus groves are examples of perennial agricultural operations. Tax deductions for these kinds of farming program include deductions of costs incurred before production and deductions for depreciation of the trees or groves. Since the planted trees or vines will produce every year for a specified length of time (e.g., 25–30 years), the cost of planting trees and vines is a capital cost and cannot be deducted as an expense in the first year. These costs must be depreciated over their ACRS life.

Annuals are commonly known as *row crops.* These plantings have no lasting value from year to year. Seeds must be planted and the plants regrown every year. For example, wheat, corn, and most vegetable farming involves plants that have a useful life of less than one year. Therefore, all costs involved in planting, seeding, and growing these crops are not considered capital assets and become immediately deductible.

Sources Of Income And Profits

Annuals and perennials provide three sources of income and profits:

1. In a profitable operation, ordinary income is realized when the agricultural products are sold.
2. Appreciation in land values produces profits from the sale of farmland.
3. Profit may be realized through commercial, industrial, or residential development of the farmland.

In addition, a tax deduction of 130–170 percent can be realized by deducting preproduction costs of development. These costs include such items as fences, buildings, farming equipment, irrigation equipment, etc., that are capitalized and depreciated over the appropriate ACRS period. Generally, the equipment as well as the trees and groves are also eligible for the investment tax credit.

Tax Considerations For Agricultural Investments

Tax deductions for perennial crops and annual (row) crops differ in two important ways. With perennial crops such as citrus groves, all expenses required to develop the grove prior to production must be capitalized. That is, they cannot be deducted in the year incurred but must be written off over the ACRS period of the grove. In the case of annuals, all costs involved in planting and seeding are deductible in the year in which they occur because the plant has no useful life beyond one year. For both perennial and annual crops, operating costs incurred from year to year and losses in the sale of crops are deductible items. Investors should note that the deduction of expenses such as clearing land for farming, fertilizing or conditioning the land, leveling, grading, and constructing dams and ditches for irrigation, and other costs of conservation and land clearance are nondeductible capital expenditures.

Farming syndicates may not deduct payments for feed, seed, fertilizer, or other farm supplies except in the year in which these are used. Finally, an income delay results from the delay between development and production of commercial crops (e.g., five years for a citrus grove to produce fruit). For this reason, agricultural syndicated investments are not for investors who seek an early cash flow.

Pitfalls And Hazards

The potential hazards of other agricultural farming are much the same as they are in cattle farming. These include adverse weather conditions, fluctuating prices, management problems, and the like. Some investors participate in agricultural investments hoping that the income will serve as a financial stopgap while the agricultural land matures and reaches the stages for residential or commercial development. Wise investors will carefully scrutinize such a venture since land investment is considered speculative and often requires long holding periods.

TIMBER INVESTMENTS

Timber is considered a natural resource and is used in the production of paper products. Many investors think that a current or future shortage of available timber lands will increase the value of timber investments. Although the huge demand for various paper products has continued to increase, often the increase in consumption is not as large as predicted. New technology, more efficient methods of producing paper from better chemical usage, and other developments have meant that more paper is being produced from less fiber.

Often, timber investments are syndicated, and a limited partnership is formed. Sometimes timber certificates are sold to investors by sponsors. Since timber is considered a natural resource, when it is cut *and* sold, cost depletion is allowed. Timber is not allowed percentage depletion allowances. An investment syndicate often sells cutting rights to its timberland. The sale can be a long-term capital gain (more than six months), but depletion allowances are not allowed because the syndicate actually did not cut the timber. After the trees have been felled by the investors or their manager, or because cutting rights were sold, often the remaining stumps, called *stumpage,* are sold to a company that has special equipment for pulling stumps out of the ground.

The types and quality of timber vary greatly in the U.S. For instance, an investor will find that timber in the South (e.g., southern pine) will grow faster, but the fiber content will be lower than that of northern-grown pine. Slow growth generally means the fibers are tighter or closer together, and fast growth means they are farther apart. However, faster growth is often desired. As tree or forestation grows, it is said to be *accreting* (growing). This accretion is taking place, becoming more valuable through natural growth, while at the same time depletion allowance can be used with timber. This is a good combination for the investor.

HORSE INVESTMENT SYNDICATES

Once the private investment area of the rich, horse investments have always carried potential tax advantages. Some DPP offerings now exist for horse-racing enthusiasts. A purchased racehorse is eligible for depreciation deductions (five-year ACRS) and investment tax credit. Maintenance, training, and operation expenses are deductible as incurred, if reasonable.

Racehorses must be owned for more than 24 months for capital gains taxation. As with purebred cattle, all depreciation deductions are recaptured up to the gain upon the sale of the animal. The "hobby loss rules" pertain to racehorse investments, but a profit must be shown (generally from purse winnings or stud fees) only in two out of every seven years for horse investment businesses.

SUMMARY

Cattle and other agricultural investments offer good tax benefits, but they also entail significant risk due to uncontrollable factors such as weather and consumer demand. Consequently, prospective investors should understand the various mechanisms by which risk in these ventures can be reduced. One of the greatest benefits that limited partnerships in these types of investments can enjoy is the tax status of a farmer. Long-term land speculation augments the tax benefits achieved through cattle investment, and profits can be made by selling or developing farmland.

17

Entertainment, Mining, and Other Exotic Tax Shelters

A great number and variety of entertainment and other nontraditional tax shelters have surfaced on the market in the last few years. Many of these have come to be known as "exotic" tax shelters. Some are considered exotic because of the lack of any realistic possibility to make profits, while others are considered exotic because of the tax and accounting approaches used to make them tax shelters.

In the entertainment world, many of these unconventional programs center around:

- movie production
- master videotape production
- master recording production
- cable TV production

Others—entertaining for sure, but of a more exotic nature—are limited partnerships investing in:

- master art paintings
- lithographs
- Bible productions
- jojoba beans
- books
- photographic masters
- gemstones

Before we discuss coal-mining investments, let's take a look at a few of the more exotic variety.

MOVIE SYNDICATIONS

Two types of movie syndications are available to the tax shelter investor. The first is called the *production service transaction,* with the production service company as an example, and the second is called the *amortization transaction,* with the negative pickup syndication as an example.

In the production service transaction, the production service company will actually finance and produce a film, but it will not own the property rights to the film. This means, for example, that costs for production delays or contract disputes must be borne by the investor. It is the investor, through the general partner, who will be arguing with a recalcitrant major movie star who wants to walk off the set!

A negative pickup syndication is an arrangement whereby the limited partnership purchases a completed film for a fixed price. In this arrangement, everyone knows what the final cost will be. The expected revenue from movie sales is, of course, unknown.

Tax benefits from this type of investment are generated by investment tax credits and depreciation deductions on the film or other valuable property owned by the partnership. The IRS looks closely at these movie and entertainment tax shelters, as well as at tax shelters for books, lithographs, records, and art, because of past abuses involving such investments.

The basis of these exotic tax shelters is that they can frequently be used as collateral for loans, both recourse and nonrecourse. The master is valuable property, and its purchase allows for depreciation and investment tax credits to be taken. If the limited partners want to use the indebtedness in these tax shelters to add to their cost basis, the at-risk rules apply. That is, the investors must be at risk and use recourse financing.

The best-suited investor for a movie tax shelter is a regular corporation, if less than 50 percent of the stock is owned by more than five individuals, because the corporation is *not* subject to *at-risk* rules. Individuals may be suited to this type of investment if they are satisfied with an initial write-off only slightly in excess of 100 percent and have carefully weighed the costs and the risks. Of course, anyone investing in movie syndications must be willing to assume certain tax risks (IRS audits and contests) as well as the unknown future revenue stream, after expenses, of this industry.

PROCEDURES FOR MOVIE SYNDICATIONS

In a production service transaction, the production service company is formed as a partnership to produce a film for a motion picture studio or someone else who owns the property rights to a particular movie. The production service company obtains funds to produce the movie by putting up cash and borrowing the balance on a *nonrecourse* basis (most commonly), with the loan frequently being guaranteed by the movie studio or by the future distributor of the movie. A fee, which is partly fixed or guaranteed payable in installments, and a deferred fee, partly dependent upon box office performance and gross receipts, are paid to the production company upon completion and delivery of the film.

With the negative pickup syndication, the limited partnership purchases a completed film. The purchase is accomplished partly through a down payment and partly through a recourse promissory note. Generally, the producer will receive a share of the film's profits. Arrangements are made with the distributor, who receives 40 - 50 percent of the net after cost receipts. The excess write-offs are gained through depreciation and investment tax credits applied to the entire leveraged price with the depreciation and the qualified U.S. production cost with the ITC.

RECENT RULINGS ON MOVIE SYNDICATIONS

With the introduction of the Tax Reform Act of 1976, the at-risk limits now make it difficult for an individual taxpayer to secure the multiple write-offs that movies have previously offered.

Also, IRS Section 280, as a result of the 1976 act, now states that a production service company must capitalize its production costs to all noncorporate partners. Thus means that production costs and income must be prorated, and, therefore, deductions may not be taken merely because they were incurred or accrued.

IRS Ruling 77-125 holds that borrowing does *not* constitute an indebtedness of the production service company when the loan is guaranteed by the producer. Thus, interest payments are not deductible as they normally would be, and such nonrecourse financed amounts may not be added to the limited partners' basis in the property.

Revenue Ruling 81-283 fatally wounded the shifting recourse note, once a very popular vehicle, by holding that the taxpayer is not at risk.

Revenue Ruling 82-224 bears reading for its determination of the taxpayer's basis for purposes of depreciation and the investment tax credit.

Finally, a continued thorn in the side of taxpayers is the question of the reasonable fair market value of the film. In Revenue Ruling 69-77, the IRS announced that it will attack the includability of a nonrecourse obligation whose amount exceeds the fair market value.

PHANTOM INCOME PROBLEMS

Investment in movie syndications can sometimes create phantom income for the partners. One such problem arises when net receipts are paid to the syndicate, creating taxable income, but are then applied as debt repayment to satisfy the nonrecourse note, which is a nondeductible expenditure. Another problem may arise if the nonrecourse or recourse note has not been satisfied by its due date. In this case, foreclosure of the note will create additional phantom income in an amount equal to the unpaid balance of the loan.

Tax Risks of Movies

Due to a history of abuse, the IRS has attacked movie shelters for years, and it's safe to assume this practice will be continued in the future. As a result, there are at least three important tax risks associated with motion picture syndications if the amortization transaction (negative pickup syndication) does not properly structure the arrangement as a sale:

1. If the structure is not set up properly, the investment may be treated as a loan to the producer rather than a purchase of the film.
2. The IRS may rule that investors have entered into a licensing arrangement, which would eliminate the depreciable base and the ITC.
3. If the price at which the movie is sold to the syndicate is deemed excessive, the syndicate will lose the right to take depreciation and the ITC.

TAX SHELTER INVESTMENTS IN BOOKS, RECORDS, AND ART MASTERS

A number of elements make up the typical investment in books, records, photographs, lithographs, and art. The purchase price is paid partly in a cash down payment with the balance normally paid through notes—one a recourse note due in a specified number of years and the other a nonrecourse note with an agreed-upon maturity. The investor purchases all rights to a *master* from which the books, records, or art can be produced. The nonrecourse note is secured by a first lien on the master, plus a specified percentage of the proceeds. Deductions are produced by accelerated depreciation write-offs and by interest paid on the note or notes. A tax credit is created by the ITC.

CABLE TELEVISION (CATV) TAX SHELTERS

Cable television tax shelters are more appropriately categorized as equipment-leasing tax shelters. In a typical CATV limited partnership investment, the partnership is not the owner or producer of the movie itself. The partnership owns the cable, subscriptions, rent/royalty income, and other installation and studio equipment. In the solicitation of cable TV subscribers, costs of solicitation can be written off currently with income deferred until earned (e.g., when an annual subscription is paid for). The equipment and cable receive ACRS depreciation deductions and investment tax credits. This type of equipment is normally excellent as collateral for both recourse and nonrecourse loans.

MINING SHELTERS

General Considerations

Mining tax shelters run hot and cold in the United States. Because the costs of developing a mine are upfront costs, expenses in *excess* of income are created. Because removal of natural resources as a wasting asset can create depletion allowances, income can be sheltered from current taxation. These two elements make for a potential tax shelter. Most natural resources could be used for this type of program. Mining operations for gold, silver, coal, copper, tin, and zinc have all been put together on a tax shelter basis. Needless to say, a thorough understanding of the industry, an awareness of potential risks, and a competent operator/general partner are all ingredients for which the investor searches when considering a mining investment.

Investments in Coal

Coal-mining investments have been structured as tax shelters. It is crucial for the person considering an investment in coal mining to be completely familiar with coal-mining operations and the attendant risks. Major risks are that coal prices will fluctuate in the future and that the contracts to sell the coal produced may not be available. Labor and environmental considerations in coal mining are substantial. Also, the investor must be confident that the syndicator has properly done the necessary homework in determining the amount and quality of the coal reserves.

Advance Royalty Payments Often the sponsor or general partner in a coal-mining operation will pay a fixed sum in advance of mine development to act as a down payment on future royalties that have been granted to the mine operator. The deduction for the payment of these advance royalties must be deferred until the year in which the minerals are sold. Advance deductions are permitted for one-year prepayment of advance minimum royalties, payable uniformly over the life of the lease, when that is a period of at least 20 years. Since TEFRA-1982, mineral exploration and development operations are allowed to deduct only 85 percent of these costs (i.e., advance royalties). The remaining 15 percent must be capitalized and amortized over five years.

Preinvestment Analysis It is crucial that prospective investors conduct a thorough analysis before investing in a coal tax shelter. The price to be paid for coal properties and engineering analyses should be determined and verified by drilling and property appraisal reports. The investor should ask (and receive satisfactory answers to) the following questions:

1. Does the analysis include a laboratory report of a sufficient number of coal samples?
2. Does the syndicate have a carefully detailed and properly thought out mining plan?
3. Is the contract miner truly experienced and properly equipped to perform the mining function?
4. Do the syndicate contracts require that the contract miner produce the established minimum production requirement necessary to comply with lease obligations and to produce volumes of coal sufficient to attain the economic objectives of the program?
5. Is the contract miner ready and able to satisfy these obligations?
6. Have adequate long-term *end user* contracts been entered into with reasonable purchasers for large percentage of the coal, and, if not, does it appear likely that adequate *spot markets* for the coal will exist?

The investor also needs to know what type of coal is involved: bituminous or anthracite. Bituminous coal is the soft coal found closer to the earth's surface. It is particularly applicable to strip mining and is used for utilities and other areas where a high sulfur content is allowed. Most utilities now have scrubbers in smokestacks to reduce air pollution.

Anthracite coal is a harder coal that burns hotter and cleaner. It is referred to as "metallurgical" coal because it is used in making steel. Anthracite is found deeper under the surface and is a more valuable coal.

Another commonly used term is "coke." Coke is preburned coal that can be burned again; it can be bituminous or anthracite.

The Mining Operation Mining is traditionally accomplished in one of two ways: strip mining or deep-shaft mining. Strip mining is subject to stringent land use regulations, and land that has been stripped away must be reconstructed. The land over which the coal has been disrupted or stripped is called the *overburden*. The cost incurred in replacing the overburden is immediately deductible because the investor is complying with local law.

In deep-shaft mining, the miner is seeking *seams* of coal. The deeper the seam is located, the more difficult it is to mine.

In either mining operation, the coal is ultimately dumped into a machine called a *tipple* to be washed, graded, and sized. Once it is processed in the tipple, it becomes part of inventory and is ready for sale. It is then shipped, via hopper railroad cars or truck, and sold. The coal that is ultimately sold falls into one of three size categories. From the smallest to largest, these are pea coal, nut coal, and lump coal.

SUMMARY

So-called "exotic" tax shelters may appeal to adventurous investors who like the idea of participating in glamorous businesses such as the movie industry. However, that exotic nature carries with it unusual risks, and you, as a salesperson, should duly caution your clients about them. Investors in limited partnerships of this type may receive little or no profit from their investments, and these tax shelters often draw unfavorable attention of the IRS.

Only brief discussions of the various tax shelters available have been included in this chapter. Prospective investors should *thoroughly* investigate the pitfalls of movie syndications, coal-mining operations, and other such shelters before investing their hard-earned dollars in these high-risk ventures.

18

Understanding the Limited Partnership Offering Document

This chapter is designed to provide you with an understanding of a limited partnership offering document. The offering documents of the programs you will be marketing provide the specific information you will need to discuss the economic and tax benefits provided by each program. What follows is a discussion of a typical offering document, providing representative section samplings, explanations of the information provided in each section, and an interpretation of how this information will affect your client's financial plan.

Though the format of offering documents varies, you will find that much of the information is similar in nature from document to document. The material presented in this chapter will be applicable to other documents you will encounter.

OFFERING DOCUMENT SECTION OVERVIEWS

Figure 18.1 provides a brief description of the limited partnership offering, the nature of the investment, and the location of the property. In addition, note that the "total limited partnership equity" is indicated together with the number of units to be sold, the investment amount of each unit, and the fact that half-units are available.

Figure 18.1 Summary of Offering

Green Garden Apartments Associates, A Limited Partnership	Total Limited Partner Equity $1,725,000 17 Units at $101,500 each (Available in half-units)

A Mass. limited partnership formed to acquire, own, and operate an existing 185-unit apartment complex—Green Garden Apartments—located in Southborough, MA. The apartment complex receives government assistance from the U.S. Department of Housing and Urban Development, and its mortgage is insured under Section 221(d)(3) of the National Housing Act.

Figure 18.2 Pay-in Period and Tax Benefits

Year	**Limited Partner Capital Contribution**	**Projected Taxable Loss**	**Tax Loss Ratio**
1984	$ 20,600	$ 41,406	2.0:1
1985	20,300	40,948	2.0:1
1986	17,000	34,131	2.0:1
1987	16,500	30,908	1.9:1
1988	14,700	26,961	1.8:1
1989	12,400	12,400	1.8:1
Total	$101,500	$196,797	1.9:1

This section describes, in chart form, the tax benefits that would accrue to your client (assuming a 50 percent tax rate) during the pay-in period. Note that in 1984 the limited partner contribution would be $20,600. The next column indicates the projected tax loss of $41,406 accruing to the individual limited partner. Note that the final column indicates the tax loss ratio of 2.0:1. As indicated, the total subscription price of the unit, $101,500, is paid in during a period of six years.

When describing a program to your client during a sales presentation, it is important that you indicate the tax loss ratios for each year during the pay-in period. Also note that the combined tax loss ratio during the entire six-year period would be 1.9:1. Stated another way, an individual contributing $101,500 to this program would receive tax benefits over the term of the pay-in period of $196,797.

Figure 18.3 Summary of Program Structure

Green Garden Apartments Associates, a limited partnership, has been selected for marketing by ETS Investments, Inc., because we feel this program represents a sound real estate investment that can provide:

- A long stream of tax deductions
  —1.9:1 over pay-in
  —3.2:1 over 15 years
- Projected high total return: 289% after tax-over 15 years (this protection assumes a 6% rate of property value appreciation and reinvestment of net benefits in a sinking fund yielding 8% after tax)
- Low risk
  —Vacancy rates minimal (0.4%) due to government rent supplements
  —Mortgage guaranteed by HUD
  —Government requirements provide a strong incentive for thorough property maintenance, a key factor with regard to property value and capital appreciation

Investors will benefit from a strong sponsor and general partner.

- Sponsor, the STT Group, Inc.
  —has structured over 400 placements representing over $500 million in early commitments
- Developer/general partner with 35 years of successful performance
  —has built over 20,000 housing units

This section provides a brief summary of the program's structure. Note in the first item that "a long stream of tax deductions" is provided throughout the life of the program. The pay-in period tax loss ratio is 1.9:1. Over the life of the program, which is 15 years, the tax loss ratio amounts to 3.2:1, which amounts to a total dollar benefit of $326,459. In the next part it is noted that the "projected high total return" would amount to 289 percent after tax over the program's life, assuming a 6 percent rate of property value appreciation and the reinvestment of net benefits in a sinking fund yielding 8 percent after tax, amounting to $293,075.

The fact that this is considered a low-risk real estate investment is outlined in the next part of this section. Note that the vacancy rate is anticipated to be at a minimum level due to government rent supplements. The mortgage is guaranteed by HUD, and the government provides incentives for "thorough property maintenance," which will enhance property values and capital appreciation.

In the next part it is noted that the program sponsor, the STT Group, Inc., has had extensive experience with this type of program. Then it is pointed out that the developer/general partner has 35 years of successful performance, having built over 20,000 housing units.

Figure 18.4 Project Specifics

Green Garden Apartments	• 185 one-bedroom apartments —7 one-story buildings; 1 two-story building —Complex includes a community building and 13 acres of land • Woodframe construction with brick veneer; modern appliances • Complex completed in 1974 • Located 2 miles from downtown Southborough, MA. A community shopping center and other commercial facilities are nearby.

This section of the offering document outlines the specifics of the proposed project. The size of the apartment complex, building construction, and other details are presented.

Figure 18.5 The Community

Market Area: Southborough, Mass.	• 40 miles northwest of Boston • Wide industrial base • Tourist and recreational attractions: 18 area lakes, 2 major rivers, extensive beaches, redeveloped marina • Modernized downtown area includes 29-acre enclosed mall and major hotel convention center.

This section outlines the nature of the community in which the project will be located. It is pointed out that this community has a wide industrial base and recreational facilities and is located near shopping facilities. These features will affect the anticipated project occupancy rate.

Figure 18.6 Government Assistance Programs

Government Assistance	• Financed under FHA and 221(d)(3) to provide housing for low- and moderate-income tenants. • Rents supplemented by HUD —Tenants pay the greater of 30% of their income or 70% of the rent as set by HUD. —Government supplement covers the difference between tenant payment and rent. • Government requirements in return for rent supplements —Cash flow over specified amount must be allocated to a cash reserve account. —HUD approval necessary for sale or refinancing (requirement expires in 10.5 years).

The information found in Figure 18.6 on page 249 describes various government assistance programs that will affect the low-risk nature of this limited partnership offering. It is noted in the first part that government financing is available. The next part indicates that tenants' rent is supplemented by HUD, which would enhance the project's occupancy rate. Finally, details concerning the government's requirements in return for rent supplements are outlined.

Figure 18.7 Appraisal and Marketability

Appraisal and Marketability Study	Durkin & Porchelli Associates, Inc., an independent appraiser, concluded: • The Limited Partnership is purchasing the apartment complex at fair market value. • The quality of construction is above average as compared to most conventional apartment complexes in the area and is presently in good condition with no significant deferred maintenance. • The complex's future prospects for conversion to a conventional complex appear good. • Occupancy rates over the past 7 years have averaged 99.6%.

An appraisal and marketability study, as shown in Figure 18.7 above, provides an opinion submitted by an independent appraising firm evaluating the feasibility of purchasing a property. This section notes that the apartment complex is being purchased for its fair market value.

Next it is pointed out that the quality of construction is above average and, finally, that occupancy rates over the past seven years have averaged 99.6 percent. These are all factors that affect cash flow, property appreciation, and marketability at project disposition.

Figure 18.8 provides specific information about the program's sponsor and the general partners. Information concerning the sponsor's experience is presented in the first part; the general part-

Figure 18.8 Sponsor and General Partners

Partnership Management

Sponsor: STT Group, Inc.	• Organized in 1969 • Primary activities include —Financial consulting to developers and investors —Structuring limited partnership investments and serving as co-general partners • STT has arranged over $500 million in equity for over 400 projects with approximately 73,000 housing units costing in excess of $2 billion.
General Partners: William Tinkelenberg and Susan Ricci	• William Tinkelenberg has 35 years of experience in housing development and construction and a net worth in excess of $3 million. • He is the principal stockholder of several corporations engaged in development, construction, and/or operation of rental housing in 12 states. • Since 1964 his company has built over 16,000 units for low/moderate-income housing and over 4,000 units of market rent housing.
Track Record	STT has over 75 Tinkelenberg properties in its portfolio dating back to 1970. These real estate investments have, on average, produced the following percentages of projected benefits.

Actual Benefits as a Percentage of Projected Benefits

Limited partner tax deductions	Cash flow	Total benefits (50% bracket)
103%	124%	107%

ner's experience with housing development and construction is outlined in the next part.

It is noted that STT has over 75 Tinkelenberg properties in its portfolio, dating back to 1970. Note the chart that depicts the average performance of these properties in terms of actual benefits as a percentage of projected benefits. On the *average,* Tinkelenberg properties produced limited partner tax deductions that amounted to 103 percent of those benefits, which were projected in the various offering documents from past programs. The cash flow amounted to 124 percent of what was projected, and, finally, the total benefits amounted to 107 percent of those projected. Though no guarantees can be made for the program outlined in this offering document, certainly this track record will lend some credibility to the projections being made here.

Figure 18.9 Limited Partners' Equity

PROJECTED CAPITALIZATION

LIMITED PARTNER EQUITY	Limited Partners' Capital Contributions	$1,725,500
	Less Front-End Costs	
	Syndication Fee	$201,992
	Interest on Deferred Portion of Fee	27,068
	Interest on the Cash Purchase Note	331,634
	Organizational Expenses	5,000
	Limited Partners' Net Capital Contributions	565,694
	(in property and working capital)	$1,159,806

This section details the total equity of limited partners in the program. Note that the total contributions amount to $1,725,500. From this amount, front-end costs amounting to $565,694 are subtracted. The total limited partners' *net* capital contributions, after front-end costs are deducted, amount to $1,159,806. This is the actual net investment being made in the program. Stated another way, when your client invests $101,500 to purchase one unit, $33,276 of that contribution will be allocated to pay front-end costs and $68,224 will be allocated to the property and working capital.

Figure 18.10 Mortgages

Mortgage Financing There will be two mortgages representing total financing of $3,497,387.

1. The Partnership will assume the existing mortgage on the property, which has an outstanding balance of $2,342,387.
   The existing mortgage on the property has an annual interest rate of 7%. It is provided by the National Mortgage Association and is insured by HUD under 221(d)(3).
2. The seller of the apartment complex will take back a mortgage (called the "purchase money note") in the amount of $1,155,000.
   The seller's purchase-money note bears 12% simple interest that will accrue and not be paid until after the HUD restrictions on refinancing lapse in (10.5 years). After that, interest will be paid from available cash, and any unpaid interest will accrue.

It is noted in this section that there will be two mortgages, representing a total financing amount of $3,497,387. Specifically, the partnership will assume an existing mortgage of $2,342,387, and the seller of the apartment complex will take back a mortgage in the amount of $1,155,000. It is also noted that the seller's mortgage bears a 12 percent simple interest rate that will accrue and not be paid "until after the HUD restrictions on refinancing lapse in 10.5 years."

Figure 18.11 Total Capital Assets

Total Capital Assets	Limited Partners' Net Capital Contributions	$1,159,806
	Mortgage Financing	3,497,384
	Total Real Estate and Other Capital Assets	$4,657,190

The total capital assets listing provides a summary of the two previous sections. Note here that the limited partners' net capital contributions and the mortgage financing combine for a "total real estate and other capital assets" of $4,657,190.

Figure 18.12 Allocations and Sharing

Allocations and Sharing

	Taxable Income/ Loss	**Distributable Cash Flow**	**Net Proceeds from Sale or Refinancing**	
			Until limited partners receive return of capital contributions	Residuals
Limited Partners	99%	99%	99%	81%
General Partners/ Sponsor	1%	1%	1%	19%

The allocations and sharing section describes how the limited partners and general partners/sponsor will share the taxable income and losses together with the distributable cash flow. We note that throughout the program the limited partners are receiving 99 percent of the taxable income and loss, and the general partners are receiving 1 percent. The distributable cash flow will be subject to the same sharing arrangement. Note the last two columns; the limited partners will receive 99 percent of the net proceeds from the sale of the project or share in the refinancing up to a point at which their total capital contributions are returned. This would amount to $101,500 for each individual limited partner.

After the capital contributions are returned, the sharing agreement will change—the limited partners receiving 81 percent of the residuals, the general partners/sponsor receiving 19 percent. This arrangement assures that the limited partners will receive their initial contribution *before* the sharing percentage of the general partners/sponsor is increased.

Figure 18.13 Suitability of Investors

Suitability There are two categories of investors who may qualify:

1. Accredited Investors: Individuals with net worth in excess of $1 million, including principal residence and automobiles, or annual income in excess of $200,000 for the past two years with reasonable expectation of income in excess of $200,000 this year.
2. Nonaccredited Investors: A maximum of 35 nonaccredited investors may qualify if they meet the minimum suitability requirements:
   a. Taxable income subject to the 42% federal income tax bracket, and
   b. (i) $250,000 of net worth, exclusive of home, furnishings, and automobiles, or
   (ii) a net worth of at least $150,000 exclusive of home, furnishings, and an annual income of at least $100,000 per unit purchased.

This section, the suitability of investors entry, provides a summary of the investors' suitability requirements outlined in the offering memorandum. Note that there are two categories, accredited investors and nonaccredited investors. This section shows that accredited investors must have a net worth in excess of $1,000,000 or an annual income exceeding $200,000 for the last two years. Nonaccredited investors must be in the 42 percent tax bracket or higher and have a $250,000 net worth, excluding their home, furnishings, and automobiles, *or* a net worth of at least $150,000 and an annual income of at least $100,000 per unit purchased. It is essential that your client and/or prospect qualify in either of these two categories.

Figure 18.4, the wiring and professionals listing shown on the following page, describes the wiring instructions an offeree should instruct his or her bank to use and lists those professionals associated with the program.

Figure 18.14 Wiring and Professionals

Wiring Instructions	After receipt and review of the offering documents, the offeree should instruct his or her bank to wire $20,600 per unit to: The Second National Bank of Southborough 116 Middle Road Southborough, Massachusetts 01772 The wire should be marked: "Attention Cheryl Bouchard immediately available funds for STT/Green Garden (investor's name)"	
Associated Professionals	Special Tax Counsel for Limited Partners	Larry, Moe & Curly (New York)
	Escrow Agent for the Investors	The Second National Bank of Southborough (Southborough)
	Accountants for the Partnership	Mahoney & Varney (Southborough)
	Appraisal and Marketability Study	Durkin & Porchelli (Southborough)

Figure 18.15, the financial projections listing shown on page 257, outlines the various financial projections for the program based on one partnership unit and an individual limited partner who is in the 50 percent tax bracket. The left-hand column lists each of the 15 years in the program. Column (A) outlines the staggered capital contributions over the first six years of the program, amounting to a total of $101,500.

Column (B) of the same chart describes the annual taxable losses attributable to each individual's annual contribution. Note that in the first six years as shown in ths column the total taxable losses amount to $196,797, a ratio of 1.9:1. Also note that over the 15-year period of the program the total taxable losses amount to $326,459.

Column (C) specifies the tax loss ratio for each year during the pay-in period, amounting to a combined ratio of 1.9:1. The total

Figure 18.15 Financial Projections

Financial Projections

Based on One Partnership Unit ($101,500)
50% Tax Bracket

Year	(A) Capital Contribution	(B) Taxable Losses	(C) (B) ÷ (A) Tax Loss Ratio	(D) Tax Savings	(E) Cash Flow	(F) (D) + (E) Total Benefits	(G) (F) - (A) Cumulative Net Benefit	(H) Cumulative Net Sinking Fund @ 8%	(I) Tax Preferences
1984	$ 20,600	$ 41,406	2.0:1	$ 20,703	$ 781	$ 21,484	$ 884	$ 884	$15,285
1985	20,300	40,948	2.0:1	20,474	852	21,325	1,909	1,980	13,843
1986	12,000	34,131	2.0:1	17,065	852	17,917	2,826	3,055	8,652
1987	16,500	30,908	1.9:1	15,454	852	16,306	2,632	3,105	6,056
1988	14,700	26,961	1.8:1	13,480	852	14,332	2,264	2,985	3,461
1989	12,400	22,443	1.8:1	11,221	852	12,073	1,937	2,897	865
	101,500	196,797	1.9:1						
1990		19,406		9,703	852	10,554	12,493	13,683	0
1991		16,490		8,245	852	9,097	21,589	23,875	0
1992		15,166		7,583	852	8,435	30,024	34,220	0
1993		15,879		7,939	852	8,791	38,815	45,749	0
1994		15,744		7,872	710	8,582	47,397	57,991	0
1995		12,690		6,345	0	6,345	53,742	68,975	0
1996		12,246		6,123	0	6,123	59,865	80,616	0
1997		11,768		5,884	0	5,884	65,749	92,949	0
1998		10,275		5,137	0	5,137	$70,886	$105,522	0
Totals	$101,500	$326,459	3.2:1	$163,229	$9,156	$172,385			

tax loss ratio over the life of the program is indicated as 3.2:1. According to this, your client can write off $3.20 for each $1.00 invested.

Tax savings are indicated in Column (D). Note that this applies to individuals in the 50 percent tax bracket and amounts to one-half of the taxable losses. This, coupled with the cash flow indicated in Column (E), would provide the investor with total first-year benefits of $21,484. You should note the the cash flow indicated for each year of the program subsequently amounts to $9,156.

Column (F) provides a total benefits projection for each of the 15 years, amounting to $172,385 at program disposition. The cumulative net benefit, as shown in Column (G), amounts to the difference between the total benefits outlined in Column (F) and the capital contributions indicated in Column (A). The cumulative net benefit is then projected for each year of the program using these figures.

Page 1 of the offering document indicated that net benefits would be reinvested in a sinking fund yielding 8 percent to the investor after taxes. Column (H) indicates the annual contributions to the sinking fund for a total amount, in the 15th year, of $105,522. This provides the investors with some assurance that their capital contribution, at a minimum will be returned at program disposition.

Column (I) indicates the dollar amounts that would be considered tax preference items. The alternative minimum tax for individuals is calculated by adding the adjusted gross income plus any items of tax preference. Accelerated depreciation in real estate that is in excess of straight-line depreciation deductions is considered subject to the alternative minimum tax calculation. You should note, however, that there is a tax preference item exemption of $40,000 for individuals filing joint returns and a $30,000 exemption for single people. If the amount in Column (I) is added to other tax preference items beyond the exemption amounts, a flat 20 percent tax applies. Note that beginning in 1985, interest that will be excluded from gross income by the special 15 percent net interest exclusion rule will also be considered a tax preference item.

Figure 18.16 describes the after-tax benefits at the sale of the partnership property in 1998. Note again that the assumption is based on an individual in the 50% tax bracket. The compound appreciation rate ranging from 0 percent through 6 percent is outlined. It should be noted that the projected high total return of 289

Figure 18.16 After-Tax Benefits

Total After-Tax Benefits at Sale

Based on Sale in 1998
One Partnership Unit
($101,500)
50% Tax Bracket

Compound appreciation rate	0%	4%	6%
Gross sales proceeds**	$ -0-	$174,776	$293,526
Tax liability* at sale	- 47,268	- 82,223	-105,973
Net after-tax Sale Proceeds	(47,268)	92,553	187,553
Cumulative 8% sinking fund	105,522	105,522	105,522
Total net after-tax benefit	$ 58,254	$198,075	$293,075

**Based on an appraised value of $4,503,000.

* A small portion of the gain from sale will be subject to recapture (taxed at the ordinary 50% rate), while most will be taxed at capital gains rates (20%).

percent after tax over the 15-year span of the program is based on a projection assumption of 6 percent. Note in the first column that, if the property sells for its appraised value of $4,503,000 (with zero appreciation), the total net after-tax benefit to the limited partner would amount to $58,254. This figure includes a tax liability of $47,268, subtracted from the cumulative 8 percent sinking fund, which has grown to $105,522. In the last column it is noted that, if the projected appreciation does occur at 6 percent, the gross sales proceeds would be $293,526 per limited partner. Subtract from this figure the tax liability at sale of $105,973, and there would be a net after-tax sale proceeds amount of $187,553. If you then add to this figure the sinking fund amount, the total net after-tax benefit realized would be $293,075 per limited partner.

SUMMARY

While offering documents will vary somewhat, all contain similar information. In the sales process, you will use the offering document for the specific investment you are recommending to your client to summarize the benefits and risks of that investment. Therefore, it would be wise for you to gain a solid overall understanding of the types of information presented in offering documents.

Glossary

ADR (American Depository Receipt)—A negotiable share issued by an American bank in a block of foreign stocks or bonds held in trust by a foreign branch of an American bank. Thus, for the individual investor, it is an approximate counterpart to the stock or bond certificate held for investment in an American corporation.

Advisor—The organization employed by a mutual fund to give professional advice on its investments and management of its assets.

Alpha measurement—*See* Beta coefficient. A statistical measure to indicate or anticipate how the performance of a security differs from its beta. The alpha is considered to reflect how a security is overvalued or undervalued in relation to the market.

Arbitrage—The process of buying and simultaneously selling the same or equivalent securities in different markets. The purpose is to take advantage of temporary price differentials.

Assessment bond—A state or local bond payable from specific levies to be collected from each property in a specified district.

Auction market—A market in which the highest bidder buys securities from the seller who offers the lowest price. All bids and offers are audible to the crowd at the trading place. The New York Exchange is the world's largest auction market for securities.

Authority—A state or local agency authorized to conduct a public business, such as a toll road or a water supply project, and to sell bonds payable solely from its business funds.

Automatic reinvestment—The option available to mutual fund shareholders whereby fund income dividends and capital gains distributions are automatically put back into the fund to buy new shares and thereby build up holdings.

Banker's acceptance—A draft drawn upon a bank and accepted (i.e., signed) by it on behalf of a customer; hence, it is equivalent to a promissory note of the bank, usually payable within 90 days.

Basis point—One-hundredth of a percentage point. Term used in quoting bond and money market yields.

Beta coefficient—A statistical measure showing how fast an individual stock or portfolio has moved up or down relative to the general market over a specified period. Theoretically, the higher the risk, the higher the beta. The beta coefficient is used to predict or anticipate how a stock should perform in a given market.

Bid and ask (or offer)—In securities terminology, a bid is a proposal to buy a specific quantity at a named price; an ask or offer is the corresponding proposal to sell.

Blue List—The title of a daily publication that lists tax-exempt bonds for sale, naming offer and asking price.

Blue sky laws—An expression that refers to state laws regulating the securities business. They describe the rules that must be met in order to issue and sell securities within a given state.

Board lot—The standard trading quantity in stock exchange transactions, usually 100 shares or one $1,000 bond.

Bond—A certificate of debt or negotiable promissory note of a corporation or public body, which promises to repay on a maturity date some years distant and to pay periodic interest until then.

Bond fund—A mutual fund whose portfolio consists primarily of bonds. The emphasis of such funds is normally on income rather than growth.

Bond indenture—The complete contract for a bond issue, covering the rights and duties of the corporation, trustee, and bondholders.

Bond issue—The entire block of similar or related bonds sold under one indenture.

Book value—The overall net worth of a corporation. It is equal to the corporation's total assets (less intangibles) minus its liabilities.

Broker—A securities firm or representative of such a firm, which acts as an agent to execute customers' orders to buy and sell securities.

Broker-dealer—A firm that retails mutual fund shares and other securities to the public.

Business risk—The chance that a business may fail or become significantly less profitable.

Call—Contract giving the holder the option to buy, from another party, a specified quantity of a specified security at a specified price within a specified time. Also, a notice to a bondholder that a debtor is exercising its contractual right to pay off the bond.

Call provisions—The terms in a bond indenture that govern the debtor's right to pay off all or portions of the issue before maturity.

Capital—To an economist, an accumulation of goods useful in productive processes or for future consumption. To a corporation, the excess of net assets over all liabilities.

Capital gain—The gain realized when the net selling price received on the sale of a capital asset is more than its cost. A capital gain is short-term if the asset was held less than a year and long-term if it was held a year or more.

Capital-gains taxes—Federal and state income taxes levied on capital gains. Currently only 40 percent of long-term capital gain is taxable. Therefore, long-term capital gains are, in effect, taxed at lower rates than ordinary income.

Capital growth—An increase in market value of a mutual fund's securities that is reflected in the net asset value of fund shares. This is a specific long-term objective of many mutual funds.

Capital loss—A loss that occurs when the net selling price of capital asset is less than its cost.

Capital value risk—One type of money-rate risk accompanying income-bearing securities, where a long-term bond or preferred stock may decline in price because of interest-rate increases.

Certificate of deposit—An interest-bearing time deposit in a bank. Consumer CDs (under $100,000) usually mature in six months to three years. Penalties, in the form of reduced interest rates, are imposed for early withdrawal. Commercial bank CDs ($100,000 and up) pay higher interest rates than consumer CDs and usually mature in one to six months.

Charter (corporation)—The authority to do business granted by a state or federal government to a corporation.

Chartist—One who predicts stock market behavior by **means** of graphic presentations of stock prices.

Churning—An excessive amount of trading in a customer's account, to generate additional commissions for an unscrupulous broker.

Closed-end company (for fund or trust)—An investment company that operates as an ordinary corporation in that its shares are traded on a securities exchange. After the initial issue, a closed-end company neither redeems its shares nor sells new ones.

Collateral trust bonds—Bonds that are secured by deposit of other bonds and stock rather than by real property. The pledged securities are generally assigned and delivered to the trustee of the collateral trust bonds, but the rights to receive the income and to exercise the voting powers of pledged securities are usually retained by the debtor corporation.

Commercial paper—Promissory notes of major corporations, maturing within 270 days or less and sold by dealers to banks and other short-term investors.

Commission—The brokerage fee paid by stockholders to a securities firm for buying or selling securities as an agent.

Common stock—The basic ownership equity in a corporation, having no preference as to income or assets.

Common stock fund—A mutual fund whose portfolio consists primarily of common stocks. The emphasis of such funds is usually on growth.

Common trust fund—A pool of investments administered by a bank and used as joint diversified investment outlets for small trusts.

Competitive bidding—The submittal of written bids by underwriting groups for new issue of bonds or stocks, usually municipal or public utility issues.

Concession—A small discount from public offering price allowed to securities firms that forward orders to offerors of new issues, municipals, or open-end funds.

Conglomerate—A corporation that operates or controls several business activities in unrelated industries.

Consolidated statement—A financial statement that combines the affairs of a holding company and its subsidiaries as though there were one business.

Constant ratio plan—An investment management plan that attempts to make market profits by adjusting stock-bond proportions to a planned ratio.

Contractual plan—A program for the accumulation of mutual fund shares in which the investor agrees to invest a fixed amount on a regular basis for a specified number of years. A substantial portion of the sales charge applicable to the total investment is usually deducted from early payments.

Convertible bond—A bond that the holder may convert, at his or her option, into a stated amount of common stock of the same company at a fixed price.

Coupon bond—A bond bearing interest coupons, usually semiannual, which are collectible like checks when due.

Credit union—A state or federally chartered association of individuals that receives savings deposits from, and makes loans to, its members.

Current assets—Business assets, such as cash, inventory, and receivables, which normally will be converted into cash within one year.

Current liabilities—Outstanding short-term debts, such as merchandise payables, bank loans, and accrued taxes.

Current ratio—A ratio of a firm's current assets to its current liabilities.

Custodian—The organization (usually a bank) that holds in custody and safekeeping the securities and other assets of a mutual fund.

Dealer—A securities firm that makes a market by standing ready to buy or sell certain securities as a principal.

Debenture—A bond *not secured* by mortgage or collateral.

Default—Failure to observe terms of a contract, especially failure to pay bond interest or principal.

Dilution—Reduction in actual or potential earnings or asset coverage for bonds or stock through issuance of more securities or options to obtain the additional securities.

Disintermediation—A withdrawal of savings by investors from deposit-type financial intermediaries in order to buy higher-yielding marketable securities.

Diversification—Making investments of varied types and maturity dates in various industries and localities to reduce the risks inherent in investing.

Dividend—A corporate distribution to shareholders, usually from earnings and usually in cash.

Dollar-cost averaging—The investing of equal amounts of money at regular intervals, regardless of whether the stock market is moving upward or downward. This reduces average share costs to the investor who acquired more shares in periods of lower securities prices and fewer shares in periods of higher prices.

Dow Jones average—An index of stock prices compiled daily by Dow Jones & Co. The index averages the prices of about 65 stocks, including 30 industrials, 20 transports, and 15 utilities.

Dow Theory—The theory that the general medium-term direction of stock price change is indicated by certain aspects of short-term price fluctuation.

Earnings per share (EPS)—Corporate earnings for a stated period, after preferred dividends have been paid, divided by the adjusted average number of common shares outstanding during the period.

Earnings yield—Earnings per share expressed as a percentage of the stock price.

Equipment obligations—Notes or certificates that are, in effect, bonds secured by pledge of airplanes, railway cars, or other movable equipment.

Estate planning—The process of planning, often through an insurance plan, assets, bequests, and estate disposition to assure liquidity, provide for family needs, minimize confusion, and avoid unnecessary taxes and forced sales.

Estate taxes—The taxes levied by the federal government and nearly all states, based on the total size of a decedent's taxable estate.

Eurodollars—U.S. dollars held (as by a bank) outside the United States and especially in Europe.

Exchange privilege—Enables a mutual fund shareholder to transfer investments from one fund to another within the same fund group if the investor's needs or objectives change, generally with a small transaction charge.

Ex-dividend—Without the pending dividend. When stock is sold ex-dividend, the seller retains the dividend. Thus, on the day a stock goes ex-dividend, its selling price per share generally declines by the dividend per share amount.

Federal agency bonds—Bonds issued by federal corporations, such as federal land banks or TVA. Some are guaranteed by the government; some are not.

Federal securities acts—A series of acts under which the securities business is regulated by federal authorities.

Finance company paper—Promissory notes issued by finance and personal loan companies for time periods up to 270 days. An important money-making investment.

Fixed assets—Business assets of a long-term nature, such as land, buildings, and machinery.

Fixed charges—Expense charges for interest, amortization of bond discount, and, in some cases, lease rentals.

Flat quotation—A bond quotation that indicates that the acquisition of the bond includes no accrued interest.

Foreign dollar bonds—Bonds issued by foreign corporate or public borrowers that are payable in the United States in dollars.

Formula plans—The plans for the making or managing of stock/bond investments through a system or formula that is expected to result in market profits.

General obligation bond—A state or municipal bond, which is an unconditional obligation to pay and is issued by a government unit with power to levy taxes.

Gift taxes—Taxes levied by the federal government and several states on donors of noncharitable gifts.

Growth fund—A mutual fund whose primary investment objective is long-term growth of capital. It invests principally in common stocks with growth potential.

Growth stock—A stock whose earnings and price have increased and are expected to increase consistently over a number of years.

Guaranteed bond—A bond whose interest and principal payments are guaranteed by a firm other than the issuer, usually a lessee of the issuer's property.

Hedge fund—Either a private investment partnership, exempt from registration as an investment company, or a registered mutual fund that uses margin trading, short selling, option writing, and other speculative methods to achieve quick market profits.

Holding company—A corporation that owns a controlling interest in the stock of at least one other corporation.

Income bond—A bond on which the interest payment is not mandatory unless earned, though it is usually cumulative if unpaid in previous periods.

Income fund—A mutual fund whose primary investment objective is current income rather than growth of capital. It usually invests in stock and bonds that normally pay higher dividends and interest.

Income risk—One type of money-rate risk in which the holder of a short-dated debt may be unable to renew it at its former high interest rate.

Indenture—A legal document that constitutes the agreement between the parties in a bond contract.

Individual retirement account (IRA)—A retirement program in which individuals may contribute and deduct from their income tax an amount up to $2,000 per year. An individual retirement account may be funded with mutual fund shares.

Industrial average—An index of several industrial stock prices compiled by Dow Jones & Co. Standard and Poors also compiles an index of industrial stock prices.

Inflation hedge—An investment whose earnings, dividend payments, or price is expected to rise at least as much as the general price level.

Inheritance taxes—State taxes levied on inheritances received by heirs from the estate of a decedent.

Institutions (financial)—Investment companies, pension funds, bank trust departments, insurance companies, and endowments whose large transactions sharply affect the securities markets.

Internal Revenue Code—The federal tax law.

Investment analysis—The study of investment characteristics and trends and the consequential estimation of values, relative values, or probable market performance.

Investment company—A corporation, trust, or partnership in which investors pool their money to obtain professional management and diversification of their investments. Mutual funds are the most popular type of investment company.

Investment Company Act of 1940—The purpose of this act is to provide for the registration and regulation of investment companies, a term that includes mutual funds and variable annuities. While this act establishes the guidelines, requirements, and restrictions for establishing mutual funds and their various features, little in the act speaks directly to sales or service activities.

Investment credit—A provision in federal tax laws since 1963 that subsidizes new plant construction and many other investments by permitting up to 10 percent of the cost of certain outlays to be deducted from the year's income tax.

Investment objective—The goal (e.g., long-term capital growth, current income, etc.) that an investor or a mutual fund pursues.

Joint tenancy—Joint ownership of securities or property under state statutes that make the survivor the full owner after the first death.

Keogh plan—Also known as *H.R. 10 Plan.* A retirement program for self-employed individuals and their employees based on tax-saving provisions. A Keogh plan may be funded with mutual fund shares.

Leasehold mortgage—A mortgage on a building and/or fixtures affixed to land leased (not owned) by the debtor.

Legal list—A list of bonds approved by state authorities for investment by savings banks or trust funds.

Legal list state—A state whose laws restrict investment of certain funds to legal lists of bonds.

Legal opinion—A written opinion by a qualified attorney that a registration of securities or an issue of municipal bonds does or does not conform to law.

Lettered stock—Unregistered shares that a mutual fund or other holder can dispose of only through private placement or by completing the entire registration process before offering the shares for public sale.

Leverage—The ratio of common stock to total capitalization of a company. The greater the proportion of fixed obligations, the higher a company is leveraged. In a highly leveraged company, there is a tendency for net profits per share to change at a faster rate than revenues.

Limit order—A customer's order to buy or sell securities at a stated price "or better."

Liquidity—The capacity to be sold for cash or to be borrowed against without delay and for full value.

Listed security—A security that is fully accepted for trading on a stock exchange.

Living trust—A trust established by a trustor while trustor is living and competent.

Margin—Owner's net equity in a brokerage account or owner's initial payment on a margin transaction.

Margin account—A brokerage account in which the owner furnishes a property equity and is lent, by the broker, the balance needed to pay for the owner's trades.

Margin trading—Buying or selling securities in a brokerage account that owes a balance to the broker.

Market average—Barometers of stock or bond prices, such as the Dow Jones average and the Standard & Poors 500 stock average.

Market risk—The risk that security or property may not be saleable or pledgeable at a fair price when money is needed, owing to some defect or disruption of the market in which it is traded.

Maturity—Time of completion, especially the time when the principal of a bond or note is due.

Merger—A combining of two or more firms into a single entity that retains all the assets and liabilities of the constituent firms.

Minority interest—The portion of the common stock (and possibly the preferred stock) not controlled by a holding company, controlling group, or individual that dominates the firm's affairs.

Money market fund—Also called a *liquid asset or cash fund.* A mutual fund whose primary objective is to make available higher-interest securities for the average investor who wants immediate income and high investment safety. This is accomplished through the purchase of high-yield money market instruments such as U.S. government securities, bank certificates of deposit, and commercial paper.

Money-market securities—High-grade, short-term securities or notes used as temporary investments.

Money-rate risk—The risk that income-bearing securities, especially long-term bonds or preferred stock, may decline in price because of interest rate increases (capital value risk) or that the holder of a debt may be unable to renew the debt at its former high interest rate (income risk).

Mortgage—A lien on property to secure a debt.

Mortgage bond—A bond that is part of a bond issue secured by a mortgage.

Municipal bond—A bond that is issued by a state or lesser governmental unit or authority. Municipal bond interest is currently exempt from federal income tax and, in most cases, from taxation by the issuing state.

Municipal bond fund—A mutual fund that invests in a broad range of tax-exempt bonds issued by states, cities, and other local governments. The interest obtained from these bonds is passed through to shareowners free of federal tax. The fund's primary objective is current tax-free income.

Mutual fund—An open-end investment company that characteristically stands ready to issue new shares or redeem existing shares.

Mutual savings bank—A bank without stockholders that receives deposits and pays interest on those deposits but, in most states, does no checking account business.

NASDAQ—National Association of Securities Dealers Automated Quotations, an organization that compiles and publishes, in a daily service, dealers' bids and offers on thousands of over-the-counter stocks and bonds.

National Association of Securities Dealers (NASD)—A quasi-governmental association formed to develop and enforce standard procedures and ethics in over-the-counter securities business.

Net asset value per share—Value of a firm's assets, minus liabilities, divided by the number of shares outstanding. The term generally applies to firms holding securities and receivables rather than tangible assets.

Nonrecurring item—A special gain or expense item, such as a capital gain or a fire loss, which makes an income statement atypical.

Odd lot—A small quantity of shares, usually *less than 100* shares of stock or $1,000 face value of bonds, sold or bought by a special procedure on a stock exchange.

Odd-lot differential—A small surcharge to compensate the odd-lot dealer. The surcharge, usually $12^1/_2$ centers per share, is added to a customer's purchase price or subtracted from a customer's selling price for odd lots of shares.

Odd-lot index—The ratio of odd-lot sales to purchases. A rise in index is considered bullish; a decline, bearish. This leads to the odd-lot theory that the odd-lot investor is usually wrong.

Open indenture—A bond indenture under which additional bonds may be issued subject to any self-contained limitations.

Open-end investment company—The more formal name for a mutual fund, indicating that it stands ready to redeem its shares (buy them back) on demand.

Open order—An order, valid until filled or canceled, to buy or sell a security, usually at a limited price.

Operating expense ratio—The ratio of operating expenses to gross revenue.

Option—In the securities business, a written contract permitting the holder to buy from, or sell to, the maker a stated quantity of stock at a stated price before a stated date.

Option income fund—A fund whose objective is to seek a high current return by investing primarily in dividend-paying common stocks on which call options are traded on national securities exchanges. Current return generally consists of dividends, premiums from expired call options, net short-term gains from sales or portfolio securities on exercises of options or otherwise, and any profits from closing purchase transactions.

Outstanding stock—The number of shares in stockholders' hands, not including unissued or reacquired shares or any held for future bond conversions or executive stock options.

Over-the-counter market—A market operated by dealers and brokers by telephone and advertised lists, through which securities are traded without the use of stock exchanges.

Participating preferred—A preferred stock that receives extra dividends under stated conditions, usually when common stock receives large dividends.

PHA (Public Housing Act) bond—An obligation of a local housing authority whose interest payments are tax-exempt but on which interest and principal are contractually payable by the federal government.

Pooling of interests—An accounting method for mergers and other corporate combinations under which assets are recorded by the acquiring concern at book value.

Portfolio—A collection of securities and other assets representing the entire holdings of an individual, a trust, or an institution.

Preferred stock—The ownership shares in a corporation that are entitled to stated priorities as to income or assets, ahead of all other shares. Preferred stock normally pays a fixed dividend, regardless of the experience of the corporation.

Present-value tables—Mathematical tables indicating the present value at compound interest of sums or annuities payable in the future.

Price-earnings ratio ***(P/E)***—A popular measure for evaluating stock prices, computed by dividing per-share annual earnings figure into the price of the stock.

Prospectus—The official booklet that describes the mutual fund and offers its shares for sale. It contains information as required by the Securities and Exchange Commission on such subjects as the fund's investment objectives and policies, services, investment restrictions, officers and directors, how shares can be bought and redeemed, its charges, and its financial statements.

Purchasing power risk—The risk that the principal and income from investments will lose their purchasing power because inflation occurs faster than investment growth.

Put—A contract giving the holder the option to sell to the signer a specified quantity of a specified security at a specified price within a specified time period.

Qualified retirement plan—A private retirement plan that meets the rules and regulations of the Internal Revenue Service. Contributions to a qualified retirement plan are, in most cases, tax-deductible, and earnings on such contributions are always tax-sheltered until withdrawal.

Ratio analysis—A technique of investment analysis that evaluates a firm's position by studying ratios developed from certain accounting figures and comparing them to ratios developed by other firms within the same industry.

Recapitalization—A corporate process through which certain securities are retired in exchange for others.

Receivership—Situations in which a court-appointed receiver takes control of a corporation to conserve its assets until troubles can be resolved.

Record date—The date designated by directors to determine the list of stockholders who are to receive rights, voting privileges, dividends, or other distribution.

Redemption price—Also known as *bid price.* The amount per share that the mutual fund shareholders receive when they cash in their shares. The value of the shares depends on the market value of the fund's portfolio securities at the time.

Registrar of stock—An agency in a bank or trust company that countersigns stock certificates to assure validity.

Registration—The required process of filing with the SEC in order to issue a new public offering of securities or to trade existing securities on the national securities exchanges.

Regulated investment company—An investment company that meets certain statutory requirements and is, therefore, exempt from paying corporate income taxes on income distributed to stockholders.

Regulatory risk—*See* **Social** risk.

Reinvestment privilege—A service provided by most mutual funds for the automatic reinvestment of a shareholder's income dividends and capital gains distributions in additional shares.

Reorganization—The court-supervised process of creating a successor corporation and issuing that corporation's securities to security holders in a bankrupt corporation.

Repurchase agreement (REPO)—A contract under which an owner sells securities to another and pledges to repurchase the securities within a few weeks at a stated price.

Revenue bond—A state or local bond, whose interest and principal payments come exclusively from a business project such as a toll road or a water system; also, in some jurisdictions, from a specific tax or revenue source.

Rights—A negotiable privilege, evidenced by a saleable certificate, to buy securities (usually common stock) from a company at below market prices; usually distributed to common stockholders in proportion to the number of shares held. Rights are sometimes issued also for the purchase of debentures.

Roundlot—The standard trading quantity in stock exchange transactions, usually 100 shares or one $1,000 bond.

Savings bond—A small or medium-sized federal obligation sold to individuals either on a discount basis to compound to par or at par to pay semiannual interest.

SEC (Securities and Exchange Commission)—The federal agency that regulates the securities business.

Secondary distribution—The organized sale by security dealers of a substantial block of existing securities, usually stocks.

Secondary movements—The upward or downward price trends in a single security or in market indexes, usually a few weeks to a few months in duration.

Securities Exchange Act of 1934—The purpose of this act is to provide for the regulation of securities exchanges and the over-the-counter market. This act also provides for the creation of the SEC and, indirectly, for the creation of the NASD. While the act contains numerous provisions regarding sales activities, most of these provisions are of more concern to representatives who are selling all kinds of securities and not just mutual funds and variable annuities.

Selling group—A group of securities dealers who purchase new securities from a purchasing syndicate and retail them.

Serial bonds—Bonds with the same issue date, which mature in installments over the life of the issue, each bond having its own due date.

Settlement date—The date on which sold securities, or the purchase price for them, must be delivered, usually on the fifth business day after a transaction.

Short interest—The aggregate outstanding number of shares of a specific stock that have been sold short.

Short sale—Any sale of a security that is completed by delivery of borrowed shares or bonds; the sale of unowned securities in anticipation of their market decline before it is necessary to buy the same securities to be returned to lender.

Sinking fund—A periodic payment by a debtor corporation to a bond trustee, usually used to buy back the debtor's bonds or call them by lot for retirement.

Small business investment company (SBIC)—A federally chartered, closed-end investment company with special tax privileges and access to government loans; chartered to assist in financing small and medium-sized corporations.

Social risk—Also known as *regulatory risk.* The risk that an otherwise profitable business or security will be impaired by adverse regulation, legislation, or other public policy.

Special offering—A technique for selling a large block of stock on a stock exchange floor through exchange member brokers.

Special situation—A security that promises unusual gains if certain developments occur.

Specialists—A stock exchange member who is appointed to handle other brokers' limit orders in certain stocks when so requested and who is obligated to prevent unnecessary price fluctuations in assigned stocks by interposing personal bids and offers.

Speculation—The acceptance of risk in owning or trading securities in the hopes of achieving capital gains or large income.

Standard and Poors Index—An index of stock prices published daily that includes prices of approximately 500 stocks.

Stock dividend—A pro rata distribution to stockholders of additional shares of stock.

Stock power—A separate piece of paper, signed by the owner of a security, which carries the same weight or authority as the investor's signature on a stock certificate.

Stock split—A process that divides each share into a larger number of shares, usually to reduce the price per share by diluting the equity per share. It makes the purchase of the stock more attractive due to the reduced price per share. A *reserve split* is a reduction in the number of shares by combining shares. This has the opposite effect of a split.

Stock (loss) order—A stock exchange order to buy or sell that becomes a market order when a transaction occurs at a stated "triggering" price.

Stopping stock—A stock exchange specialist's action in earmarking an open order to cover a stop order when the latter becomes effective.

Straddle—The simultaneous writing of put and call options on the same security.

Street name—A broker or brokerage firm in whose name stock certificates are held for the owner.

Subordinated bonds—A bond with terms that remain junior in rank, or priority for payment, to other company debt.

Support point—A price, somewhat below the present level, at which numerous bids may halt a price decline.

Tax selling—Sales made to realize gains or losses for income tax purposes.

Third market—An over-the-counter market in listed securities, wherein large blocks are at times bought and sold by dealers.

Transfer—The process of removing a securityholder's name from an official list of stockholders or registered bondholders and substituting another's name.

Transfer agent—The organization that is employed by a mutual fund to prepare and maintain records relating to the accounts of its shareholders.

Treasury bill—A type of United States government obligation that is sold at a discount from the face amount, pays no interest, matures at par in most cases within a year's time, and is traded in great quantities as a liquid money market investment.

Treasury bond—A United States government bond of the usual type that has ten or more years before maturity at time of first issue.

Trust—An arrangement under which a bank or other trustee takes title to and possession of another's property under legal obligation to administer that property as directed and pay income or principal to designated beneficiaries.

Trust deeds—A substitute for a mortgage in corporate bond transactions and personal real estate loans in some states, in which the debtor's property is technically deeded to a trustee instead of to the creditor.

Trustee—A bank, group, or individual that undertakes administrative obligations under a trust or a bank that holds title as security for a bond issue or real estate loan.

Underwriting—Securities firms agreeing to buy new securities not sold by a projected selling effort or the process of buying a block of securities with the intent to market them immediately.

Underwriting commission—A fee paid to a securities firm for assuring the success of the securities offering or the firm's gross markup in a purchase and sale transaction.

Unlisted market—The over-the-counter securities market for securities not traded on an exchange.

Variable annuity—A life annuity with reserve funds invested in whole or in part in common stocks or other securities and whose annuity payments will be based on the value of such holdings.

Variable-ratio plan—A mechanical plan for managing a stock-bond portfolio, wherein the percentage of stocks is increased when the formula shows the market price level to be low and vice versa.

Warrant—A long-term certificate from the corporation evidencing a holder's right to buy an indicated quantity of new stock at a stated price; also the certificate evidencing stock rights.

When-issued contract (W.I.)—A contract entered into by investors, through securities, to be completed when and if the securities are issued.

Working capital—The net liquid assets with which a firm does business, measured roughly as current assets minus current liabilities, and thus provided from long-term or equity sources.

Yield—The current or prospective stock dividend rate expressed as a percentage of the price; the total rate of return on a bond held to the maturity date, considering the initial price paid, the interest received, and the price received when the bond is paid off at its maturity date.

Index

COMPOUND INTEREST
ONE DOLLAR PER ANNUM IN ADVANCE

The sum of which One Dollar per annum, paid at the beginning of each year, will **increase** at compound interest in any number of years not exceeding fifty.

Years	2.5%	3%	4%	5.5%	6%	7%	7.5%	8%
1	1.0250	1.0300	1.0400	1.0550	1.0600	1.0700	1.0750	1.0800
2	2.0756	2.0909	2.1216	2.1680	2.1836	2.2149	2.2306	2.2464
3	3.1525	3.1836	3.2465	3.3423	3.3746	3.4399	3.4729	3.5061
4	4.2563	4.3091	4.4163	4.5811	4.6371	4.7507	4.8084	4.8666
5	5.3877	5.4684	5.6330	5.8881	5.9753	6.1533	6.2440	6.3359
6	6.5474	6.6625	6.8983	7.2669	7.3938	7.6540	7.7873	7.9228
7	7.7361	7.8923	8.2142	8.7216	8.8975	9.2598	9.4464	9.6366
8	8.9545	9.1591	9.5828	10.2563	10.4913	10.9780	11.2298	11.4876
9	10.2034	10.4639	11.0061	11.8754	12.1808	12.8164	13.1471	13.4866
10	11.4835	11.8078	12.4864	13.5835	13.9716	14.7836	15.2081	15.6455
11	12.7956	13.1920	14.0258	15.3856	15.8699	16.8885	17.4237	17.9771
12	14.1404	14.6178	15.6268	17.2868	17.8821	19.1406	19.8055	20.4953
13	15.5190	16.0863	17.2919	19.2926	20.0151	21.5505	22.3659	23.2149
14	16.9319	17.5989	19.0236	21.4087	22.2760	24.1290	25.1184	26.1521
15	18.3802	19.1569	20.8245	23.6411	24.6725	26.8881	28.0772	29.3243
16	19.8647	20.7616	22.6975	25.9964	27.2129	29.8402	31.2580	32.7502
17	21.3863	22.4144	24.6454	28.4812	29.9057	32.9990	34.6774	36.4502
18	22.9460	24.1169	26.6712	31.1027	32.7600	36.3790	38.3532	40.4463
19	24.5447	25.8704	28.7781	33.8683	35.7856	39.9955	42.3047	44.7620
20	26.1833	27.6765	30.9692	36.7861	38.9927	43.8652	46.5525	49.4229
21	27.8629	29.5368	33.2480	39.8643	42.3923	46.0057	51.1190	54.4568
22	29.5844	31.4529	35.6179	43.1118	45.9958	52.4361	56.0279	59.6933
23	31.2490	33.4265	38.0826	46.5360	49.8156	57.1767	61.3050	65.7648
24	33.1578	35.4593	40.6459	50.1526	53.8645	62.2490	66.9779	72.1059
25	35.0117	37.5530	43.3117	53.9660	58.1564	67.6765	73.0762	78.9544
26	36.9120	39.7096	46.0842	57.9891	62.7058	73.4838	79.6319	86.3508
27	38.8598	41.9309	48.9676	62.2335	67.5281	79.6977	86.6793	94.3388
28	40.8563	44.2189	51.9663	66.7114	72.6398	86.3465	94.2553	102.9659
29	42.9027	46.5754	55.0849	71.4355	78.0582	93.4608	102.3994	112.2832
30	45.0003	49.0027	58.3283	76.4194	83.8017	101.0730	111.1544	122.3459
31	47.1503	51.5028	61.7015	81.6775	89.8898	109.2182	120.5659	133.2135
32	49.3540	54.0778	65.2095	87.2248	96.3432	117.9334	130.6834	144.9506
33	51.6129	56.7302	68.8579	93.0771	103.1838	127.2588	141.5596	157.6267
34	53.9282	59.4621	72.6522	99.2514	110.4348	137.2369	153.2516	171.3168
35	56.3014	62.2759	76.5983	105.7652	118.1209	147.9135	165.8205	186.1021
36	58.7339	65.1742	80.7022	112.6373	126.2681	159.3374	179.3320	202.0703
37	61.2273	68.1594	84.9703	119.8873	134.9042	171.5610	193.8569	219.3159
38	63.7830	71.2342	89.4091	127.5361	144.0585	184.6403	209.4712	237.9412
39	66.4026	74.4013	94.0255	135.6056	153.7620	198.6351	226.2565	258.0565
40	69.0876	77.6633	98.8265	144.1189	164.0477	213.6096	144.3008	279.7810
41	71.8398	81.0232	103.8196	153.1005	174.9505	229.6322	263.6983	303.2435
42	74.6608	84.4839	109.0124	162.5760	186.5076	246.7765	284.5507	328.5830
43	77.5523	88.0484	114.4129	172.5727	198.7580	265.1209	306.9670	355.9496
44	80.5161	91.7199	120.0294	183.1192	211.7435	284.7493	331.0645	385.5056
45	83.5540	95.5015	125.8706	194.2457	225.5081	305.7518	356.9694	417.4261
46	86.6679	99.3965	131.9454	205.9842	240.0986	328.2244	384.8171	451.9002
47	89.8596	103.4084	138.2632	218.3684	255.5645	352.2701	414.7533	489.1322
48	93.1311	107.5406	144.8337	231.4336	271.9587	377.9990	446.9348	529.3427
49	96.4843	111.7969	151.6671	245.2175	289.3359	405.5289	481.5299	572.7702
50	99.9215	116.1808	158.7738	259.7594	307.7561	434.9860	518.7197	619.6718

COMPOUND INTEREST
ONE DOLLAR PER ANNUM IN ADVANCE

The sum of which One Dollar per annum, paid at the beginning of each year, will increase at compound interest in any number of years not exceeding fifty.

Years	8.25%	8.75%	9%	10%	11%	12%	13.5%	15%
1	1.0825	1.0875	1.0900	1.1000	1.1100	1.1200	1.1350	1.1500
2	2.2543	2.2702	2.2781	2.3100	2.3421	2.3744	2.4232	2.4725
3	3.5228	3.5563	3.5731	3.6410	3.7097	3.7793	3.8854	3.9934
4	4.8959	4.9550	4.9847	5.1051	5.2278	5.3528	5.5449	5.7424
5	6.3823	6.4760	6.5233	6.7156	6.9129	7.1152	7.4284	7.7537
6	7.9914	8.1302	8.2004	8.4872	8.7833	9.0890	9.5663	10.0668
7	9.7332	9.9291	10.0285	10.4359	10.8594	11.2997	11.9927	12.7268
8	11.6186	11.8854	12.0210	12.5795	13.1640	13.7757	14.7468	15.7858
9	13.6597	14.0128	14.1929	14.9374	15.7220	16.5487	17.8726	19.3037
10	15.8691	16.3265	16.5603	17.5312	18.5614	19.6546	21.4204	23.3493
11	16.2608	16.8425	19.1407	20.3843	21.7132	23.1331	25.4471	28.0017
12	20.8498	21.5787	21.9534	23.5227	25.2116	27.0291	30.0175	33.3519
13	23.6524	24.5544	25.0192	26.9750	29.0949	31.3926	35.2048	39.5047
14	26.6863	27.7904	28.3609	30.7725	33.4054	36.2797	41.0925	46.5804
15	29.9704	31.3096	32.0034	34.9497	38.1899	41.7533	47.7750	54.7175
16	33.5254	35.1366	35.9737	39.5447	43.5008	47.8837	55.3596	64.0751
17	37.3738	39.2986	40.3013	44.5992	49.3959	54.7497	63.9681	74.8364
18	41.5396	43.8247	45.0185	50.1591	55.9395	62.4397	73.7388	87.2116
19	46.0491	48.7469	50.1601	56.2760	63.2028	71.0524	84.8486	101.4436
20	50.9307	54.0997	55.7645	63.0725	71.2651	80.6987	97.4154	117.8101
21	56.2150	59.9210	61.8733	70.4027	80.2143	91.5026	111.7015	136.6316
22	61.9352	66.2516	68.5319	78.5430	90.1479	103.6029	127.9162	158.2764
23	68.1274	73.1361	75.7898	87.4933	101.1742	117.1552	146.3199	183.1678
24	74.8304	80.6230	83.7009	97.3471	113.4133	132.3339	167.2081	211.7930
25	82.0864	88.7650	92.3240	108.1828	126.9988	149.3339	190.9162	244.7120
26	89.9410	97.6194	101.7231	120.0989	142.0766	168.3740	217.8248	282.5688
27	98.4436	107.2486	111.9682	133.2099	158.8173	189.6989	248.3662	326.1041
28	107.6477	117.7204	123.1354	147.6209	177.3972	213.5828	283.0306	376.1697
29	117.6112	129.1084	135.3075	163.4240	198.0209	240.3327	322.3748	433.7451
30	129.3966	141.4929	148.5752	180.9434	220.9132	270.2926	367.0303	499.9569
31	140.0718	154.9610	163.0370	200.1378	246.3236	303.8477	417.7144	576.0105
32	152.7102	169.6076	178.8003	221.2515	274.5294	341.4294	475.2409	663.6655
33	166.3913	185.5358	195.9823	244.4767	305.8374	383.5210	540.5334	764.3654
34	181.2011	202.8577	214.7108	270.0244	340.5896	430.6635	614.6404	880.1702
35	197.2327	221.8952	235.1247	298.1268	379.1644	483.4631	698.7519	1013.3457
36	214.5869	242.1810	257.3759	329.0395	421.9825	542.5987	794.2184	1166.4975
37	233.3728	264.4594	281.6298	363.0434	489.5106	608.8305	902.5729	1342.6222
38	253.7086	288.6871	308.0665	400.4478	522.2667	683.0102	1025.5552	1545.1655
39	275.7221	315.0347	336.8824	441.5926	580.8261	766.0914	1165.1404	1778.0903
40	299.5516	343.6877	368.2919	486.8518	645.8269	859.1424	1323.5691	2045.9359
41	325.3471	374.8479	402.5281	536.6370	717.9779	963.3595	1503.3859	2353.9969
42	353.2708	408.7346	439.8457	591.4007	798.0655	1080.0826	1707.4780	2708.2465
43	383.4981	445.5864	480.5218	651.6408	886.9627	1210.8125	1939.1225	3115.6334
44	416.2192	485.6627	514.8587	717.9048	985.6386	1357.2300	2202.0391	3584.1285
45	451.6398	529.2456	573.1860	790.7953	1095.1688	1521.2176	2500.4493	4122.8977
46	489.9826	576.6421	625.8628	870.9749	1216.7474	1704.8838	2839.1450	4742.4824
47	531.4886	628.1858	683.2804	959.1723	1351.6996	1910.5898	3223.5646	5455.0047
48	576.4190	684.2396	745.8656	1056.1896	1501.4965	2140.9806	3659.8808	6274.4055
49	625.0560	745.1981	814.0836	1162.9085	1667.7712	2399.0182	4155.0997	7216.7163
50	677.7056	811.4904	868.4411	1280.2994	1852.3360	2688.0204	4717.1731	8300.3737

COMPOUND INTEREST
ONE DOLLAR PRINCIPAL

The sum to which One Dollar Principal will increase in any number of years not exceeding fifty, at the Compound Interest Rates Shown below.

Years	2.5%	3%	4%	5.5%	6%	7%	7.5%	8%
1	1.0250	1.0300	1.0400	1.0550	1.0600	1.0700	1.0750	1.0800
2	1.0506	1.0609	1.0816	1.1130	1.1236	1.1449	1.1556	1.1664
3	1.0769	1.0927	1.1249	1.1742	1.1910	1.2250	1.2423	1.2597
4	1.1038	1.1255	1.1699	1.2388	1.2625	1.3108	1.3355	1.3605
5	1.1314	1.1593	1.2167	1.3070	1.3382	1.4026	1.4356	1.4693
6	1.1597	1.1941	1.2653	1.3788	1.4185	1.5007	1.5433	1.5869
7	1.1887	1.2299	1.3159	1.4547	1.5036	1.6058	1.6590	1.7138
8	1.2184	1.2668	1.3686	1.5347	1.5938	1.7182	1.7835	1.8509
9	1.2489	1.3048	1.4233	1.6191	1.6895	1.8385	1.9172	1.9990
10	1.2801	1.3439	1.4802	1.7081	1.7908	1.9672	2.0610	2.1589
11	1.3121	1.3842	1.5395	1.8021	1.8983	2.1049	2.2156	2.3316
12	1.3449	1.4258	1.6010	1.9012	2.0122	2.2522	2.3818	2.5182
13	1.3785	1.4685	1.6651	2.0058	2.1329	2.4098	2.5604	2.7196
14	1.4130	1.5126	1.7317	2.1161	2.2609	2.5782	2.7524	2.9372
15	1.4483	1.5580	1.8009	2.2325	2.3966	2.7590	2.9589	3.1722
16	1.4845	1.6047	1.8730	2.3553	2.5404	2.9522	3.1808	3.4259
17	1.5216	1.6528	1.9479	2.4848	2.6928	3.1588	3.4194	3.7000
18	1.5597	1.7024	2.0258	2.6215	2.8543	3.3799	3.6758	3.9960
19	1.5987	1.7535	2.1068	2.7656	3.0256	3.6165	3.9515	4.3157
20	1.6386	1.8061	2.1911	2.9178	3.2071	3.8697	4.2479	4.6610
21	1.6796	1.8603	2.2788	3.0762	3.3996	4.1406	4.5664	5.0338
22	1.7216	1.9161	2.3699	3.2475	3.6035	4.4304	4.9089	5.4365
23	1.7646	1.9736	2.4647	3.4262	3.8197	4.7405	5.2771	5.8715
24	1.8087	2.0328	2.5633	3.6146	4.0489	5.0724	5.6729	6.3412
25	1.8539	2.0938	2.6658	3.8134	4.2919	5.4274	6.0983	6.8485
26	1.9003	2.1566	2.7725	4.0231	4.5494	5.8074	6.5557	7.3964
27	2.9478	2.2213	2.8834	4.2444	4.8223	6.2139	7.0474	7.9881
28	1.9965	2.2879	2.9987	4.4778	5.1117	6.6488	7.5759	8.8271
29	2.0464	2.3566	3.1187	4.7241	5.4184	7.1143	8.1441	9.3173
30	2.0976	2.4273	3.2434	4.9840	5.7435	7.6123	8.7550	10.0627
31	2.1500	2.5001	3.3731	5.2581	6.0881	8.1451	9.4116	10.8677
32	2.2038	2.5751	3.5081	5.5473	6.4534	8.7153	10.1174	11.7371
33	2.2589	2.6523	3.6484	5.8524	6.8406	9.3253	10.8763	12.6760
34	2.3153	2.7319	3.7943	6.1742	7.2510	9.9781	11.6920	13 6901
35	2.3732	2.8139	3.9461	6.5138	7.6861	10.6766	12.5689	14.7853
36	2.4325	2.8983	4.1039	6.8721	8.1473	11.4239	13.5115	15.9682
37	2.4933	2.9852	4.2681	7.2501	8.6361	12.2236	14.5249	17.2456
38	2.5557	3.0748	4.4388	7.6488	9.1543	13.0793	15.6143	18.6253
39	2.6196	3.1670	4.6164	8.0695	9.7035	13.9948	16.7853	20.1153
40	2.6851	3.2620	4.8010	8.5133	10.2857	14.9745	18.0442	21.7245
41	2.7522	3.3599	4.9931	8.9815	10.9029	16.0227	19.3976	23.4625
42	2.8210	3.4607	5.1928	9.4755	11.5570	17.1443	20.8524	25.3395
43	2.8915	3.5645	5.4005	9.9967	12.2505	18.3444	22.4163	27.3666
44	2.9638	3.6715	5.6165	10.5465	12.9855	19.6285	24.0975	29.5560
45	3.0379	3.7816	5.8412	11.1266	13.7646	21.0025	25.9048	31.9204
46	3.1139	3.8950	6.0748	11.7385	14.5905	22.4726	27.8477	34.4741
47	3.1917	4.0119	6.3178	12.3841	15.4659	24.0457	29.9363	37.2320
48	3.2715	4.1323	6.5705	13.0653	16.3939	25.7289	32.1815	40.2106
49	3.3533	4.2582	6.8333	13.7838	17.3775	27.5299	34.5951	43.4247
50	3.4371	4.3839	7.1067	14.5420	18.4202	29.4570	37.1897	45.9016

COMPOUND INTEREST
ONE DOLLAR PRINCIPAL

The sum to which One Dollar Principal will increase in any number of years not exceeding fifty, at the Compound Interest Rates shown below.

Years	8.25%	8.75%	9%	10%	11%	12%	13.5%	15%
1	1.0825	1.0875	1.0900	1.1000	1.1100	1.1200	1.1350	1.1500
2	1.1718	1.1827	1.1881	1.2100	1.2321	1.2544	1.2882	1.3225
3	1.2685	1.2861	1.2950	1.3310	1.3676	1.4049	1.4621	1.5209
4	1.3731	1.3987	1.4116	1.4641	1.5181	1.5735	1.6595	1.7490
5	1.4864	1.5211	1.5386	1.6105	1.6851	1.7623	1.8836	2.0114
6	1.6090	1.6542	1.6771	1.7716	1.8704	1.9738	2.1378	2.3131
7	1.7418	1.7989	1.8280	1.9487	2.0762	2.2107	2.4264	2.6600
8	1.8855	1.9563	1.9926	2.1436	2.3045	2.4760	2.7540	3.0590
9	2.0410	2.1275	2.1719	2.3579	2.5580	2.7731	3.1258	3.5179
10	2.2094	2.3136	2.3674	2.5937	2.8394	3.1058	3.5478	4.0456
11	2.3917	2.5161	2.5804	2.8531	3.1518	3.4785	4.0267	4.6524
12	2.5890	2.7362	2.8127	3.1384	3.4985	3.8960	4.5704	5.3503
13	2.8206	2.9756	3.0658	3.4523	3.8833	4.3625	5.1874	6.1528
14	3.0338	3.2360	3.3417	3.7975	4.3104	4.8871	5.8877	7.0757
15	3.2841	3.5192	3.6425	4.1772	4.7846	5.4736	6.6825	8.1371
16	3.5551	3.8271	3.9703	4.5950	5.3109	6.1304	7.5846	9.3576
17	3.8483	4.1620	4.3276	5.0545	5.8951	6.8660	8.6085	10.7613
18	4.1658	4.5261	4.7171	5.5599	6.5436	7.6900	9.7707	12.3755
19	4.5095	4.9222	5.1417	6.1159	7.2633	8.6128	11.0897	14.2318
20	4.8816	5.3529	5.6044	6.7275	8.0623	9.6463	12.5869	16.3665
21	5.2843	5.8212	6.1088	7.4002	8.9492	10.8038	14.2861	18.8215
22	5.7202	6.3306	6.6586	8.1403	9.9336	12.1003	16.2147	21.6447
23	6.1922	6.8845	7.2579	8.9543	11.0263	13.5523	18.4037	24.8915
24	6.7030	7.4869	7.9111	9.8497	12.2392	13.5523	18.4037	24.8915
25	7.2560	8.1420	8.6231	10.8347	13.5855	17.0001	23.7081	32.9190
26	7.8546	8.8544	9.3992	11.9182	15.0799	19.6401	26.9087	37.8568
27	8.5026	9.6292	10.2451	13.1100	16.7386	21.3249	30.5414	43.5353
28	9.2041	10.4718	11.1671	14.4210	18.5799	23.8839	34.6644	50.0656
29	9.9634	11.3880	12.1722	15.8631	20.6237	26.7499	39.3441	57.5755
30	10.7854	12.3845	13.2677	17.4494	22.8923	29.9599	44.6556	66.2118
31	11.6752	13.4681	14.4681	19.1943	25.4104	33.5551	50.6841	76.1435
32	12.6384	14.6466	15.7633	21.1138	28.2056	37.5817	57.5264	87.5651
33	13.6811	15.9282	17.1820	23.2252	31.3082	42.0915	65.2925	100.6998
34	14.8089	17.3219	18.7284	25.5447	34.7521	47.1425	74.1070	115.8048
35	16.0316	18.8375	20.4140	28.1024	38.5749	52.7996	84.1115	133.1755
36	17.3542	20.4858	22.2515	30.9127	42.8181	59.1356	95.4665	153.1519
37	18.7859	22.2783	24.2538	34.0039	47.5281	66.2318	108.3545	176.1246
38	20.3358	24.2277	26.4367	37.4043	52.7562	74.1797	122.9823	202.5433
39	22.0135	26.3476	28.8160	41.1448	58.5593	83.0812	139.5850	232.9248
40	23.8296	28.6530	31.4094	45.2593	65.0609	93.0510	158.4289	267.8635
41	25.7955	31.1602	34.2363	49.7852	72.1510	104.2171	179.8168	308.0431
42	27.9236	33.8867	37.3175	54.7637	80.0876	116.7231	204.0921	354.2495
43	30.2273	36.8518	40.6761	60.2401	88.8972	130.7299	231.6445	407.3870
44	32.7211	40.0763	44.3370	66.2641	98.6759	146.4175	262.9165	468.4950
45	35.4206	43.5830	48.3273	72.8905	109.5309	163.9876	298.4103	538.7693
46	38.3428	47.3965	52.6767	80.1795	121.5786	183.6661	338.6957	619.5847
47	41.5061	51.5437	57.4176	88.1975	134.1975	205.7061	384.4196	712.5224
48	44.9303	56.0538	62.5852	97.0172	149.7970	230.3908	436.3162	819.4007
49	48.6371	60.9585	68.2179	106.7190	166.2746	258.0377	495.2189	942.3108
50	52.6496	66.2923	74.3575	117.3909	184.5648	289.0022	562.0735	1083.6574